FAMILY, KINSHIP, AND SYMPATHY IN NINETEENTH-CENTURY AMERICAN LITERATURE

In *Family, Kinship, and Sympathy in Nineteenth-Century American Literature* Cindy Weinstein radically revises our understanding of nineteenth-century sentimental literature in the United States. She argues that these novels are far more complex than critics have suggested, expanding the canon of sentimental novels to include some of the more popular, though under-examined writers, such as Mary Jane Holmes, Caroline Lee Hentz, and Mary Hayden Green Pike. Rather than confirming the power of the bourgeois family, Weinstein argues, sentimental fictions used the destruction of the biological family as an opportunity to reconfigure the family in terms of love rather than consanguinity. Their texts intervened in debates about slavery, domestic reform, and other social issues of the time. Furthermore, Weinstein shows how canonical texts, such as Melville's *Pierre* and works by Stowe and Twain, can take on new meaning when read in the context of nineteenth-century sentimental fictions. Through intensive close readings of a wide range of novels, this groundbreaking study demonstrates the aesthetic and political complexities of this important and influential genre.

CINDY WEINSTEIN is Associate Professor of English at the California Institute of Technology. She is the author of *The Literature of Labor and the Labors of Literature: Allegory in Nineteenth-Century American Fiction* (Cambridge, 1995) and the editor of *The Cambridge Companion to Harriet Beecher Stowe* (Cambridge, 2004).

Recent books in this series

FAMILY, KINSHIP, AND SYMPATHY IN NINETEENTH-CENTURY AMERICAN LITERATURE

CINDY WEINSTEIN

Associate Professor of English, California Institute of Technology

February 2008

To Nancy,
with admiration

Cindy

CAMBRIDGE
UNIVERSITY PRESS

CAMBRIDGE UNIVERSITY PRESS
Cambridge, New York, Melbourne, Madrid, Cape Town, Singapore, São Paulo

Cambridge University Press
The Edinburgh Building, Cambridge CB2 2RU, UK

Published in the United States of America by Cambridge University Press, New York

www.cambridge.org
Information on this title: www.cambridge.org/9780521842532

First published 2004
Hardback version transferred to digital printing 2006
Digitally printed first paperback version 2006

A catalogue record for this publication is available from the British Library

Library of Congress Cataloguing in Publication data
Weinstein, Cindy.
Family, kinship, and sympathy in nineteenth-century American literature / Cindy Weinstein.
p.   cm. – (Cambridge studies in American literature and culture; 147)
Includes bibliographical references and index.
ISBN 0 521 84253 0 (hardback)
1. American fiction – 19th century – History and criticism.   2. Domestic fiction, American – History
and criticism.   3. Literature and society – United States – History – 19th century.   4. Sympathy in
literature.   5. Kinship in literature.   6. Family in literature.   I. Title.   II. Series.

PS374.D57W45 2004
813′.3093552–dc22   2004045923

ISBN-13 978-0-521-84253-2 hardback
ISBN-10 0-521-84253-0 hardback

ISBN-13 978-0-521-03126-4 paperback
ISBN-10 0-521-03126-5 paperback

For Jim, Sarah, and Sam

Contents

Acknowledgments

So many people have my profound gratitude that it's difficult to know where to begin. Eric Sundquist and Michael Gilmore have given me the kind of support and critique of which academics dream. They are models of discipline and generosity. Dorothy Hale's intellectual guidance and personal friendship have always inspired me to do the best work possible and have sustained me for many years and over many miles. I am grateful to Jim Astorga, Martha Banta, Sara Blair, Gregg Crane, William Merrill Decker, Wai Chee Dimock, Emory Elliott, Jonathan Freedman, Jane Garrity, Greg Jackson, Jeffrey Knapp, Robert Levine, Lori Merish, Nancy Ruttenberg, Margit Stange, John Sutherland, Lynn Wardley, and Arlene Zuckerberg, all of whom have spent time with this book and have contributed invaluable advice. Marianne Noble, Lois Brown, Xiamora Santamartin, and Mary Kelley intervened at especially helpful moments. For reading the manuscript with great care and attentiveness, I am deeply indebted to Carolyn Karcher and to Samuel Otter. Special thanks go to Sam, whose generosity of spirit and suggestion is unsurpassed. Thank you to Ross Posnock, head of the Cambridge series, and Ray Ryan, editor of the series, for finding such ideal readers and for so graciously shepherding the manuscript into print. I am also grateful to Jackie Warren, Lucy Carolan, and Mike Leach at Cambridge University Press. Thank you to my colleagues at Caltech, John Brewer, Moti Feingold, Kevin Gilmartin, Cathy Jurca, Morgan Kousser, Jenijoy Labelle, and Mac Pigman. Special thanks to Cathy, whose keen and generous readings of early versions of chapters helped me to clarify the argument. I am grateful for permission to reprint Chapter 2, "'A Sort of Adopted Daughter': Family Relations in *The Lamplighter*," which first appeared in *ELH* 68 (2001): 1023–1047. My thanks also go to the staff of the Huntington Library and Alan Jutzi, in particular. The division of humanities and social sciences, under the direction of John Ledyard, gave me the time to write this book, and Jean Ensminger provided the additional support to finish it.

Susan Davis, Megan Guichard, Margaret Lindstrom, Gina Morea, the Inter-Library Loan staff at Caltech, and Peet's coffee facilitated all matters related to this project.

I began to have the idea for this book when my father was in the later stages of Alzheimer's disease. Although the illness took away his mind, he somehow managed never to let it take away his heart. His abiding love helped me to write this book. For my mother's support and affection, I am deeply grateful. Thank you to my sister, Linda, who found my family a house to live in during our wonderful sabbatical year in Maryland, where most of the book was written, and to my brother, Lyle, for providing comfort, humor, affection, and encouragement on a constant basis. This book is dedicated to my husband, Jim, and our children, Sarah and Sam, whose love makes all things imaginable and possible.

Introduction

Family, Kinship, and Sympathy expands the critical conversation about sentimental fiction by extending our understanding of sympathy, or what Harriet Beecher Stowe famously asked her readers to do at the conclusion of *Uncle Tom's Cabin* – to *"feel right."* The imperative to "see to your sympathies" is, however, not solely a feature of Stowe's anti-slavery polemic. "Feeling right" informs virtually all sentimental fiction, regardless of political intentions. Novel after novel tells the story of children learning how to feel right about their families, selves, nation, and God in the face of great pain, which almost always takes the form of parental loss. It should come as no surprise, then, that these texts often imagine their disfigured families in relation to the institution of slavery, whose *donnée* is the fracturing of domestic order. It should also come as no surprise that Melville's *Pierre*, our most profound literary analysis of sentimental novels and the families out of which they are made, is about a character whose primary occupation is ridding himself of the parents who prevent him from joining his sentimental cohorts in learning how to feel right about families, selves, nation, and God. Surrounded by one woman who functions as both sister and wife and another who appears to be a cousin (the subject of a later chapter), Pierre finds himself "utterly without sympathy." Is the family the site where sympathy is produced or annihilated, dispensed or withheld? Is it possible that sentimental novels are making the very unsentimental point that sympathy thrives in the absence of family ties?[1]

It is no coincidence that out of the materials of mid nineteenth-century American culture, Ann Douglas and Jane Tompkins, the literary critics most responsible for establishing the terms of the debate about sentimental fiction, produced sympathy as a litmus test for assessing a text's politics. This was, after all, the very test that many antebellum Americans applied to their daily activities and the principles around which their lives were organized. Mothers read advice manuals in order to learn how to be more sympathetic; the south was sympathetic, it insisted, because it cared for slaves; the north claimed that it was sympathetic because it opposed slavery and had a system of free labor; the law aimed to be sympathetic in its decision to uphold "the best interests of the child," a legal consideration developed during this period; the literature repeatedly deployed sympathy as one of the most reliable measures of characterological virtue. Thus, sympathy is, quite rightly, the starting point for many studies of senti-mental fictions.[2]

As successful as Tompkins's defense of *Uncle Tom's Cabin* and her putative canonization of what she calls "the other American Renaissance" has been in effecting a transformation in what constitutes the antebellum literary landscape, it has been less successful in altering the ideological judgments most often leveled against writers such as Stowe, Susan Warner, and "that damned mob of scribbling women," as Hawthorne famously put it in an 1855 letter to William Ticknor. Douglas would seem to have won that particular battle. To be sure, Douglas's critique of sentimental litera-ture as "the political sense obfuscated or gone rancid" has been updated, cast in new theoretical terms, and expanded to include possibly even more trenchant accusations against sentimentalism. Her complaint is, nonethe-less, sustained, time and again, as new texts are added to the canon, which then are read primarily for their political failings. Lauren Berlant's assess-ment of sentimentalism in *Uncle Tom's Cabin*, which indicts Stowe for her "not Marxist enough cry, 'But, what can any individual do?'" is an excellent case in point. To read much of the literary criticism about sentimentalism, one might conclude that the hundreds of novels comprising the canon of sentimental fiction is, in fact, a monolithic entity, a critic's white whale as it were, to be confronted and destroyed. Laura Wexler, for example, describes sentimentalism as an "expansive, imperial project ... that aimed at the subjection of different classes and even races who were compelled to play not the leading roles but the human scenery before which the melodrama of middle-class redemption could be enacted." Amy Kaplan writes, "where the domestic novel appears most turned inward to the private sphere of female interiority, we often find subjectivity scripted by narratives of nation and empire." In a similar vein, Michelle Burnham charges *Uncle Tom's Cabin* with the "project of sentimental imperialism when it finally scripts Cassy and the rest of the Harris family into an exemplary model of domesticity." "Feeling right" always seems to be feeling (and doing) wrong. Why?[3]

These negative assessments, in large measure, derive from a particular argument about the nature of "feeling right," which claims that sympathy in sentimental fictions has the same homogenizing meaning, the same stultifying and baleful effect, the same mode of production, regardless of the context in which it is cultivated, extended, and received. Sympathy becomes a form of appropriation structurally equivalent to the appropriations of slavery. Thus, Saidaya Hartman maintains that "in making the other's suffering one's own, this suffering is occluded by the other's obliteration," but is this a fact about sympathy itself or about a particular deployment of or, perhaps, a transitory stage in a process that then moves onward and outward? Must sympathy "ultimately bring us back to ourselves" in a "narcissistic model of projection and rejection," as Elizabeth Barnes has argued? And is it accurate to maintain, along with Karen Sanchez-Eppler that all "antislavery writing responds to slavery's annihilation of personhood with its own act of annihilation"?[4] What about Stowe's claim at the beginning of the chapter entitled "The Unprotected" in *Uncle Tom's Cabin*: "no creature on God's earth is left more utterly unprotected and desolate than the slave in these circumstances [the loss of a kind master]. The child who has lost a father has still the protection of friends, and of the law; he is something, and can do something, – has acknowledged rights and position; the slave has none" (457)? Doesn't this passage suggest that antebellum writers are capable of maintaining the difference between someone who is a slave and someone who is free? And if so, what are the implications for our understanding of how sympathy might work in their texts? Is it possible that the identificatory structure of sympathy that underlies so many recent critiques of sympathy (the "I sympathize with you only to the extent that you are like me" rule of thumb) is an insufficient description of how sympathy is generated and deployed?[5]

My point in asking such questions is to suggest that much of the recent debate about sympathy in sentimental literature produces a monolithic and consistently pernicious account of sympathy for three reasons: first, it assumes that the structure of sympathy is the same, regardless of the context in which it is circulating; second, it fails to register how sympathy gets produced (and has effects) in these novels not only through a foundational moment of identification but through a recognition of difference; and third, it fails to take into account the extraordinarily rich and ideologically diverse debate about sympathy that was taking place in the antebellum period, most importantly, for my purposes, within sentimental fiction itself – a debate, interestingly enough, that anticipates the substance of current critiques. In contrast, I maintain that sentimental fictions delineate alternative models of sympathy which, when examined, enrich our understanding of the multiple ways in which sympathy was imagined and practiced. Southern expressions of sympathy on behalf of the slave, to choose the most obvious example, are structured differently from northern admonitions to "feel right" because the logic of southern sympathy disallows potential identifications across race (those who are slaves, the argument goes, have nothing in common with those who aren't) and installs difference as the foundational category of sympathy. An alternative model of sympathy is at work in the case of Mary Hayden Green Pike's novel *Ida May*, in which a white girl is kidnapped and made into a black slave. The text suggests that identification, though a necessary first step in the production of sympathy, must then be surpassed by a recognition of difference. Still different is *Pierre*, which posits the absence of familiarity, in this case understood as the absence of consanguinity itself, as the necessary condition for sympathy.

It should be apparent that I have several other objections to many of the current readings of sentimental fictions, not the least of which is a critical tendency to make very broad claims based on very few texts. Critics of this literature are as focused on New England as any conventional study of Hawthorne, Thoreau, and Emerson. The sheer quantity of antebellum sentimental fiction is enormous (Mary Jane Holmes alone wrote forty novels, E.D.E.N. Southworth's collected volumes add up to forty-two, and Anna Sophia Stephens wrote thirty books, to name just three of the genre's most popular practitioners), and critics have attempted to circumscribe it in any number of ways, whether by time period, elements of the plot, ideological import, and/or the gender of the author. My archive has been organized with several frameworks in mind. First, certain sentimental texts, such as *The Lamplighter* and *The Wide, Wide World*, have achieved canonical status (at least within the canon of sentimental fictions). My analysis of these texts, therefore, acknowledges their prominent place in recent accounts, at the same time as I demonstrate how influential readings of these canonical texts have laid the groundwork for misreadings of the genre. Second, I have chosen to focus on a particular set of novels that reveal, with exemplary force, both the genre's profound awareness of the relative fragility of the biological family and a commitment to strengthening and redefining it according to the logic of love. My goal has been to demonstrate through readings of what I take to be representative sentimental texts this heretofore unobserved yet very powerful aspect of the genre. Third, my interest in authors such as Holmes and Caroline Lee Hentz speaks not only to the ways in which their texts respond to the pressures of close reading, but also to my desire to open up the canon of sentimental fictions. Precious little commentary is to be found on some of the most widely read sentimental writers, including, for instance, the

Kentucky-born Holmes, who according to Mary Kelley was "next to Harriet Beecher Stowe probably the biggest money-maker of the literary domestics," and Hentz, who grew up in New England and then spent most of her adult life living in the south and defending its institutions.[6] The lack of attention toward Hentz speaks to a crucially missing link in our sentimental archive – the south. Moreover, it is not my contention that certain sentimental texts are not imperialist or racist or sexist in precisely the ways outlined by critics of this literature, but rather that these allegations should not be taken to be the final word on the genre. The limited usefulness of these generalizations is, in part, a consequence of the limits of the archive, but it is also the case that much criticism on sentimentalism seems unable to imagine its practitioners as operating within discrete and disparate contexts that might produce a number of competing interventions. My analysis offers an account of sentimental fictions that not only acknowledges the linkages between novels, whether thematic, structural, or political, but illuminates the surprisingly diverse ideological and aesthetic contributions made by individual texts.[7]

Indeed, much criticism on the subject of sentimentalism seems incapable of considering this body of literature for its aesthetic qualities. It is as if the Douglas/Tompkins debate has taken such concerns off of the critical radar screen, as if questions of ideology and more conventional matters of literary form were mutually exclusive. Tompkins animated our interest in Stowe and Susan Warner, but at the same time, her argument has made it extremely difficult to talk about the distinct aesthetic investments (other than stereotype) of the "other American Renaissance." Being "other" has hindered our understanding of their works in terms of irony, ambiguity, character, and narrative voice. Thus, another one of my goals is to present new readings of sentimental fictions by subjecting them to more traditional methods of literary analysis.[8]

My critical practice is guided by an attentiveness to the verbal playfulness and complexity of these texts, which I believe provides a more satisfying account both of their ideological variability and aesthetic contributions. What is absent from many of the most influential analyses of sentimental fictions is a sustained consideration of the language of these texts. In not attending to the specifics of language, critics have missed the ways in which sentimental novels are fascinated by the material implications of words and figures, including pronouns, possessives, characters' names, analogies and euphemisms, and, as a result, have simplified (and homogenized) the genre. Once these verbal features of the novels are made apparent, it becomes clear that they are conducting their thematic analysis of family through a linguistic focus upon the words designating family relations. For example, a fundamental component in many of these texts is an ambiguity about proper names, which when subject to close reading, enables us to see how the novels are working out issues about identity and family.

Family, Kinship, and Sympathy thus proposes that we must first recognize that sympathy is produced, dispensed, and received in a variety of contexts, whether regional, political, reformist, judicial, literary, that goes beyond the framework of the biological family. And each of them helps to constitute sympathy differently. As I have already suggested, pro-slavery advocates conceive of the operations of sympathy quite distinctly from anti-slavery activists. Or, writers of domestic manuals represent sympathy in the family very differently from the Perfectionists of Oneida, or the Shakers. Second, I contend that new terms are needed (or, in certain cases, a revitalization of old ones) with which to analyze sympathy's material and/ or psychic effects as well as its ideological implications. The tears that often precipitate and accompany acts of sympathy have, with good reason, drawn a great deal of critical attention. For Douglas, they exemplify the bad faith at the core of sentimentalism, inasmuch as they "provide a way to protest a power to which one has already in part capitulated" (12). For Tompkins, they (along with prayers) comprise "the heroine's only recourse against injustice; the thought of injustice itself is implicitly forbidden." For Philip Fisher, "weeping is a sign of powerlessness." When Ellen Montgomery, protagonist of *The Wide, Wide World*, cries at her relatives' house in Scotland, she is, indeed, powerless to do anything about her situation. However, when Fanny Kemble weeps over the conditions of the slaves at the Georgia plantation over which she is mistress, her next step is to break the law and teach one of them how to read. My larger claim, here, is that weeping and acting need not be cast as mutually exclusive. Tears and reason don't have to cancel one another out, an observation made by Nina Baym, who puts it this way: "woman's fiction . . . believes in effective virtue." The concise phrase, "effective virtue," registers the point that sentimental fictions don't discriminate between sympathy and action, feeling and doing, but rather the two processes are inextricably linked.[9] Many of these texts also allow us to see that irony and sympathy don't have to be conceived of in opposition to one another. One need only read the first line of *Uncle Tom's Cabin* – "Late in the afternoon of a chilly day in February, two gentlemen were sitting alone over their wine" (41) – to realize that Stowe's irony (these gentlemen are not gentlemen) is a fundamental strategy in her critique of slavery.

I also argue that not all sentimental fictions unself-consciously reproduce formulaic requirements (the child suffers the loss of her parents and is recompensed at the novel's end by getting a spouse), but rather they have the capacity to interrogate their generic foundations. Slavery is central to this self-examination as sentimental fictions register the ways in which their tales of parentless children both intersect with and diverge from the narratives of children made parentless through slavery's legalized acts of what Orlando Patterson has identified as "social death." Although much critical attention has been paid to what Sanchez-Eppler calls the "hybridization of slave and domestic narrative forms," the analysis is usually centered on the slave narrative's incorporation and subversion of the domestic narrative. This book shifts the emphasis and explores how sentimental fictions incorporate features of the slave narrative in order not only to represent the suffering of their (white) heroine, but to hierarchize her temporary suffering in relation to the slaves' potentially unending abuse. In other words, even as the analogy between white women and black slaves gets deployed, what gets written into some sentimental novels is an awareness of the racial (and racist) conditions that make the freedom of their white protagonist a convention of the genre.[10]

There are several recent studies of the genre that have complicated the ideological, authorial, and interpretive polarizations of the Douglas/Tompkins debate in an attempt to reveal how the cultural work of sentimental fictions need not travel in one straight path. For example, Julia Stern argues that "mourning is the central subtext of much American sentimental women's writing in the eighteenth and nineteenth century; multivocality plays a crucial role in communicating what such sublimated narrative material represses." Gillian Brown's reading of *Uncle Tom's Cabin* demonstrates that while Stowe's "reformulated domestic virtue" combines "love and protest, maternal duty and political action," those progressive formulations depend upon a racist ideology of what Brown calls "sentimental possession" that requires an erasure of all signs of the market economy in the middle-class home, including slaves. Glenn Hendler challenges the very discursive foundations of the Douglas/Tompkins debate by "countering theories and histories of nineteenth-century sentimentality and domesticity that describe these modes as 'private' and place the domestic sphere in binary opposition to an economic realm defined as public." In one of the most powerful critiques of the limits of binary analysis as applied to this fiction, Lora Romero makes the point that sentimental texts can occupy a variety of positions on the ideological spectrum: "we seem unable to entertain the possibility that traditions, or even individual texts, could be radical on some issues (market capitalism, for example) and reactionary on others (gender or race, for instance)." The place called home, she argues, is the place that seems to transcend such ideological variability, that permits us (as it did antebellum Americans) to stabilize the "incommensurability of political visions" that are at play in these texts.[11]

Events in sentimental novels, of course, take place in the everyday world of the home. If literary critics agree on anything (even as they assign diametrically opposed value to it), surely it would be that the everyday experiences of the domestic drive the plots, the characters, the scenes, and the meanings of sentimental literature, domestic literature, women's literature, whatever one wishes to call that body of fiction whose primary subjects, one can only conclude, are feelings and families. Fisher eloquently observes: "Certain forms of life, and with them, certain underlying economic systems – obviously, that of slavery in this case – become suicidal and temperamentally deadlocked in the face of the few inviolable facts of family and feeling to which sentimentality with its enlightenment version of a common human nature is bound" (123). Baym also makes this point in *Woman's Fiction*: "[the fiction] assumes that men as well as women find greatest happiness and fulfillment in domestic relations, by which are meant not simply spouse and parent, but the whole network of human attachments based on love, support, and mutual responsibility" (27). It is also the case that "in novel after novel, a network of surrogate kin gradually defines itself around the heroine, making hers the story not only that of a self-made woman but that of a self-made or surrogate family" (38).

The making of a family is the task that awaits most sentimental protagonists, but what makes this endeavor so interesting and important, to my mind, is that in the process of making a family, the family is being redefined as an institution to which one can choose to belong or not. Indeed, a sense of consanguinity's insufficiencies is pervasive, but it is accompanied by a productive rush to fill in the void. Generically speaking, sentimental fiction is about the relative merits of consanguineous and elective ties in the emotional life of the child, but the value and meaning ascribed to those ties is contingent upon the context in which those families are situated. A widespread cultural examination of the family is being conducted in a variety of antebellum realms, including the field of domestic relations, the debate about slavery, and the many utopian efforts to reform the family. Not only are sentimental fictions similarly absorbed in this project of redefinition but the novels are intimately connected to the larger cultural conversation about domestic reform. Although we may be accustomed to thinking about these novels as conservative exempla of bourgeois ideology, many of them fiercely challenge the patriarchal regime of the biological family by calling attention to the frequency with which fathers neglect the economic as well as emotional obligations owed to their children. To counter paternal failure, advice manuals of the period advance a theory of mother love, but the plots of most sentimental novels require that the child be motherless. The child's survival, in other words, demands that the possibilities for who counts as family be expanded. In the process, the criterion by which families are deemed capable (or not) to raise a child shifts from considerations of economy to those of affection. Sentimental fictions are about finding the right place where sympathy flourishes and understanding that place and those people as one's home and "family." They tell the surprisingly pragmatic stories of these other "parents" and their ability or lack thereof to have sympathy for children who are not, biologically speaking, theirs. To extend the meaning of family is to extend the possibilities for sympathy.

Perhaps the most sweeping claim in what follows is that the cultural work of sentimental fictions is nothing less than an interrogation and reconfiguration of what constitutes a family. This is a monumental task, a paradigm shift, whose trajectory is neither even nor consistently successful. Although sentimental fictions longingly look back to a time when families were understood as consanguineous units, novel after novel is engaged in ridding itself of the paternalism of consanguinity by replacing it with a family that is based on affection and organized according to a paradigm of contract, by which I mean that individual family members have rights that must be guaranteed and protected and that these rights increasingly come to be understood in affective terms. The generic goal is the substitution of freely given love, rather than blood, as the invincible tie that binds together individuals in a family, thereby loosening the hold that consanguinity has both as a mechanism for structuring the family and for organizing the feelings of the people in it. That most of these texts conclude in marriage and, presumably, the reproduction of the biological family would seem to suggest that their inquiries leave the institution untouched, if not even more powerful for having been investigated and pronounced worthy of another generation. Moreover, many of these novels seem capable of ending only when the biological father is reintegrated into the life of the heroine (the biological mother is usually long gone), an element of the plot which would appear to reinstall the priority of blood relations and weaken the claim for the authority of love. The fact is, however, that consanguinity becomes one more choice to be made.

It would be unreasonable, of course, to expect sentimental fictions to figure out how to demolish the biological family and patriarchy once and for all, and not all of them wish to do so. More often than not, their analysis is founded in a desire to reform the family rather than dispense with it altogether (*Pierre* being a notable exception). But the plots do such a convincing job of demonstrating the inadequacies of family that it is difficult, especially for twenty-first-century readers, to understand why its future is guaranteed in the endings of the texts. To judge these novels solely on the matter of the consistency with which they sustain their critique of the family (they would all fail because their protagonists marry) is to miss the intellectual creativity, the humor, and the difficulty of their intervention.

The strategy they share for challenging the rule of consanguinity is the application of an ideal of contract, sometimes literal but more often metaphorical, to the expression of love.[12] This linkage helps to explain why adoption and marriage play such crucial roles in the plots of virtually all sentimental novels. Selecting a parent, in many of these texts, requires intellectual and emotional skills not unlike those necessary for choosing a spouse. Having learned how to choose a parent out of necessity (dead mom, deadbeat dad), perhaps the child protagonist will do a better job of finding a loving mate and have the happy marriage that has eluded practically every adult in her world. It is important to stress, however, that while the novels consistently explore the impact of contract on family, they do not permit a unilateral conclusion about what contract means in a sentimental novel.[13] For example, to be free of consanguineous relations in *The Lamplighter* is to be free to make contracts that eventuate in self-possession. By contrast, to free oneself of consanguinity in *Pierre* so as to establish bonds based on contract is a fable of self-possession that leads to self-destruction. Still different is the case of *The Wide, Wide World,* where to be free of the obligations of consanguinity is to find oneself wanting to reproduce them in one's contractual relations. The privileging of contract, in other words, has diverse ideological implications, which are dependent upon the specific context from which the critique of consanguinity is launched. The unhinging of consanguinity as the definitional heart of the biological family produces very different ideological results.

This spectrum of interpretive possibility, however, doesn't begin to take into account what happens when sentimental novels consider slavery, where the affective value accorded to consanguineous relations has been rendered irrelevant (from the perspective of slave masters) by virtue of the economic value assigned to children born of slave mothers. Sentimental fictions' insistence on the marriage contract as the embodiment of an ideal of family based on choice also takes on different meanings when understood in relation to the fact that slave law mandated marriage as a contract into which slaves could not legally enter. The consanguineous havoc wrought by slavery is, perhaps, best exemplified in this passage by Harriet Jacobs: "My mother's mistress was the daughter of my grandmother's mistress. She was the foster sister of my mother; they were both nourished at my grandmother's breast . . . my mother was a most faithful servant to her white foster sister."[14] Obviously, the sentimental novels' language of paternal insufficiency – these dads don't simply abandon their daughters, they rape them, sell them, and sell their children – doesn't come close to capturing the real, as well as the rhetorical, predicament described by Jacobs. What kinds of connections might we make between the unmooring of the "'parental relation'" (368, the quotation marks are Jacobs's) in the context of slavery and the endless round of substitute parents in sentimental novels? In what ways do these "surrogate families," to quote Baym, intersect and diverge? Several of the chapters that follow demonstrate that slavery is the "hard fact," to invoke Fisher's title, against which sentimental fictions come up in their experimentation with alternatives to families based on consanguinity, which is one of the reasons why sentimental novels often stop short of advocating a complete abrogation of the rule of consanguinity. The recognition of the affective value of blood relations, of family conventionally understood, is precisely what slavery disallows as the one-drop rule validates only the economic value of blood (the child follows the condition of the mother). We shall see that many sentimental fictions find themselves required, at some level, to recognize the validity of consanguinity in order to distance themselves from arguments made in favor of the peculiar institution.

Chapter 1, "*In loco parentis*," examines a broad swath of antebellum sentimental fictions in order to establish both the consanguineous disarray in which these fictional families find themselves and to develop an account of how these novels arrive at a modicum of domestic stability. They do so, I argue, by questioning the absolute value ascribed to relationships based on blood. Time and again, these novels reveal the vulnerability of consanguinity as the best indicator of love and set themselves the task of arriving at a different set of criteria for constituting families. Time and again, they arrive at adoption as the most reliable expression of affection. The chapter puts a great deal of pressure on the presence of adoption in these narratives, using Holmes's *Lena Rivers* (1856) as an exemplary case, because the voluntary assumption of parental bonds generates an ideal and ideology of affiliation that clashes with the family as biologically understood. It is fascinating that at precisely the moment that the affective lives of antebellum Americans seem to be coalescing around an ideal of the biological family, these texts consistently represent its insufficiencies and the necessity of coming up with alternatives. I read the domestic disarray of Hentz's *Ernest Linwood* (1856) as exemplary of the genre's fascinating destabilization of family life conventionally understood. My goal here is to begin to challenge our assumptions about sentimental fictions by demonstrating that the very genre that has been understood as pivotal in disseminating a particularly circumscribed view of the middle-class family ought to be regarded as instrumental in the imagined reconfiguration of the family.

Chapter 2, " 'A sort of adopted daughter,' or *The Lamplighter*," develops the centrality of the adoption theme in sentimental fictions by focusing on the role of adoption in Cummins's novel. I propose that, in linking adoption with sympathy, Cummins offers an alternative model of sympathy that understands sympathy, not only in terms of tears and other bodily effects, but as a rational, humane response to the needs of others, what I call "judicious sympathy." I read this meditation on the affective and social benefits of adoption in the context of antebellum judicial decisions that, in formalizing adoption law, recognized the increasing role of contract in the family. Because the heroine Gerty has no biological relations (or doesn't learn of them until the novel's end), she gains membership in several families through verbally made contracts, primarily adoptions. Far from hindering the development of her sympathies, such contracts liberate her from potentially restrictive biological bonds. Gerty's biologically unattached status thus permits her to decide rationally what her relations with and responsibilities toward others should be. It is not, however, the case that consanguinity simply disappears from *The Lamplighter*'s understanding of family, but rather it disappears just long enough so that the novel can begin to lay the groundwork for an affective rather than an economic foundation upon which the family can be redefined.

Chapter 3, "Thinking through sympathy: Kemble, Hentz, and Stowe," explores sympathy in a range of heretofore relatively marginalized texts, including Fanny Kemble's *Journal of a Residence on a Georgian Plantation in 1838–1839* (1863), *The Planter's Northern Bride* (1854), Hentz's rejoinder to *Uncle Tom's Cabin* (1852), and Stowe's *A Key to Uncle Tom's Cabin* (1853). It is the first of three chapters that considers the mobilization of sympathy within the context of debates about slavery. Although the *Journal* and *A Key* are not sentimental fictions, per se, their self-conscious examination of anti-slavery sympathy helps to situate both my specific reading of Hentz's pro-slavery position as well as my more general reading of sentimental fictions' extension of sympathy.[15] The analysis of Hentz and other pro-slavery fiction demonstrates their strategic investment in

valorizing sympathetic attachments based on contract as a means of vindi-
cating slavery's perversion of families. Furthermore, I challenge interpretations of Stowe that charge her anti-slavery appeal with racism on the
grounds that they not only fail to consider southern contexts which clearly
distinguish her from her detractors, but they unwittingly replicate a pro-
slavery strategy that validates slavery by erasing its differences from freedom. This logic aims to disrupt anti-slavery circuits of sympathy, wresting
sympathy away from slaves and redirecting it toward their masters. Stowe's
A Key exposes such ideological brutality, proving that defenses of slavery
require an absence of sympathy, which is based on an absence of fact. *A Key*,
I argue, attempts to expand the foundation of sympathy by demonstrating
that advocates of slavery cannot distinguish between facts and lies. Anti-
slavery, she contends, is based on truth and therefore is true whereas the
pro-slavery position is based on lies and is therefore false. Like Cummins,
Stowe brings sympathy into the realm of the rational.

Chapter 4, "Behind the scenes of sentimental novels," continues to
explore how the debate about slavery informs our understanding of sentimental literature, but it does so in light of generic considerations. My
argument proceeds by juxtaposing a reading of Pike's *Ida May* (1854) and
Solomon Northup's *Twelve Years a Slave* (1853), two texts in which both
fictional heroine and non-fictional hero are kidnapped into slavery, and
explicates the generic ties that bind sentimental fictions and slave narratives. The dismantling of the biological family is their shared *donnée* and as
a consequence both genres narrate the process whereby their protagonists
find new families to which they can belong. Although their plots ineluct-
ably overlap, I am interested in demonstrating that sentimental novels are
not generically incapable of recognizing the absolute differences between a
child who has no parents because she has been orphaned and a child who
has no parents because they have been sold. In fact, even as Pike's sentimental text accumulates much of its emotional power by virtue of this
analogy (just as critics have argued that the slave narrative resonates more
powerfully through its borrowings from the sentimental novel), the novel
rejects it in order to make clear the distinctions between being free and
being enslaved, one of the most significant being that the former can enter
into contractual relations and the latter cannot.

The final two chapters of the book take the unusual step of pairing *The
Wide, Wide World* and *Pierre*. Both novels interrogate an ideal of affiliation
that links freedom with the capacity to enter into contracts by representing
chosen relations as radically limited by a number of factors, including the
pressures of psychology, sexuality, and language. Whereas contract in the

earlier chapters of my analysis represents an alternative to a world determined by consanguineous relations, contract in Warner's and Melville's
texts is a far less stable marker of freedom than in texts by Cummins,
Hentz, Pike, or Northup. Chapter 5, "Love American style: *The Wide,
Wide World*," therefore re-examines and complicates my claim that contract – adoption and the marriage contract in particular – is the sentimental
novel's most consistent and compelling strategy through which to articu-
late its generic difference from the slave narrative. Although Warner strives
to use Ellen's understanding of attachments based on contract as evidence
of her status as free, her adoptions and eventual marriage to John are less
capable of cordoning off slavery from freedom. To be sure, slaves can
neither be adopted nor marry, and it is Ellen's ability to enter into both of
these contracts that signifies her status as free. Yet the quality of those
contractual relations overlaps quite ominously with the logic and language
of slavery, as is the case with virtually all of her consanguineous relations,
and those resonances with slavery never completely go away. The excision
of two scenes from Warner's 1849 manuscript, both of which take up the
issue of race, suggests that such a context might not have been far from view
during the writing process. How is it that Ellen can both be a slave and not
be a slave? How she will be extricated from that difficult situation becomes
the entanglement from which the narrative must extricate itself. This
obstacle is, of course, the same one confronting the nation precisely at
the time that Warner writes her 1850 literary blockbuster. Whereas the
novel manages to absorb the tension of Ellen's condition and liberates its
heroine through a *deus ex machina*, the Compromise of 1850 is the nation's
(ultimately failed) resolution to the intertwining plots of slavery and
sentiment.

Chapter 6, "We are family, or Melville's *Pierre*," presents a formalist
reading of the language and narrative of ubiquitous kinship in a novel bent
on the destruction of consanguinity and desperate for relations based on
contract. *Pierre* (1852) is a pre-history (in other words, what might Gerty's
and Ellen's stories be like if their parents didn't die or disappear for a
while?) of the sentimental novel that explains why Gerty or Ellen or Ida
might be considerably happier not being enmeshed in a biological family.
Unlike theirs, his narrative is a deliberate flight from "blood relation" (218).
All of the children in *Pierre* seek to embrace an ideal of contract only to find
that biology, indeed incest, awaits them. The novel thus begins to attack
itself as the only available choices are negations of relation. But even the
negations, it turns out, become attestations of consanguinity. The only
thing left for the text to do is destroy itself, and to that extent, it admirably

succeeds. I explore the logic of the novel's undoing, beginning with its infamous narrative experimentalism and concluding with its social experimentalism. Contract in the world of *Pierre* is impossible because virtually everyone in the novel is related to everyone else; all attempts to get outside of consanguinity only reproduce it.

I end with a coda on Twain's *Pudd'nhead Wilson* (1894), a text which validates biological rather than contractual ties, even as it exposes the failures of sympathy in both. The heroine, Roxy, switches her child with her master's and is then cruelly treated by her biological son, who considers himself her master. But Roxy's relationship with the child who thinks she's his mother remains untold, because to tell it opens up the possibility that slavery might sustain loving relationships, a pro-slavery position. If Twain does Roxy a disservice, he does so in order to make absolute his indictment of slavery, which is based on establishing racial identity as socially constructed rather than biologically based. Thus, when Roxy reveals to her biological child the fact of his parentage, he "becomes" black. Roxy, though, doesn't become the mother of her master's child when she switches him, because her sympathies are not and cannot be transferred. Twain biologizes maternal sympathy in order to critique the biologism of racism. Biology, in other words, may not be the only direction in which sympathy travels, but Twain refuses to let sympathy go anywhere else. The transracial adoption story cannot be told, because to tell it would be to allow the possibility that loving relations could develop under the regime of slavery in much the same way they do in the plots of sentimental fictions. It is to those plots that I now turn in order to establish how the rupturing of the biological family produces at once a new familial ideal – contented children without biological parents, ubiquitous sympathy without consanguinity – at the same time as that ideal is contested by slavery, where the reunion of the biological family is the slave's foremost *desideratum* and the absence of sympathy her primary human condition.

CHAPTER I

In loco parentis

> O, there is affection stronger than any of this earth. It has a power, a
> beauty, a holiness, like no other sentiment.
> (The Reverend E. H. Chapin, "A Mother's Love")[1]

The Mother's Assistant and Young Lady's Friend was one of many popular
advice manuals in the mid nineteenth century which presented its primarily
female audience with a menu of articles, short stories, poems, and adages to
aid them in the strenuous work of raising children. Its pages instruct her in
a variety of childrearing departments, such as the proper forms of discipline, the ideal educational regimen, and the implementation of Christian
values and practices. Titles range from "The Influence of a Sister," "Family
Education," "Obedience of Children," or "Maternal Assistance," but the
message to mothers is always the same: "the mother must watch carefully,
that she does not mistake here." The "here" is, of course, everywhere,
making the task of mothering not only monumental but monumentally
difficult. The necessity of constant watchfulness, of her own behavior as
well as her children's (not to mention her husband's), signifies both her
power within the domestic realm and, as many have argued, her contain-
ment within it. She must consider her every action, every look, every
feeling because, as one article entitled, "The Silent Ministry of Example,"
reminds her: "an inconsistent word, a sullen look, a contention with her
husband, or her servants; petulance from an error, or an unhappy lot, will
dash in pieces the lessons of months."[2] No wonder she needs assistance.

My interest in antebellum advice manuals derives from the fact that
they, like the sentimental novels I shall be discussing, revolve around the
question of the family. The preservation and perfection of the biological
family, with the ideal mother at its helm, is usually taken to be the shared
cultural mission of both discursive forms, and ample evidence exists to
suggest that both are committed to instilling in their readers the notion that
"the mother is the child's oracle in life, language, and action." The manuals

do so by creating an atmosphere of crisis so as to ensure that the institution of the family continues to uphold its function as the nation's political, affective, and religious nursery. While reassuring mothers of their essential place and central role within the biological (and national) family, however, the cumulative effect of the articles is to undermine mothers by conveying the sense that they are failing to understand, appreciate, and perform their assigned roles in the household. "Awake, then, mothers, to a true consciousness of your responsibility to God for the manner in which you discharge the high and holy mission committed to your trust!" But as insistent as the advice manuals are on the cosmic significance of the mother's every move to the welfare of the child's physical and emotional development, even they, on occasion, acknowledge the fact that persons other than mothers (or fathers) might have the care of children either on a temporary or permanent basis. For example, in an article called "Influence of Early Instruction," the Reverend Hubbard Winslow admonishes parents against naively assuming that their domestics are properly raising their children: "if parents cannot secure such [truly virtuous domestics], let them forego other demands, and give their own time more unreservedly to their children." In another piece entitled, "Home," the Reverend Harvey Newcomb envisions an ideal family, "a miniature representation of heaven . . . [where] all their affections centre," and then remarks, "the wise parent or guardian will take delight in seeing children enjoy themselves." Even amidst the glorification of the biological mother and child, whom Lydia Sigourney strikingly describes "as this fragment of yourself," we find a piece entitled, "The Step-Mother," which celebrates "the magic power of her sympathy and presence." Another essay, "Family Education," contends that "a very young child will sympathize with the feelings of those who have the care of it."[3]

Sympathy is, as many scholars have correctly observed, the coin of the emotional realm in the antebellum period, and it is an attribute inextricably yoked to the figure of the biological mother. The Reverend Jacob Abbott, frequent contributor to *The Mother's Assistant* and author of many full-length advice manuals, writes that "the wonderful influence of sympathy shows the importance of the careful culture of our own hearts." The careful culture of our own hearts is, of course, conducted by our mother, that "sympathizing friend," to whom "young affections are given her to train, and young minds to imbue with lofty and generous sentiments." Thus, to invest oneself with the powers of sympathy is to lay claim to being right, ethical, disinterested, and, above all, maternal. There is, however, in these last quotations that refer to domestics, guardians and step-mothers, an underlying admission – one that will become a governing principle in the novels – that should mothers and fathers become unable to fulfill their child-raising tasks, others will be able to do so. Indeed, one might reasonably argue that these manuals, by virtue of their tireless attention to the minutiae of childrearing, make it possible for individuals who find themselves unexpectedly in the position of mother to learn how to perform the part, how to "cultivate a spirit of holy sympathy," to quote an anonymous article entitled "Sympathy."[4] The birth mother, from the point of view of these manuals, has nature going for her and thus has the best chance of successfully fulfilling her maternal obligations, but others can take her place, sometimes achieving even better results than the biological parents.

I HOUSES DIVIDED

Sentimental fictions of this period take as their *donnée* the hazardous health of the biological family (sick mothers and irresponsible fathers abound) and seek to establish alternatives to it that depend not exclusively on a traditional notion of family as defined by consanguinity but increasingly on a more modern sense of family as understood, indeed practiced, as contractual. In fact, their very plots are brought into being by the breakdown or the break-up of blood relations, catapulting their protagonists, often "discarded daughters" (the title of E.D.E.N Southworth's 1852 novel, as well as the designation given to the main character of Caroline Lee Hentz's *Eoline*) into "a wide, wide world" of strangers, where new replacement families emerge based on choice.[5] These novels are full of fascinating and ambiguous terms designating relations that are and are not familial, as the following list demonstrates: "my more than mother," "a sort of cousin," "a sort of adopted daughter," "a sort of elder brother-in-law," "some indirect cousinship, "some distant relation, or dependant of father's," "brother-like", "my *foster* child-lady."[6] They are replete with attestations and denials of consanguinity, as if desire rather than DNA were the decisive factor in establishing the proper criteria for kinship: "I will not have you call me 'uncle' – I am your father," "I will no more have a father," "I will stay here and be your little girl, Uncle Charles," "I will call you papa, if you like," "Come with me and be my sister," "she gladly consented to be to her a mother," and "he shall be your brother too, Gabriella."[7] And last, their plots consistently register a sometimes playful, sometimes dangerous ambiguity about names: "I have worshipped you as L'éclair, adored you as Florence, but I love you most of all as the gentle Rosa," "He had no legal name," "Yes, here is a name, – *the name*, – Ida May!'" "she had, in reality, no surname of her own," "There is no Miss Lynn here; it is Gabriella – *our Gabriella* – that is her name; you must not call her by any other."[8] As these quotations suggest, sentimental protagonists alternate between having an absence and a plethora of first and last names; their nominative undecidability signifies identities in flux and families in transition. Because the biological family and the father in particular are no longer providing the children of sentimental fictions with the structural coherence that will give them definitive last names, these novels devote themselves to discovering a new kind of coherence for their fictional children, one that is based more on affection than affinity, more on sympathy than on salary.

To begin to think about sentimental fictions in this way – that is as an extension rather than a structural and affective contraction of family – is to go against the grain of contemporary interpretations. Richard Brodhead's theory of "disciplinary intimacy" is, perhaps, the most influential. He argues that sentimental fictions, like the domestic manuals of the period, helped to inculcate "the disciplinary practices of the new model family," which meant that acts of love as opposed to corporeal punishment became the preferred mode of producing social normativity. These texts, he writes, "quite overtly posit as their audience a family closed off from extended relations." My objection to this analysis has less to do with his account of how discipline becomes privatized in relation to public displays of punishment and more to do with his characterization of antebellum families. These hypothetical families are far more unstable and porous than Brodhead's examination suggests, which means that the production of "American 'normality'" is neither as normal nor as settled as he maintains. One could even argue that extended domestic arrangements of sentimental fictions not only hearken back to eighteenth-century family formations, but also resonate with some of the more radical alternatives to family that were circulating in the mid nineteenth century, a point to which I shall return in my discussion of *Pierre*.[9]

Indeed, antebellum writers are preoccupied with the question, what is a family? They pose it time and again from a variety of ideological and institutional perspectives. Whereas some authors ask the question with the explicit goal of establishing a regime of ideal responsibility and affection between individual family members, others concentrate on defining the entity itself with the aim of producing culturally sanctioned family units by discouraging, if not disciplining, less acceptable ones. One might even think of the question – what is a family – as, quite literally, a cultural *idée fixe* in which the idea of family is constantly trying to be "fixed," as if it were in need of definitional repair, as if idea and practice have become unhinged. One need only look at abolitionist accounts of the ravaged family life (both black and white) on southern plantations or pro-slavery accounts of family life among workers in the industrialized north to see that, at least from the point of view of many Americans in the antebellum period, the family *was* in deep trouble. The sense that the family isn't what it used to be is the starting point for an impressively diverse range of textual offerings. To prove this point, one might peruse the speeches and writings of Frances Wright and John Humphrey Noyes, to name just two of the era's most (in)famous radical reformers, who sought to undermine the monogamous and exogamous cornerstones of the American family. Or, one could review the burgeoning advice literature of the period that instructed mothers and fathers, sisters and brothers, on their proper relations both within the family and without (sisters should be their brothers' consciences; brothers should be their sisters' protectors). Or, one might analyze the legal treatises that helped to develop the field of "domestic relations" law. Or, one could examine the many fictional attempts that aimed to translate into and make sense of a cultural experience of uncertainty within domestic relations through the realm of literary artistry, a realm ever hospitable to representations of precisely this kind of experience.

The unhinging of the biological family, whether through death, disagreement or *deus ex machina*, is a narrative fact as well as requirement underlying all of the novels I shall be discussing. I want to begin to outline my sense of the potential complexities of sentimental fictions by examining Hentz's *Ernest Linwood*, a classic example of a sentimental novel that so effectively and damningly diagnoses the instability of family relations that the damage done seems virtually incapable of being resolved, even as it tries to make the case for the future happiness of Gabriella, the main character, based on her marriage and motherhood. "Is domestic happiness a houseless wanderer?" (225), Gabriella asks her "second mother" (118), Mrs. Linwood, during a particularly difficult patch with her crazed husband, Ernest, her "adopted brother" (106) en route to becoming "a faithless guardian" (266) and eventually declaring himself "not worthy to be called thy husband" (459). Characters are profoundly unsure of what their relations are to one another, and with good reason. The plot of Hentz's novel hinges on two connected facts. The first, and one that will make its appearance in Lydia Maria Child's *The Romance of the Republic* and Mark Twain's *Pudd'nhead Wilson*, is that Gabriella's father's mother "was not able to distinguish the one [twin brother] from the other" (436) – Gabriella's father is named Henry Gabriel; her uncle is named Gabriel Henry. And, the second is that Gabriella's mother, Rosalie, when confronted with a marriage certificate that seems proof positive of her husband's bigamy, doesn't read the evidence carefully enough (nor do most readers, I would venture to guess), not "notic[ing] in the marriage certificate the difference between the names of Henry Gabriel and Gabriel Henry St. James" (440). So an identity between brothers makes possible the future confusions, which include Gabriella mistaking her uncle for her father, Richard (the child of Gabriel Henry) mistaking Gabriella for his sister, and a litany of relational ambiguities that is rivaled, perhaps, only by *Pierre*.

Before moving on to them, though, it should give one pause that in a novel where the grief over the loss of a mother is described as "immortal, as the love of which it is born" (16), the plot originates from the fact that a mother can't distinguish between her twin children. Although it is the case that Richard, Gabriella's childhood friend, who has himself been adopted, remarks, "I had a mother once, – she, too, is gone. The world may contain for us many friends, but never but one mother, Gabriella" (76), the truth of the matter is that mothers are ubiquitous, and so are brothers, sisters, and fathers. Gabriella says, Ernest "watched me as the fond mother does the child" (272); elsewhere she describes herself in relation to her former teacher, Mr. Regulus, as "a child again, in my mother's presence" (312). As much as the novel fetishizes blood relations in passages such as "he was *my brother*" (386); "my sister, my dear sister" (391); "the sacred name of 'Father'" (430); "My daughter! let me repeat the name" (431), the fact is that the language of the text is working equally hard to destabilize and problematize the meaning of those designations. This is accomplished by making those terms that designate biological relations apply less to individual persons in a family and more to particular types of behavior that can be learned by anyone and applied to anyone.

That is to say, this inability not only to know what it means to be one's brother or sister, but even to be able to know who is one's brother or sister (or child or father) pervades the narrative, wreaking havoc on the characters who are trying to define the nature of their relatedness even as the available language to do so incessantly registers both its insufficiencies and excesses of meaning. "I don't know exactly how a brother feels," (86) says Richard. Gabriella similarly reflects, "I thought I regarded him as a brother; till now Edith convinced me I am mistaken" (122). In a fit of jealous rage, Ernest accuses Gabriella, "he was to you in the relation almost of a father" (332). At the novel's end, Gabriella tells Richard, "My father could not love you better if you were his own son; and surely no own brother could be dearer, Richard, than you are and ever will be to me" (454). The language of this last passage strains, through its negatives and hypotheticals, to get the connections (and the affections underlying them) right. This is best exemplified by the repetition of "own," a word that pervades a novel that is at once deeply suspicious of Ernest's allegedly "rightful owner[ship]" (288) of Gabriella, while at the same time clinging to an ideal of ownership that doesn't leave one feeling "annihilated" (17, 79, 161, 202, 294, 343).[10] Is it any wonder that Gabriella describes herself as if "I walked as one in a dream, doubting my own identity" (191)?

It seems clear that Hentz's concern with what is one's own has everything to do with losing one's name, specifically the moment when a woman marries, loses her name, becomes a possession of her husband and metamorphoses, in the words of eighteenth-century legal writer William Blackstone, into a *feme couverte*.[11] In considering the appropriateness of Edith's suitor, Julian, Mrs. Linwood remarks: "she loses her own identity in his ... but my daughter must take a stainless name, if she relinquish her own" (349–350). The legal status of *feme couverte* is explicitly invoked by Mrs. Linwood when she tells Gabriella, "well is it for you, that your own [name] is covered with one, which from generation to generation has been pure and honorable" (335). To be covered by the "exclusive Ernest Linwood" (282) – he says to Gabriella, "I claim you as my own" (230) – is, however, tantamount to being destroyed as he wipes out everything and everyone in his path, including Gabriella. In contrast to the "sympathy and compassion" (408) of Mrs. Brahan, or "the heartfelt sympathy and affection" (416) communicated to Gabriella by Mrs. Linwood, or Edith's "sweet, unaffected sympathy" (54), all of which make Gabriella stronger, "to dwell in sympathy" (128) with Ernest is to be loved "almost to suffocation" (241). Rather than a "golden chain of sympathy which binds together the great family of mankind" (46), Ernest's sympathy can only extend itself to one person who is then rendered incapable of receiving sympathy from or dispensing sympathy to anyone else. Indeed, in one of the novel's many climaxes, Mrs. Linwood's "guardianship" (363) of Gabriella must be reestablished in order that the "exclusive and jealous" (253) Ernest can learn how to live in a world where consanguineous relations are constantly being "supplanted" (189, 325, 359, 442) by relations based on affection, even as those relations based on blood are continually being offered up as ideal.

To counter the annihilation of identity experienced by Gabriella, the novel strives to produce identity as inherently multiple and unlocatable: if identity is no longer distinguishable (the problem that catapults the plot to begin with) by the novel's end, it is not because persons can't be told apart as much as because what tells them apart is not a matter of consanguinity but love. When Gabriella sees her father she states, "I knew it was my father, because he met all the wants of my yearning filial nature, because I felt him worthy of honor, admiration, reverence, and love" (433). And when Gabriella describes Richard to her father, she says, "He is gifted with every good and noble quality, every pure and generous feeling – friend, brother, cousin – it matters not which – he will ever be the same to me" (433). Even gender is potentially complicated as Richard "combine[s] the tenderness of a daughter with the devotion of a son (447), and Gabriella's father clasps her to his bosom "with all a father's tenderness, and all a mother's love" (445). This multiplicity of identity (and identifications) allows Gabriella to escape the logic of ownership that produces in her a sense that "I wanted room" (191) and in Ernest a sense that "there is no room for more" (251) – even for children.[12] Only by relinquishing what is, perhaps, one's "own" (one's self, one's mother, one's place in a family) can one escape being possessed by others. That is why at the end of the novel, Richard is welcomed into the Linwood home "like a long absent son and brother" (356), Gabriella is treated by Mrs. Brahan "as if she were another Mrs. Linwood" (405), the same woman whom Gabriella has earlier described as a "second mother" (118), and Julian, Edith's fiancé, "seemed to cherish for him [Gabriella's father] even parental affection" (449). The fungibility of relations is sympathy's ideal manifestation.

In fact, all along Gabriella has wanted Richard to "transfer to Edith the affections given to me" (304). That specific wish has not been granted, but the more general *desideratum* has been accomplished, as the novel concludes with him waiting to "find another Gabriella" (465). Although Ernest calls Gabriella "my own and only love" (459) at their moment of reconciliation, suggesting that a problem persists, we are meant to believe that Ernest has made peace with this new world order. Mrs. Linwood hopefully forecasts that Gabriella's "second bridal morn will be fairer than the first" (448), and this seems to be corroborated by the birth of their daughter, a second Rosalie. Gabriella is now mother to her mother, at least in name, and Ernest has made room for someone else, all of which suggests the necessity of supplanting the first order of things, whether it is one's marriage, one's mother, or one's self, in order to find happiness the second time around.

Although I shall go into greater length about the potential ideological consequences of Hentz's validation of the secondary order of relations in Chapter 3 (she was an avid defender of slavery), it is important to register here that slavery represents the perverse culmination of such domestic disorder. It functions, at times, although not in the case of *Ernest Linwood*, within sentimental fictions as a dark reminder of the potential consequences of denying the affective value of consanguinity. In developing the case against the family as biologically understood, sentimental fictions risked a critique of family that overlapped with defenses of slavery which sought to validate the institution on precisely the grounds that affections could be disarticulated from blood or, to put it another way, that affections could be transferred from biological parent to *in loco parentis*. This is exactly the position occupied by *Uncle Tom's Cabin*. The text is torn between advancing an argument which, on the one hand, upholds the limitless capacity of persons to love one another regardless of race, gender, age, politics, biology, as we assert our collective membership in the family of Christ, and, on the other hand, an argument which urges the sanctity of individual families and the absolute validity of the bonds of blood. The tension is particularly keen because Stowe's critique of slavery absolutely demands a withdrawal from the sentimental novels' experimentation with alternative kinds of family. For Stowe, the only available model for a family that is not based on the affective ties of consanguinity is the family (or non-family) produced by slavery.

Uncle Tom's Cabin is thus preoccupied with the point at which affection will not be transferred, even as it makes the case for the transferability of love. For example, Mammy loves Eva, and it is Mammy, not Mommy, who unconditionally accepts the little girl's repeated embraces. But only pages later, we learn that Marie has separated Mammy from two children of her own, and she "has always kept up a sort of sulkiness about this."[13] Similarly, at the same time as Tom and Eva's relationship deepens, and Tom appears content with his life at the St. Clare mansion, the narrator reminds us that "Tom's home-yearnings had become so strong" that he undertakes to write a letter to "my poor old woman and my little chil'en" (348). Although Tom tells George Shelby that "the Lord gives good many things twice over; but he don't give ye a mother but once" (172), the machinations of slavery declare otherwise.

The incessant circulation of slave children and their mothers and fathers, along with the claim that their affections are easily redirected, enacts a defiant refusal to respect the consanguineous ties of slaves except insofar as the blood of the slave mother can be marketed for the master's profit. Topsy is, of course, the most powerful example of this. Not only does she respond to Miss Ophelia's question, "who was your mother?" with the words, "never had none" (355), but Topsy even states on two occasions that she "never was born" (355, 356).[14] In response to this devastating negation of the slave's bodily origins, Stowe insists upon their validity, indeed their absolute value and thus, the definitive rule of consanguinity. This stance has been taken to indicate Stowe's inability to move beyond the racial (and racist) essentialism of her day, and I do not dispute the presence of textual evidence that reveals Stowe's inability to transcend problematic aspects of her cultural context, whether it be her representation of mulattos and full blacks or her suggestion that freed slaves, once educated, go to Liberia.[15] I would like to suggest, however, that another way to read her insistence upon the racial make-up of slaves' bodies is to see it as an attempt to halt the pernicious traffic in slavery that attempts to erase the biological (black) mother's love for her children (and vice-versa), even as that traffic fully depends upon cashing in on the visibility of her body. It is crucial for Stowe, that slavery not appropriate everything – even as it is "*appropriating . . . body and bone, soul and spirit*" (340), to quote St. Clare's brother, Alfred – particularly the child's love for his/her biological mother. As critics have noted, this defense of consanguinity all too easily maps onto racist presumptions of biological destiny and therefore qualifies what Elizabeth Barnes calls "Stowe's version of political correctness" (16). Yet, to claim as Barnes does, that Stowe's appeal to "feel right" is "an ultra-conservative move" (16) by virtue of "sympathy's homogenizing function" (97) simplifies her position because racial difference is the sign of the black maternal body and as such is indispensable to Stowe's critique of slavery. Slavery's most heinous appropriation, from Stowe's perspective, is the theft of the love between a mother and a child. George Fitzhugh, to take one of the more influential defenders of slavery, argues for the benevolent necessity of abrogating the mother/child bond and replacing it with the master/slave bond in order to protect the slaves' "natural and inalienable right to be slaves." Louisa McCord similarly contends that, "we love our negroes; not as a miser loves his gold; but rather as a father loves his children . . . The grey-haired negro, who watches with pride the growth of his baby-master, exulting in his lordly air, and glorying, more perhaps even than the parent."[16] With love like this, the pro-slavery argument goes, what child needs her mother or father (in cases where the father is not the master)? Stowe's deployment of sympathy fixes this misappropriation and perversion of inalienable rights by restoring that love to its rightful owners.

II "WE ARE ALL ORPHANS." (*RENA; OR, THE SNOW BIRD*)[17]

There is a compulsive absence of mothers and fathers in antebellum literature. Ishmael lays claim to being America's most renowned literary orphan; Pearl, the most well-known bastard; Topsy, the most bereft slave child who "never had no father nor mother" but "was raised by a

speculator" (356). From the most canonical to the least, from the protagonist to the most minor of characters, the configurations of domestic
disarray are virtually endless. Gerty begins life without a mother and a
father, or so it seems, until the very end of *The Lamplighter* when her absent
father resurfaces to claim his daughter's love. The opening chapter of Mary
Jane Holmes's *Ethelyn's Mistake* explains that Ethelyn lives with her Aunt
Barbara, the "half-sister of Julia [Ethelyn's biological mother]" who, eighteen years earlier, "had come home to die."[18] The premature death of
Marcus Warland's mother means that his alcoholic father raises both son
and daughter until Mr. and Mrs. Bellamy come to their rescue, demanding
in exchange for their guardianship that Marcus obliterate his biological
paternity (at least in public) in order that he "should be considered as his
[Mr. Bellamy's] adopted son" (117). E.D.E.N. Southworth's *Ishmael, or in
the Depths* presents yet another tale of paternal failure in which Ishmael's
mother dies in childbirth after having been abandoned by the man she
married in a secret ceremony, leaving the child with only his mother's last
name and the tarnish of bastardy. Even when parents start out alive and
well, it is only a matter of time (usually just a few pages, at most a few
chapters) until the child loses one or both of them. Ellen's mother's illness
requires that she and Mr. Montgomery leave their daughter, in effect
bringing about a figurative death before their actual one. Ida May is barely
introduced to the reader before we learn of the "impending separation
from [her] mother" (10). The first paragraph of Holmes's *Dora Deane*
concludes with the words, "she looked upon that pale, sick mother, and
thought how soon she would be gone!" (1) Similarly, even before her
mother dies, Gabriella feels "as if the doom of the motherless were already
mine" (30). Sometimes the separation makes little sense, other than to get
the child away from the parents by whatever means necessary, as in the case
of *Vara, Child of Adoption*, where Vara's parents send her away from what
seems to be a perfectly delightful home in the Pacific Islands to be raised by
strangers in America. And this list doesn't even begin to take into account
the narratives of slaves for whom the dissolution of domestic bonds was the
constant threat and often painful reality of their lives.

These separations of parent and child constitute the foundational plot
mechanism upon which so many sentimental texts depend.[19] They provide
the conflict which initiates the protagonist's journey from child to adult,
from psychic despair to emotional confidence, from the bonds of consanguinity to affections based on choice. This is not to say, however, that there
are not plenty of other characters more than willing to take the place of the
temporarily lost or permanently departed parents; in fact, quite the reverse

is true. There are far more aunts and uncles, guardians and wards, adoptive parents and adopted children than living biological mothers and fathers. Why?

Perhaps the most obvious response would be to quote the famous opening sentence of *Anna Karenina,* "Happy families are all alike; every unhappy family is unhappy in its own way."[20] From Cinderella to Lemony Snicket, literature is preoccupied with families in shambles and children bereft of loving parents. Without some kind of tension within the family there would only be happy families and boring novels, leaving authors precious little with which to work. To be sure, conflict is a necessary ingredient in any fiction, but there is a compelling specificity to the conflict and resolution imagined by this body of literature. If one were to take a sampling of sentimental texts from this period, it is not so evident that, as Tolstoy would have it, these families are individuated by virtue of their unhappiness. In fact, quite the opposite seems to be true. With Pierre being a notable exception, the nature of their unhappiness is rather uniform. Biological parents are missing in action, for a variety of reasons, which leaves children in a state of unattached affiliation, forcing them to develop their inner resources with the external assistance of a second (sometimes, third, fourth, and so on) set of parental figures. Novel after novel, as the following chapters will demonstrate, takes as its primary subject matter this cast of substitute parents and their abilities to raise these newly made orphans. What particularly intrigues me is how their relative successes and failures as guardians, adopters, foster-mothers and father-figures tend to line up with the absence or presence of consanguinity. Once the biological bond with the parent is ruptured, the principle of consanguinity itself no longer has the force of destiny or the presumption of affection. The preferred "new parents" (51), to use Vara's phrase, are often those with whom no blood is shared.

The question of who should care for the child is thus a crucial one and provides us with a second reason for the ubiquitous presence of replacement parents. If the biological parent is unavailable, dead, or incompetent, who is most fit to educate, support, and develop the character of the child? When asking this question about the fiction, it is helpful to remember that this is the same period of time in which Elizabeth Peabody first advocated kindergarten as a necessary extra-familial mechanism that would facilitate the development of the child's character. Education reformer Horace Mann went so far as to demand that state schools "step in and fill the parent's place."[21] Also, it is worth keeping in mind that this is the era in which the legal notion of the "best interests of the child" was introduced as a means of establishing objective standards in order that judges could better determine where and to whom the child belonged. The preponderance of parental figures begins to make more sense and to take on greater cultural relevance if we think about sentimental fictions as similarly committed to ascertaining the "best interests of the child" and to implementing them. Thus, when Rena is removed from her parental roof to the home of her aunt in Hentz's *Rena; or, the Snowbird*, the narrator poses one of the central and ineluctable questions of the genre: "was Aunt Debby qualified for the charge"? (31)

Significantly, the novels do not recommend a state-sponsored system which would place children in orphanages, asylums, or poor houses. Rena's conniving foil, Stella Lightner, never recovers (until the last few pages of the novel) from the characterological damage done to her by spending her early years in an orphanage. Nor do the novels, for that matter, suggest communal structures such as those proffered by followers of any number of reform groups, including the Fourierists, the Shakers, or the Mormons. That is not to say, however, that the fictional community at large isn't caring for the child as various replacement parents undertake the responsibility of giving her their love and their home. That is to say that the middle-class home is *always* the proper place for the child, and it is just a matter of finding the right one. I should add that the right one does not necessarily come complete with its own set of biological parents. Ellen's eventual home is with the widower Mr. Humphreys and his two children; Gerty's with the widower Mr. Graham, who will remarry in the course of the narrative, and his daughter, Emily; Effie's (the main child in Hentz's *The Planter's Northern Bride*) is with her father and step-mother, Eulalia. Like the child's original family, which has been broken by separations of all kinds, the new one similarly bears evidence of damage, and it is often the case that its reconstitution, though well underway before the heroine appears, is fully effected through her incorporation into their household.

Given that a wrecking ball has seemed to make its way through a large percentage of fictional families, the inevitable question arises: what is it about the antebellum family that, in spite of its structural vulnerability and emotional imbalance, makes it the right place for the child? How can these novels both make the case for the insufficiency of the family and its insuperability? The fictions answer these questions by reconfiguring the organizational structure of the family and arriving at an expanded (and extended) definition of what a family is. Sentimental fictions make the argument that the production and dispensation of sympathy – also called feeling, sentiment, or affection – is the *raison d'être* of the family, and then decimate it by generic fiat. Yes, blood relations remain, usually in the form of aunts and uncles, but more often than not, they function as obstacles to the child's desired family, where consanguinity is happily missing. Love becomes the decisive criterion for the child's family, and biology, rather than being the surest indicator of love, acts as a hindrance to it. Cummins gently puts the case this way, "the tie of kindred blood is not always needed to bind heart to heart in the closest bonds of sympathy and affection" (141). Sentimental novels like *The Lamplighter*, and many others that I'll be discussing, then, establish a conflict between the family as defined according to the dictates of consanguinity as opposed to the family as organized according to a paradigm of contract. To put it baldly, the family's vulnerabilities are the consequences of blood; its strengths are the results of choice. The family thus remains the ideal institution in which to care for the child, but the fiction repeatedly represents the biological family as either inadequate (or unavailable) to the task. As I have already begun to suggest, this reconceptualization of what might be called the cultural work of the family is by no means limited to the sphere of antebellum literary production. Nor is the literature alone in helping to shift the value ascribed to family from an economic to emotional one or, as legal historian Michael Grossberg convincingly maintains, from a paternal to a maternal one. What is distinctive about the literature is its relentless representation of children being put in the position of having no viable biological parent to supervise their sentimental education.

As the above implies, a third reason is that the novels are reflecting a number of realities about family life in mid nineteenth-century American culture. People died at a much younger age in the antebellum period than at present. Women died more often in childbirth than they do today. Children died of diseases which now mean little more than a day in bed.[22] In addition, children more frequently served as apprentices in other families. Interestingly, these employment arrangements not only gave a child the opportunity to acquire skills which could then be used to increase the economic viability of her biological family but could have the additional effect of instilling in the child a sense that consanguinity need not be a requirement for family. This resulted, in some cases, in the child's desire to transform an apprenticeship into a parental relation. The broken, patchwork, permeable, even expansive condition of families in much of this literature thus suggests the limited availability of the ideal, biologically coherent family. What interests me about the fiction from this perspective is its willingness to explore alternative models of family given the inherent frailties of the human beings constituting it. Rather than reading the project of the literature as a preservation of an ideal bourgeois home, these texts concede its implausibility and then work to develop new structures of and criterion for affiliation, the most important being the sympathetic capacities of those stepping up to the childcare plate. Yes, a standard feature of these texts is the protagonist's nostalgic look back at the good old days of familial coherence, but there is a competing and overriding pragmatism in what they have to say about choosing new families. If the biological family must be broken in order to tell a story, as Tolstoy contends, many of these novels make the case that it need not, indeed cannot, be repaired in order to complete it. And good riddance to it.

This takes me to a fourth reason for the plethora of substitute parents in the fiction of the antebellum period. The literature is not simply reflecting a cultural preoccupation with defining the family but is participating in that project in an attempt to make sense of the changing complexion of the family, understood both as an institution and as constituted by the individual members within it. Like the production of adoption within domestic relations law, like advice manuals to new mothers, and like reformist tracts urging a shake-up in family organization, the novels take as their primary subject matter the fluctuating boundaries of the family and what, if anything, to do about them. Sometimes the novels arrive at conclusions similar to those offered in other areas of cultural production; sometimes they don't. *The Lamplighter* and *The Wide, Wide World*, though in different ways, embrace adoption as the mechanism that most effectively reflects the best interests of the child. *Pierre*, by contrast, represents an experimental household, on the order of utopian societies like John Humphrey Noyes's Perfectionists or Anne Lee's Shakers, in order to expose the impossibility of domestic arrangements based on anything other than consanguinity. Melville's, however, is no endorsement of traditionally configured families. Those fail too, leaving us with a novel that not only takes up the problem of the family but analyzes the problems with the solutions to it.

My point is that the generic parameters of literature, unlike the normative requirements of, say, advice manuals or judicial decisions, are flexible enough to mean that just because the novel comes to an end doesn't mean that all of the novel's relational ambiguities must be resolved. To be sure, many of these texts do just that and, as a result, tax our capacity for romantic coincidence and the timely resurfacing of yet one more deadbeat dad. Sentimental novels are often denounced on the grounds that their generic prescription requires an unthinking and conservative allegiance to marriage and the restoration of family order. Specifically, this interpretation fails to understand the complexities of these novels because it mistakes the texts' preoccupation with the lost biological family for a commitment to its preservation. More generally, the dominant position regarding sentimental fictions is unwilling to credit the genre either with the possibility of ideological complexity and range (other than the complexities of hegemony) or the capacity for critical self-consciousness. As a result, readers have become unable to see how sentimental novels might work with (and against) the demands of their genre and sometimes exceed their structural and ideological limitations.

Representations of marriage are a case in point, in that they are profoundly mixed. "Her marriage was a great mistake" (217) is the assessment of Ethelyn's marriage to Richard Markham in *Ethelyn's Mistake*, but this statement just as accurately represents a central fact about so many sentimental novels, for example, *'Lena Rivers, Ernest Linwood, Ishmael, or Self-Raised, Hagar, the Martyr*, and *The Wide, Wide World*. Many of these texts are not only predicated upon the failure of the marriage contract but are profoundly committed to establishing an alternative, expanded vision of family which loosens the tethers of consanguineous affiliation. In what follows, I shall consider several sentimental texts with the intention of delineating a set of narrative and rhetorical conventions that haven't been observed or appreciated by many readers of sentimental fictions, the most important being their willingness to entertain the possibility that the child's emotional life is best satisfied within relationships that are chosen according to the criterion of affection rather than those that are mandated by blood. Furthermore, I shall demonstrate that, like *Ernest Linwood*, these texts not only relish the ambiguity of family relations, but they enjoy the signifying possibilities of language, and even leave the reader with a sense of what Melville in *Billy Budd* called "the ragged edges" of human experience. Sentimental novels open themselves up to this kind of discursive analysis through their persistent manipulation of the terms of familial relations, which establishes the necessity for and the vocabulary of new structures of affiliation.[23]

III "AND YOU ARE 'LENA – 'LENA NICHOLS, THEY CALL YOU, I SUPPOSE."[24]

The question of 'Lena's name – "what is your name" (346) – drives the plot of Holmes's novel *'Lena Rivers*: "she calls herself 'Lena, but the 'tother name I don't know" (350). 'Lena's name has talismanic properties throughout the text. Characters don't simply call her 'Lena; they tell the reader that they are calling her 'Lena, as if, on some level, they are in doubt about the accuracy of the designation, as if aware of a mystery contained within it, as if cognizant of its basic lack and fundamental plethora of meaning. Thus, when characters refer to 'Lena, their words are marked by self-consciousness: "That young girl – 'Lena, I think you call her" (121) or "I called her by her name, 'Lena Rivers" (60). When Durward, 'Lena's love interest, comforts a melancholy 'Lena, the narrator writes, "he drew her gently toward him, trying to soothe her grief, calling her *'Lena*" (137) and later, while sleeping, he "breathes the name of *'Lena* in his dreams" (164). The words with which this section begins are spoken by 'Lena's uncle, who refers to his niece as 'Lena Nichols because, even though the child "was christened HELENA RIVERS; – the *'Lena* of our story" (13), the identity of 'Lena's father remains a mystery. When 'Lena is brought into her uncle's household, her well-disposed cousin, Anna, similarly observes, "Why, I thought her name was 'Lena Nichols" (60). We quickly learn that 'Lena's father abandoned the mother in the days before the birth of their child, but because they were married in a secret ceremony, doubts persist about the legitimacy of the marriage and, by extension, 'Lena. Interestingly, we also discover that 'Lena's uncle has changed his name from "*Mr. John Nichols*" (23) to Mr. John Livingstone because his baleful fiancée disliked his birth name. His father, upon his deathbed, issues this reproach: "how could you do so? 'Twas a good name – *my* name" (21).

The names of persons are a constant subject of inquiry, whether among the novel's characters or on the part of the narrator, who calls attention to names through italics, bold print, quotation marks, or repetition.[25] For example, when Mr. Graham, who marries 'Lena's mother using his middle name, Rivers, as his last name and turns out to be 'Lena's biological father, first meets 'Lena, we are told that "she wondered why he looked at her so long and earnestly, twice repeating her name – 'Miss Rivers – *Rivers*'" (119). The following exchange captures a similar preoccupation with names, but here the issue is their changeability. Upon overhearing Mr. Livingstone's son "calling her '*Lena*,'" Mr. Graham observes that she "is a fine-looking girl – 'Lena, I think your son called her?" The two men continue their conversation:

"Yes, or *Helena*, which was her mother's name."
"And her mother was your sister, Helena Livingstone?"
"No, sir, Nichols. I changed my name to gratify a fancy of my wife." (120)

Nichols is Livingstone, Graham is Rivers, and 'Lena is alternatively, Helena Rivers, 'Lena Nichols, 'Lena Rivers, *Miss Graham* (389), *Miss 'Lena Rivers Graham* (380), and, in the words of one of the slaves on Mr. Livingstone's plantation, "Miss 'Leny Yivers Gayum" to which Mr. Livingstone's son adds the name of 'Lena's fiancé, "Bellmont" (384) who, as sentimental convention would have it, turns out to be Mr. Graham's stepson, which is to say that 'Lena will be marrying her step-brother.

It should be noted that *'Lena Rivers* takes place on a Kentucky plantation called Maple Grove, upon which are found slaves like Corinda, who "didn't know what a *surname* meant" (56). 'Lena's grandmother, the elderly and crotchety Mrs. Nichols, accompanies the child from Massachusetts to a slave state and fancies herself an abolitionist, although she ends up abusing the slaves and believes that "we shall all be white in heaven" (69). Nevertheless, her allegedly progressive political beliefs are meant to be registered by her resolution to call the various slaves with whom she comes in contact by their full names. Thus, when Aunt Polly tells her that she was married to a man named Jeems, "this was not definite enough for Mrs. Nichols, who asked for the surname" (69). In a subsequent conversation with the Livingstones, she then refers to Aunt Polly as "*Miss Atherton*" (71), and the residents of Maple Grove have no idea to whom she is referring because, from their perspective, a slave could not possibly be a Miss Atherton. The self-conscious proliferation of the names of white characters, especially surnames, is countered by an aborted and somewhat feeble attempt to expand the names of black slaves, but Holmes seems to be unwilling, unable, and uninterested in developing a critique of a system that denies people a last name other than their master's.[26]

There are several more general things to say about this group of characters, a group whose numbers are small but whose names are many. First, the focus on names and their seemingly endless multiplication are standard fare for much sentimental fiction. Similar questions, as we shall see, circulate around Gerty's name in *The Lamplighter*, Ishmael's in *Ishmael, or in the Depths*, Ida's in *Ida May*, Ellen's in *The Wide, Wide World*, L'éclair's (or is it Florence or Rosa?) in *Marcus Warland*, and Hagar's in *Hagar, the Martyr*, whose last name we never learn. Second, the ambiguity of names is an obvious means both of generating the plot and its complications – if only Harry had the courage to reveal to 'Lena's mother his real last name! – and, I would submit, a mechanism for permitting characters an opportunity to generate themselves or, more precisely, new selves. For example, when John Nichols becomes John Livingstone, he leaves behind him the plodding ways and provincial manners of his New England parents to embrace the patrician world of the southern slaveowner; when Harry Graham first transforms himself into Harry Rivers, "he had no particular reason, except that it suited his fancy, and Rivers, he thought, was a better name than Graham" (359). Spurning his father's name clearly allows him to fall in love with Helena, a woman whom Harry Rivers can marry but not Harry Graham. In reversing that process, he then becomes the man who will marry the woman his father chooses for him, leaving behind the woman he loves.[27] The act of changing one's name, in other words, often represents an attempt to free oneself from the fetters not only of one's past actions but of one's biological origins, which are perhaps best signified by one's birth name.

Such nominative liberations are, however, usually reserved for men. That's not to say that women don't get to change their names. They do. This is, of course, an issue we have already seen in *Ernest Linwood* and one that will play a significant part in Fanny Kemble's *Journal*. But as these women writers make clear, the context is almost always the marriage ceremony in which she takes her husband's last name and becomes, in Blackstone's infamous theory of legalized female invisibility, a *feme couverte*. Overseen by the state, this change in a woman's name signifies a profound revision of her identity which, among other things, establishes her and her possessions as her husband's, and thus radically differs from the assertions of new identity of the "Call me Ishmael" variety that we see in much antebellum fiction. The uncertainty surrounding 'Lena's last name is the direct result of the ambiguity surrounding her mother's status: did she or didn't she marry Harry Rivers? Did she or didn't she legally assume Harry's last name? If she did, then 'Lena's paternity is (sort of) resolved and her last name is her father's (whatever that is); if she didn't, then 'Lena is a bastard.[28]

The answers to these straightforward questions are, obviously, not so clear-cut. Yes, she did marry, but she married a fictional someone who called himself Harry Rivers. And yes, she assumed what she assumed to be his last name, Rivers, but she kept the marriage a secret, which presumably means that she continued to go by her original surname. Certainly, there is a warning in all of this to Holmes's female audience. Don't marry on the sly because, like 'Lena (the mother), who, even though she "take[s] the precaution to procure from the clergyman, who had married her, a letter, confirming the fact" (11), you too will stand accused of unspeakable crimes. Furthermore, any evidence you might marshal in your defense will be undermined and subject to the accusation of forgery, which is what happens with 'Lena's mother's proof. Also, don't agree to a secret marriage because men can't be trusted to fulfill their husbandly obligations, unless they are made to by the combined pressures of the wife's family, the community, and the legal system.[29] Such pressures cannot be exerted if the marriage remains a secret. The message seems to be that one is better off taking one's chances with the legal protections of a *feme couverte*, inadequate as they may be, than trusting oneself to a husband who avoids publicly acknowledging his wife. I don't mean to suggest that the novel is making the case for remaining single, but the consummation of 'Lena and Durward's marriage is surrounded by so many unhappy and ill-fated unions, including their own parents', that there seems to be as much of a narrative pull away from as toward marriage. For example, not only does Mrs. Livingstone wish that "she had never married John Nichols" (47), but Mrs. Graham spends much of the novel in a jealous rage, convinced that both her husband and son are in love with 'Lena (215). As far as marriages among the younger set go, 'Lena's insidious cousin, Carrie, marries the much older Captain Atherton (who was willing to marry Anna, then 'Lena, then Carrie – so much for true love), only to spend the rest of their days occupying different residences. In addition, 'Lena's friend, Nellie, is "transformed into Nellie Livingstone" (409) when she weds John Livingstone, Jr. ('Lena's cousin). But this is only after 'Lena's other friend, Mabel, who was John Livingstone's Jr.'s first wife, is dead, having been destroyed by her husband's cruelty.

Thus, even though the plot of *'Lena Rivers* is clearly about solving the mystery of 'Lena's paternity, and it does so with the requisite amount of coincidence and completeness typical of sentimental fictions, it is also about the uncertainty, the vulnerability, and the unhappiness that can come with marriage, both for men and women, but especially for women. Although Mr. Graham is given the opportunity to right his paternal wrongs, his husbandly misdeeds cannot be fixed. Indeed, at the very moment of the absolute resolution of the child's parentage – "*that man* – was – 'Lena's father" (399) – the novel calls attention to the profound indeterminacy of his relation with 'Lena's mother. He is "the husband or something of Helleny Nichols" (399). Even at the conclusion of the novel, then, 'Lena's mother is still referred to by her original surname, as if all the clarifications in the world don't have the power to legitimate her secret marriage and bestow upon her a new name. And, of course, the phrase, "or something," captures perfectly an ambiguity in 'Lena's parent's marriage that won't go away, no matter how neatly the novel has tied up the confusing history of her paternity.

IV "A RELATION OF YOURN, MEBBY?" (*'LENA RIVERS*, 366)

When 'Lena arrives at Maple Grove, she feels that there is "no affinity whatever between herself and the objects around her" (57). This applies to persons as well for when 'Lena attempts to befriend her cousin, Carrie, and is promptly rejected, the narrator remarks, "there was no affinity between

them" (104). In a novel in which characters are identified and identifiable
only through the language of family relation, it is simply not possible for
there to be no affinity. Virtually everyone in *'Lena Rivers* is related ('Lena
and Carrie are cousins), if not by blood than by marriage and if not by
marriage than by choice. For example, Joel Slocum, a minor character with
major impact, not only is able to explain away Durward's anxieties about
his father's seeming romantic interest in 'Lena but, in the process, reveals
himself to be Durward's fourth cousin. "Captain Atherton is related to
Nellie" (66), Mabel is "a sort of cousin" (66), Durward "was Nellie's
cousin" (184), Nellie's father refers to Nellie and Mabel as "both his
daughters" (204), even though Mabel is an orphan, and Mary always called
Nellie, "her sister" (197), even though they're not sisters. A funny instance
of the inescapability of consanguinity (real or imposed) or more precisely,
the language of consanguinity, occurs when 'Lena's grandmother hears that
Durward has "got *Noble* blood in him" and remarks, "I used to know a
family of Nobles in Massachusetts, and I think like as not he's some kin!"
(86) Such discursive assumptions of kinship are, as we shall see, a standard
feature of sentimental fictions. Indeed, in the case of 'Lena and Mr.
Graham, the question is not whether they are related, but how. Thus,
when they first lay eyes on each other, 'Lena thinks that he is "just such a
man as she could wish *her* father to be" (35) and later wishes "that she were
[Durward's] sister, and the daughter of his father" (36). When 'Lena has
finally been exiled from the Livingstone household, on the grounds of her
alleged affair with Mr. Graham, Durward finds her in a state of manic
despair. The narrator reports, "it was in vain Durward strove to convince
her of his identity . . . he finally desisted, and suffered her to think he was
her cousin" (354). The passage ends with his temporary departure and
'Lena "stretching her arms toward him as a child toward its mother" (354).
In the course of the narrative, Durward has morphed from brother to lover
to cousin to mother to husband. Mr. Graham has a similar relational
trajectory. When Durward finds his father visiting 'Lena and expects to
receive confirmation of their mutual love, he is surprised to discover that
"her face was as calm and unruffled as if the visitor had been her uncle"
(220). Mr. Graham goes from fantasy father to alleged lover to uncle to
"near relative" (236) to biological father.

Amidst this panoply of identities, another kind of relation presents itself
and is roundly rejected: Mr. Graham as the adoptive father of his biological
daughter. His cowardly reluctance to tell Mrs. Graham (who, by the way, is
on her second husband and had a child with her first) not only that she's
not his first wife but that he had 'Lena with a woman he secretly married,

leads him to the conclusion that adopting 'Lena might solve the problem of bringing 'Lena into his family and avoiding the unpleasant consequences of exposing her (and his) true identity to Mrs. Graham. Thus, in a conversation with 'Lena's grandmother, he announces, "I should be proud to call her my daughter" (128). Shortly thereafter he tells Mrs. Livingstone, "I have taken a great fancy to Miss Rivers, and would like to adopt her as my daughter" (143), and then informs his wife that 'Lena is "just the kind of person I would like to have round – just such a one as I would wish my daughter to be if I had one. In short, I like her, and with your consent I will adopt her as my own" (143–144). To be sure, Mrs. Graham's rationale for opposing the adoption reveals the limitations of her character. She assumes that he wants 'Lena in his house so as "to make love to" (144) her and should his suit be unsuccessful, she alludes to 'Lena's "doubtful parentage" (144), and the threat she poses should Durward want to make love to her. Notwithstanding these obstacles, the fact is that adopting his biological daughter solves Mr. Graham's problem but not 'Lena's. On the one hand, he would become her father and, legally speaking, she would be transformed into his daughter. She, on the other hand, would get to call him her father and even get the right last name that her mother never got – Graham – but the "dark mystery of her birth" (83) would continue to haunt her and compromise her marital prospects. She would become 'Lena Graham not because that is who she is (although *that is* who she is) but because that is who the act of adoption makes her. She would remain unacknowledged and the cowardly Mr. Graham would maintain his secret as the unacknowledged biological father and miscreant husband of 'Lena's mother. Adoption is the mechanism that allows the first marriage to be kept a secret, and therefore it must be rejected. Mr. Graham can't be permitted to say, "if I had a daughter," because the denial of paternity contained in that phrase perpetuates the lie that has caused so much of 'Lena's misery. He can't be allowed to pretend that she is not his (in a biological sense) in order, then, to claim her as his (in an adoptive sense). In refusing adoption as an option, the novel forces Mr. Graham not only to claim his daughter but to acknowledge his first marriage with 'Lena's mother.

Sentimental fictions are fascinated with adoption. Although my close reading of *The Lamplighter* in Chapter 2 will examine the legal history of adoption law, an antebellum development that occurred at precisely the moment that so many of these novels were being conceptualized and written, I want here to suggest some of the many ways in which the literature explores the narrative and ideological possibilities presented by adoption. It appears in virtually every text in the genre, and although this observation has been made before, its importance has yet to be fully examined.³⁰ The case of 'Lena is instructive because it so clearly enforces the line between a biological and adoptive parent. Simply put, when it comes to your own child, if you're one, you can't be the other. To try and adopt your own child is to reject the claims of consanguinity. Thus, although Mr. Graham's desire to adopt 'Lena, in part, indicates his love for her, it also reflects his wish to avoid the consequences of his abandonment of 'Lena's mother. This is not to imply that consanguinity trumps adoption as the deepest form of love. Indeed, the fact is that an adoptive parent can fill the place of a biological one, but the reverse is not true. In much of this fiction, adoption functions as signifier of ideal affection. Adoption signifies the most profound expression of an adult's love for a child, because it is based on choice rather than necessity, and as such is it what biological parents can't do.³¹

Mr. Graham is the exception that proves the following rule: the desire to adopt the child protagonist stands as one of the most powerful and reliable means of registering an adult character's integrity and capacity for love. Not wanting to adopt the heroine, as in the case of Mrs. Graham and Mrs. Livingstone, is the outward manifestation of a deeply flawed interior. It is also true that the worth of the child's character can be measured by what we might call her "adoptability." Her (or his) moral and spiritual value can be gauged by the extent to which she creates in the adults with whom she comes in contact the desire to adopt her.

The chapters that follow will devote much time to a reading of the fascinating stories of Gerty's, Ellen's, and Ida May's adoptions, but let me briefly allude to some other texts in which adoption plays an important part so as to give some idea of its generic centrality. In the first moments of Marcus Warland's meeting with the Bellamys, no sooner does Mr. Bellamy speak the words, "if I had such a son" (25) and Mrs. Bellamy "has been entreating me to adopt a little girl" (55), than the discursive and affective groundwork has been established for Marcus and Katy to become their "adopted children" (68). The threads of Hagar's story are disentangled at the conclusion of *Hagar, the Martyr,* once we learn that Hagar's uncle "adopted her [, and] his wife became a mother to her" (341). When a baby boy, who has survived an accident at sea, and his less fortunate dead mother wash ashore the Maine coast in Stowe's *The Pearl of Orr's Island,* the question of adoption is soon raised – "I should n't wonder, said Miss Roxy, if Cap'n Pennel should adopt it" – and quickly resolved. The child is given, appropriately enough, the name of Moses, and the narrator remarks, "what change of destiny was then going on for him in this simple formula of adoption, none could tell." No sooner has the childless and kind-hearted Countess Hurstmonceux, in Southworth's *Ishmael, or in the Depths*, solved the mystery of Ishmael's paternity than she claims him as "my son by marriage and by adoption" (vol I, 142). Although this adoption is rejected by Ishmael's Aunt Hannah (for reasons having to do with the preservation of Ishmael's mother's integrity), the "motherly" (318) Countess does manage to adopt Claudia, another main character in the novel: "I adopted her. I told her that I should be her mother until the arrival of her father" (vol. II, 333). The true character of Aunt Debby in *Rena* is established through the mechanism of adoption. Although at first, she seems like an unfeeling and unlovable old crank, the fact is that "she had conceived the idea of adopting the child [Rena] as her own" (32). Therein lies the key to her character, and in the course of the narrative we see her rediscover her capacity to love and be loved, as she becomes Rena's "other mother" (177) and Rena becomes "the child of her adoption" (272). In fact, the depravity of Rena's adversary, Stella, is registered not only by the unwillingness of others to adopt her, but by her misguided hope that adoption will prove her ticket out of poverty: "some rich gentleman might take pity on her and adopt her" (154).[32]

We are accustomed to reading sentimental novels in terms of their commitment to an enclosed biological family, but the essential status accorded to adoption suggests that other ideological commitments are in play. Maternity may be the originary *ne plus ultra* of affection, as many of the advice manuals suggest, but novel after novel insists not only on the absolute unavailability of mother love (she's dead), but then goes on to posit the love signified by the act of adoption as a secondary order of ideal love; sometimes, even going so far as to maintain the superiority of adoptive love precisely because it is not based on consanguinity. To be sure, *'Lena Rivers* insists on a recognition of affinity in the face of denial, but it also produces adoption as a trope for ideal affection. Establishing the presence of consanguineous ties is, in other words, different from affirming their superiority. Many of these narratives are being pulled in two opposite directions, both of which seem to be generic inevitabilities. On the one hand, the requirements of consanguinity must be satisfied and, on the other, contractual forms of affection, like adoption, must be incorporated.

V "WHICH LOT WOULD YOU CHOOSE FOR A CHILD?" (*THE SABLE CLOUD*, 126)[33]

This is the question posed in Nehemiah Adams's politically noxious novel *cum* Socratic dialogue which outlines the merits of slavery in a series of didactic conversations between the barely disguised Adams, the Mr. C. of the narrative, and a Massachusetts family with abolitionist inclinations. Adams, a New England minister turned southern sympathizer, offers the usual menu of explanations and justifications as to why slavery is a superior system of governing people who have been cursed by God, who are more able to endure hard labor than whites, who become better Christians by virtue of slavery, and who were slaves anyway when they were first kidnapped from Africa. In this passage, he asks the northern parents, allegorically named A. Freeman North and his wife, Mrs. North, whether they would prefer that their daughter be "a servant in a Southern family, brought up as a playmate with the children, a sharer in many of their gifts, a partner with their parents, as the children grew up, in the pride and joy of the parents, an honored member of the wedding party . . . [and] not in a pauper establishment, but in her owner's home, and when the parents die, if she survives, taken by some branch of the family" or "for the sake of 'priceless liberty,' 'heaven's best gift to man,' would you prefer to see her seated under the iron fence of a park . . . and sleeping you not know where" (125–126). The words designating possession are instructive of Adams's larger aim. There is a purposeful ambiguity, for example, in Adams's use of "the" and "their." Exactly whose parents is he talking about? And if "their" parents are the parents of the white family, where are the slave's parents? And why would slave children give up the biological partnership with "their parents" in order to be partners with the parents of the white children?

Clearly, Adams wants to render the slave children's parents irrelevant to the economic and psychic well-being of the slave child. Far better to have the certainty of being in one's "owner's home" than trying to preserve or to make one's own, at least in the case of slave children. Adams thus uses the vulnerabilities of the northerner's white child to make the argument that "it is far better for them [slaves] to be owned than to be free" (130). The analogy, in other words, gets deployed in order to argue for the benefits of slavery and the liabilities of freedom, but only, it turns out, in the case of blacks. Black children and white children, in this example, are similar only up to the point at which they become adults and the former become the latter's slaves. The notion that slavery is the best expression of sympathy for an unprotected child gets produced first by a momentary recognition of likeness (white children and black children are similarly vulnerable), which is then disavowed by claims of their absolute difference: "some are so constituted by an all-wise God that they are happier to be in subordinate situations" (151). In the words of the anti-slavery turned pro-slavery

Mrs. North, "He is not persuading us to be slaves rather than free" (133). The "us" is, of course, key in that it constitutes a "them" for whom freedom is a dangerous and ill-conceived proposition. Given the protections afforded by their master's parents, slaves and slave children (there is no difference between them from Adams's point of view, because clearly all slaves *are* children, and "it is a privilege to the blacks to have owners" [122]), have the good fortune never to find themselves in the position of the sentimental protagonist, ejected into the wide, wide world of strangers who are also potential loved ones and adoptive parents. Having had the luck to be visited upon by the curse of Ham, to invoke a popular pro-slavery sentiment, the slave gets to have a master who "is a guardian and provider" (130) for life.

The sentimental story of a child being adopted by a set of substitute parents is thus rendered irrelevant in Adams's view of slavery because all slaves are, in effect, adopted. Such a sleight of hand is beyond insidious because, legally speaking, adoption, like marriage, was a contract not extended to slaves who were considered chattel and therefore incapable not only of making contracts but of being members of legally recognized families.[34] It is, therefore, particularly interesting that Adams begins his defense of slavery, a defense that holds that "there is no form or condition of service in the world which has more effect than slavery to keep families together" (142), with a classically sentimental tableau of a mother stricken by the death of her child. The stricken mother, Mary, however, is not Kate, the biological mother, but rather her owner, and it is Mary's tearful response to the death of Cygnet, the slave child, that becomes the jumping-off point for Adams's pro-slavery polemic. Mr. C. sends his friend, Mr. North, a letter in which Mary grieves over Kate's loss. Puzzled and somewhat undone by the representation of "this lady's tears for the mother of this little black babe" (9), Mr. North seeks to understand how it is possible for this owner of slaves to have "these yearnings of compassion" (5) for slaves. Initially, Mr. North "cannot conceive how being 'owned' is anything but a curse" (15), although he is eventually converted to the idea that far from inhibiting attachments and sympathies from being formed, the ownership of (black) persons helps to develop the sympathies of their (white) masters. Mary's sympathies are, after all, prompted by the fact that she, too, has lost a child. And yet we are also told that it is wrong when, "on thinking of being 'a slave,' we immediately make the case our own, and imagine what it would be for us to be in bondage to the will of another" (73). Sympathy seems to be operating according to a transgressive model of identification, until we realize that what Mary's sympathy does is to turn the black child into, quite literally, her own. Not only is Kate's child as much, if not more than, Mary's child, Kate herself "is a slave-mother belonging to" (3) Mary and, since the child follows the condition of the mother, Cygnet is Mary's too: her child and her slave. Thus, she mourns. Stowe's iconic belief in motherhood as the embodiment of a universal sympathy that ought to bring about the end of slavery is here translated into the disappearance of black motherhood and the universalization of white motherhood.[35] Although Mr. North initially rejects the view that "Kate's relation to [Mary] is as gentle and pleasant, almost, as that of an adopted member of a family, who is half attendant, and half companion" (20), he comes to accept the view that masters are the guardians of the slaves whom they've adopted. Slaves are, for all intents and purposes, always already "almost" adopted. According to Adams, they are best served by remaining in a perpetual state of guardianship, even as they themselves become mothers and fathers. Until they escape or, in the case of Child's *The Romance of the Republic*, until they are adopted.[36]

What happens when the adopted child is a slave is the question around which Child's story of racial "entanglement," to borrow an often-used term from the novel, revolves.[37] The intricacies of the plot mirror the perversions of slavery as Rosa and Flora, the two protagonists, grow up in what seems to be a world elsewhere only to discover, upon the death of their father (their mother is, of course, already dead), that they are slaves. Indeed, Child takes the opportunity, on several occasions, to invoke the pernicious law which states that "'the child follows the condition of the mother'" (50, 182, 390). Initially, the women are saved from the auction-block by Rosa's beloved, but treacherous, Gerald Fitzgerald, who marries her in a sham wedding ceremony and takes the two sisters to a hidden cottage near his Georgia plantation where he will eventually bring his legally recognized Caucasian wife, Lily Bell, and keep the two sisters – his slaves – as his concubines. Once his perfidious intentions make themselves apparent (his affections for Rosa wane as his interest in Flora increases), both girls manage to escape, though to separate destinations and without knowledge of one another's whereabouts (in fact, Rosa thinks Flora is dead). In time, they are reunited. First, they are adopted.

Although several chapters of my analysis will be devoted to an in-depth analysis of how slavery is a key player in the self-imaginings of sentimental novels, the issue is relevant here for several reasons. First, it is worth pointing out that the generic conventions of sentimental novels become the logical messengers for Child's anti-slavery polemic. Biological parents die, names change, and substitute parents assume center stage with the primary intention of making the case against slavery. Rosa and Flora's father must die in order to critique a system that puts the fate of children in the hands of masters who will do anything for profit. The girls are constantly changing their names, not because their paternity is in doubt, but to escape the consequences of their maternal ancestry. And replacement parents emerge so as to contrast true expressions of parental love from the bastardization of that love, which is the effect of slavery.

Second, adoption is the fictional mechanism that begins the process of healing the racial crimes perpetrated in the name of slavery. It should come as no surprise, given our discussion above, that adoption plays a key role in Child's story and that it represents the distillation of sympathy's potential. When Flora escapes from Gerald's clutches, she becomes the "adopted daughter" (146) of the puritanical, but kindly, Mrs. Delano, a Bostonian who has thought little of slavery until she meets Flora while in Georgia, becomes enchanted with her, and then learns of her family connection with Alfred Royal, the man with whom she, as a young girl, fell in love but was forbidden to marry. Mrs. Delano's confession, "Ah, Flora, I wish you were my daughter," (94) is soon followed by the announcement, "you shall live with me, and be my daughter" (105). Despite Flora's anxiety that her identity as a slave makes her unadoptable – and legally speaking, it does – Mrs. Delano doesn't hesitate to become her "dear new Mamita" (105). Child uses the mechanism of adoption to portray the radicalizing possibilities of sympathy.

The case of Rosa is similar. She, too, gets away from the horrible Gerald and flees to Europe with old family friends, Mamma Balbino (née Madame Guirland) and Papa Balbino (née Signor Papanti), who pronounces himself Rosa's "adopted father" (236) while fending off Gerald's intrusions. The plot gets even more complicated when we learn that Rosa, in a fit of what she "hope[s] was insan[ity]" (352) has switched her baby, who is destined for a life in slavery, with Lily Bell's. Rosa's husband, the heroic Alfred King, takes care that all of these "entanglements" get resolved: not only does he accept Rosa's biological son (who has been raised by Lily Bell), saying "you are my step-son, you know . . . you may rely upon me as an affectionate father" (359), but he embraces Lily Bell's biological son and his wife (who have been living as fugitive slaves) and makes them a part of the family. Adoption is both an admission that the family is in ruins because of slavery at the same time as adoption is, from Child's point of view, an antidote to the ravages inflicted upon the domestic lives of slaves. Unlike Twain's vision of racial relations in *Pudd'nhead Wilson*, which I shall take up in the Afterword, Child's novel visualizes a fully miscegenated and liberated national family, with adoption playing a pivotal role in bringing about that ideal.

Third, adoption is an essential aspect of the cure because it represents, as it does in the context of *Marcus Warland, Rena, Ishmael, or in the Depths,* and *'Lena Rivers,* the deepest expression of sympathy. But even more so in the case of Child, I would maintain, because slavery signifies the most complete absence of sympathy conceivable. If the recognition of related-ness constitutes the first step in the sympathetic process, then slavery doesn't even get that far as whites get to be human beings while blacks are consigned to the category of chattel. Adoption, by contrast, extends the sphere of who counts as related by transcending the limits of consanguin-eous identification. Thus, if one understands slavery as the willful perver-sion, disavowal, and rupture of the bonds of consanguinity, adoption might well be considered slavery's opposite. Child's novel represents a vision of family no longer burdened by the cruel mandate of blood or, more precisely, the one-drop rule, as the adoptive assumption of kinship leads to the expansion of family, its reconfiguration based on choice, and the seemingly unexpected linkage of contract and sympathy. Once con-tracts in which African-Americans were not permitted to enter, such as adoption, as well as marriage, now become available to all, then sympathy becomes an attribute not solely (or necessarily) underwritten by biology but entered into by choice.

Sentimental fictions are about the relative merits of consanguineous and contractual ties in the emotional life of the child. They are about finding the right place where sympathy flourishes and understanding that place and those people as one's home, as one's family. The *locus classicus* of sympathy may be in the arms of one's biological mother, as *Uncle Tom's Cabin* tirelessly points out, but the more relevant issue for the preponder-ance of sentimental novels seems to be what to do and where to go in the absence of that maternal embrace. In response to that lack, sympathy is mobilized on behalf of the orphaned child, traveling across blood lines, geographical lines, and even across racial ones in the case of Child.[38] The accession of contract as an ideal of sympathy is, in fact, the story told in Cummins's sentimental blockbuster *The Lamplighter,* which, incidentally, makes an appearance in *'Lena Rivers* when the narrator describes one of the main characters as "so absorbed in the fortunes of 'Uncle True and little Gerty'" (251). Those fortunes are the subject of the next chapter.

CHAPTER 2

"A sort of adopted daughter": family relations in
The Lamplighter

The title of my chapter comes from a passage in Maria Cummins's *The Lamplighter* (1854) where the question of Gerty Flint's (or is her last name Grant, Graham, or Amory?) identity is raised. She is alternately Trueman Flint's "adopted child" or the child of True and Emily Graham who have "adopted her jointly."[1] She is both a "doubly-orphaned girl" (176), according to Mr. and Mrs. Arnold, and she is an "orphan child" of the "good foster-mother" (278) world. Exactly what it means to be an adopted child in Gerty's world, or to be doubly orphaned, is tantalizingly imprecise. The array of relational possibilities is quite stunning, whether from the parental perspective or the child's. This imprecision has significant consequences in terms of Gerty's development in the novel, most importantly in producing her capacity to dispense what I shall be calling "judicious sympathy"; that is, an ability not only to recognize and respond to the multiple claims people make upon her sympathy, but more importantly, to prioritize those claims and to mete out her sympathy accordingly. Gerty exercises her sympathy the way she goes about making her family – freely, rationally, and contractually.

Cummins's inconsistent vocabulary is, however, part of another story, and that is the development of what legal historian Michael Grossberg has called "the legal category of domestic relations," specifically divorce and adoption, which was being formulated and debated during the historical moment of *The Lamplighter* and sentimental fictions more generally.[2] Gerty's story, in fact, *is* the story of the production of domestic relations law. *The Lamplighter* produces a paradigm of family based on chosen affections rather than biologically determined ones, and as such both intersects with and departs from antebellum formulations of the family, especially in the nascent sphere of domestic relations law. This notion of family, in which the rules of contract apply to biological relations, reflects a republican ideal, where each family member possesses individual rights which are guaranteed, not by one's status in the family, but by the contractual obligations family members have toward one another.

The Lamplighter functions as an exemplary sentimental text because it so clearly explores the increasingly central role played by affections in the constitution and definition of what it means to be in a family (in the north) during the antebellum period. Although my analysis of adoption law focuses on Cummins's novel as a means by which to analyze sentimental fictions' investment in many of the issues being raised in the judiciary and legislature, it should be evident from the previous chapter that the plots of virtually all of these novels are about "the best interests of the child," and adoption figures as a key mechanism by which those interests are established and protected. The history of legal cases concerning adoption and guardianship indicate that judges were increasingly willing to separate children from their parents in instances of clear parental negligence, oftentimes granting custody to an aunt or grandparent. To give the child to a blood relation, in other words, was still a *desideratum* of the court, even though the courts were making arguments that began to dislodge consanguinity from its assumed connection with affection. These cases reflect a developing skepticism about the degree of consanguineous attachment being a guarantee of childrearing ability. Biological parents were not necessarily the best parents of their biological children.

It was up to sentimental novels, like *The Lamplighter*, to finish the job (though not quite, as we shall see) and to make the case that being related to someone and loving them might have very little to do with one another. *The Lamplighter* thus captures in literary form the moment when courts were attempting to make sense of this new idea of family, when judges were struggling to define terms such as adoption and guardianship, as well as trying to formalize and codify domestic arrangements, which were based on contracts, sometimes verbal, sometimes written, rather than biology.

Were these families, or weren't they? Could families now be chosen and, if so, what rules governed the choice? The legal narrative is, as we shall see, as uneven and unstable as Gerty's, which is to say that both the law and the novel profoundly waver about affirming the very reconstitution of the family that their narratives seem to advocate – families based on choice. Many of the most significant legal cases of the antebellum period having to do with custody and adoption sought to resolve the conflicts produced by, on the one hand, a residual model of the family, which conceived of its members in biological relation to one another, as opposed to, on the other hand, an emergent model of family, which envisioned its members in contractual relation with one another. Cummins's novel, like the law, reproduces these conflicts, sometimes coming out in favor of blood ties, sometimes in favor of adopted ones, and also like antebellum law slowly and unevenly moves toward a recognition, indeed a validation, of the claims of contract.

But Gerty's story is also radically different from her legal analogues. Whereas the law demands a verdict which, in delivering a child to one person meant separating a child from another, Gerty's judicious sympathy produces a much happier outcome. In the course of the narrative, we witness Gerty's gradual possession of her sympathy, enabling her to choose how, when, and to whom her affections will be given. Although Gerty gets to be everyone's eventually – that is, virtually every adult character in the novel adopts her at some point – her sympathy produces a family economy where one person's gain is not another person's loss.

The term judicious sympathy responds to June Howard's timely call for a "transdisciplinary" approach to the study of sentimental novels and the role of sympathy. Heeding her warning that no "account of the form [can] end discussion and produce a consensus for a single definition of senti-mentality," this chapter challenges recent readings of sentimental fictions, *The Lamplighter* in particular, such as that of Amy Kaplan who urges us to consider female subjectivity in sentimental novels as "underwritten by and abet[ting]the imperial expansion of the nation." She uses Gerty as a case in point: "[she] must become her own first colonial subject and purge herself of . . . her origin in a diseased uncivilized terrain." A key piece of evidence is the fact that "she was born in Brazil to the daughter of a ship captain, who was killed by malaria." But in Kaplan's effort to make the case against Cummins's text as exemplifying the imperialistic logic of antebellum sentimentalism, she has misread the novel. In its conclusion, we learn that Gerty's father didn't die but rather "after an almost interminable illness . . . made [his] way, destitute, ragged, and emaciated, back to Rio" (384), and eventually back into Gerty's life at which point she learns and embraces her past. Far from purging her origins, Gerty must confront them. Indeed, the debate being staged in the novel between the claims of biological as opposed to contractual families necessitates his return.[3]

My point is that the operations of sympathy ought not to be reduced (because they are not reducible) to hegemonic claims about the hegemony of sentimental novels. Sympathy in *The Lamplighter* is a contextually fluid category which sentimental fiction and the law each deploy to establish the parameters of northern middle-class families and the legal identities of the persons therein. Yes, there are lots of tears, key players in these texts, but there are also considered decisions about how best to weigh competing claims to one's sympathy. In addition, far from abandoning a "commitment to social justice," to quote Amy Lang's assessment of *The Lamplighter*, the text's preoccupation with Gerty's multiple positions within a variety of chosen families intersects with legal cases similarly concerned with adjudicating children's rights within an array of domestic arrangements. In fact, it is through her multiple arrangements that Gerty at once becomes everyone's and yet loses nothing (of) herself. What she gains *is* herself. Gerty's self-possession is, in other words, established on the foundation of her multiple adoptions.[4]

My account of the *Lamplighter*, then, begins with the problem of indefinability and concludes with a reading of indefinability's virtues. The narrator doesn't know how to name Gerty's relation to the various people who care for her, whether it be Nan Grant, Trueman Flint, Emily Graham, or Mr. Graham. Gerty's power both to help others and to take care of herself, to dispense sympathy judiciously, comes from precisely the fact that her identity is productively unstable and always expanding. Like so many sentimental protagonists, she is, we might say, biologically unattached. *The Lamplighter* forces a consideration of the presence of contract in the domestic sphere because there are very few complete biological families in the novel. As a result, there is a revealing self-consciousness about how one goes about making one's domestic arrangements, and the responsibilities incurred thereupon. If "every contract," as William Story claims in his *Treatise on the Law of Contracts* (1844), "is founded upon the mutual agreement of the parties," *The Lamplighter* asks the question, to what have the parties mutually agreed?[5] And if they no longer agree, what are the consequences? But at the same time as Gerty's chosen families configure an ideal republican family, where each family member possesses commensurate rights, the ending of the novel seems to challenge that configuration. Gerty's long-lost father's rights seem to be more important than all of the fathers Gerty has chosen throughout the course of the narrative. Quite simply, Gerty must learn the identity of her real father before she can marry Willie Sullivan, and thus start her own family. She can't take Willie's name until she's legally and biologically gotten one of her own. *The Lamplighter*, then, simultaneously advances an argument in favor of blood not contract even as it seems to give contract not blood the last word.[6]

I "WHO ARE YOU?" (53)

Gerty's story takes place in Massachusetts (where Cummins was born and where the first adoption law was enacted in 1851), and her beginnings are anything but auspicious. Having lost her mother five years before we are introduced to her, the eight-year-old girl is protected by no one, and physical and mental abuses are heaped upon her by the wretched Nan Grant. Nan finds herself "keep[ing] the child" (3), although her reasons for doing so remain unclear even when the novel tries to explain them in the conclusion. When Trueman Flint, the lamplighter, first discovers the awful conditions in which Gerty lives, he asks her, "Who do you belong to, you poor little thing," to which she replies, "Nobody." He then slightly rephrases the first question and asks again, "But who do you live with, and who takes care of you?" (12). The possibility that Gerty might live with someone to whom she doesn't belong allows True to intervene and become "her kind protector" (16), and later to become her "Uncle True, for that was the name by which True had told her to call him" (17). Shortly thereafter, Gerty is identified in the narrative as True's "adopted child" (38). Although Gerty will "live with" many people throughout the course of the novel, the answer to the first question remains the same. She will belong to "nobody," that is, nobody will possess her, except eventually herself. She can belong to True only because she doesn't belong to Nan, but she can also belong to Emily, only because she doesn't belong to True, and so on.

Inasmuch as Uncle True announces his desire to "be a father to that child" (21), the wish seems to fall short of the reality. When Gerty meets Emily Graham, the woman who will be the maternal presence in Gerty's life, their conversation echoes her earlier words with True and calls attention to the ambiguity of their familial relation:

"Who are you?"
"Gerty."
"Gerty who?"
"Nothing else but Gerty."
"Have you forgotten your other name?"
"I have n't got any other name." (53)

Is her last name Flint? Not quite, because even as the narrator assures us that "the old man could not have loved the little adopted one better had she been his own child" (66), she nevertheless calls attention to the fact that Gerty is *not* his child in any formal way, or at least in such as a way as to give her his last name. What does it mean for True to have "adopted" Gerty and yet not to have legally given her his name? First, it means that she lives with him but does not necessarily belong to him, and second, it means that someone else can (and several people will) subsequently "adopt" Gerty. Thus, being "adopted" according to the procedures, or lack thereof, of *The Lamplighter* underscores the likelihood of being adopted again.[7]

Family ties, as I have begun to suggest, are elastic and transferable to the point of meaninglessness in the novel; that is, almost everyone in Cummins's novel, as in many of the sentimental fictions discussed in the first chapter, has multiple relational identifications. For example, Willie, upon first meeting Gerty, introduces himself as her "cousin" because "Uncle True's your uncle, and mine too" (30). Elsewhere, Willie's mother posits a fraternal relationship between the two, as "if they were own brother and sister" (97). Still later, when Willie prepares to depart for India, he asks his cousin/sister, "Gerty, dear, for my sake take good care of *our* mother and grandfather – they are *yours* almost as much as mine" (107). These passages are particularly interesting in that they both collapse the difference between biological and non-biological ties by addressing Gerty as a member of the family and call attention to that very difference by the word "almost" and the hypothetical "if they were." What this allows, I think, is a tremendous amount of flexibility in one's relations. Thus, Gerty, who is alternately described as a "foundling" (21), a "little charge" (34), and an "orphan" (36), has the capacity to become True's "childish guardian" (88), as well as a "guardian" (133) to Willie's grandfather when both men become ill and require her care. Gerty's guardianship involves taking care of other people and can therefore be seen as exemplifying women's limited options in antebellum culture, but in the world of *The Lamplighter*, all worthy characters, regardless of gender, willingly choose to care for others, whether it's Mr. Miller kindly attending to Willie's senile grandfather, or Willie taking care of the financial needs of his mother, or True offering Gerty a home. Becoming her guardian's guardian signifies both Gerty's moral fibre and her equal status within the family. It is not the case, moreover, that not having an "other name" consigns oneself to a less powerful position in the world of *The Lamplighter*; rather, being in the perennial place of "almost" this and not quite that produces Gerty's most admirable quality – her ability to act upon a sympathy that excludes no one because "[the world] has been a good foster-mother to its orphan child, and now I love it dearly" (278).

Let us return to the question True first poses to Gerty – "who are you?" This question could be asked of virtually any character in the novel because biological categories are either insufficient markers of identity (what do we call the relationship between Willie and Gerty once True has adopted them both?) or unavailable (there is an alarming shortage of biological mothers – Gerty's, Emily's, Belle's – and biological fathers – Willie's, Ben's). That this question still remains unanswered even after True has adopted Gerty is evident in the following exchange between Gerty and her unsympathetic schoolmates:

"Who's that man?"
"That's my Uncle True," said Gerty.
"Your what?"
"My uncle, Mr. Flint, that I live with."
"So you belong to him, do you?" said the girl, in an insolent tone of voice. "Ha! ha! ha!" (60)

This passage raises a possible connection between identity and possession: the fact that Gerty does not know exactly how to refer to True (is he Uncle True or Mr. Flint?) seems connected to the fact that she doesn't exactly belong to him. Not belonging to someone and not knowing who you are appear to be related problems. True's adoption of Gerty, in other words, does little to resolve the question of the child's identity. If identity is established on the grounds of parental possession, and if True's possession of Gerty is guaranteed through their mutual affection rather than any legal decree, Gerty's status as a possession (and possessor) remains uncertain.

Indeed, one of the ultimate goals of adoption law, according to the 1851 Massachusetts legislature, was to secure "for the purposes of inheritance and succession" the adopted child's right to the possessions of her adoptive parents. In addition, the law was intended to guarantee that adoptive parents possessed rights to their adopted child "as if such child had been born in lawful wedlock."[8] The legalization of adoption, moreover, had as much to do with formalizing and stabilizing the transmission of property in the form of inheritance as with recognizing and guaranteeing the smooth transmission of the child from one person to another. Children had been adopted before 1851, but in the absence of legally sanctioned procedures, the relationship between adopted children and adoptive parents remained unprotected by law. Natural parents could reclaim their biological children at any time, and adopted children were greatly disadvantaged when they tried to claim their inheritance. The law attempted to clarify everyone's rights: both biological parents, if living, had to consent to the adoption; adopting parents assumed all "legal rights whatsoever as respects such child"; and children, aged fourteen and up, had to consent to the adoption.[9] The child, however, came to assume center stage, and the legal cases narrativize the acquisition of the child's rights to choose her family and to have those rights protected in court. This narrative provides us with a crucial context through which to understand the families in sentimental fictions and how those families help or hinder the child's journey toward self-possession.

II IN THE BEST INTERESTS OF THE CHILD

The Massachusetts law was a logical step in defining and stabilizing new family arrangements that threatened a patriarchal notion of family as biologically based. It was in the courts, however, that adoption came to be constituted and protected as a legal means of creating and, as Grossberg puts it, "actually defin[ing] the artificial family."[10] As we shall see from a number of key legal cases brought before northern courts in the antebellum years, artificial families were being made through a haphazard amalgam of contractual methods. Most often, a child joined a new family because of a death, or the parents' conviction that the child would receive greater economic advantages elsewhere, or a business arrangement whereby the child became an apprentice in order to learn a trade. The legal status of these arrangements, though, was unclear. Guardians, according to nineteenth-century legal historian Lewis Hochheimer, were especially vulnerable given the fact that "considerations connected with the welfare of the child" meant that guardians, even when appointed by parents, could easily lose "custody of the child."[11] To make matters even more vexed, contracts were either written up or dispensed with altogether, and a verbal agreement was made. Oftentimes, the parties involved wanted the contract changed. Parents who had wanted informal and temporary arrangements sometimes found their children wanting those arrangements made more formal, in some instances permanent, thus necessitating judicial intervention.

It should also be noted that adoption wasn't always the endpoint. More often that not, the child simply wished to remain where she was for the time being, having established bonds and customs with her new family. In *Commonwealth* v. *Hamilton* (1810), an early Massachusetts case which helped to lay the groundwork for privileging the child's wishes, a mother attempted to reclaim her child who had been bound in service until the age of eighteen. The court responded:

as there is no evidence of any neglect of that duty on his part, but, on the contrary, the child appears to have been well treated, and to be attached to the family of the defendant, – it would be unreasonable to take her from his care, and deliver her to her mother, who, by her marriage of her present husband, ceased to have any power of controlling her own actions, or of providing for the support and education of her child. Whatever rights she might have . . . they have certainly ceased at the age of this child [about fourteen years old].[12]

Once courts began to respect the validity of these new arrangements, and the child's sentimental investment in them, parents' rights no longer seemed invulnerable. Exactly what rights, then, if any, were parents abdicating once their child left the home? How long a separation was necessary before parental rights were *de facto* relinquished? Indeed, was it even possible for a parent to relinquish her rights to her child? And at what point did the child's rights supersede all others?

Commonwealth v. *Hammond* (1830) illustrates the complex domestic scenarios which judges had to disentangle and deliberate upon. The Massachusetts case contains two competing contracts, and at least three parental figures – the mother, a "respondent" (274), and a guardian (four, if the judge is included). The child involved was eleven-year-old Margaret Holst. Her father had died and her mother "had committed [Margaret] to [Joseph Hammond], on a verbal contract for support and education."[13] This verbal contract, however, went against a previous judge's ruling which had named Ephraim Tufts the child's guardian. The court decided that because "the liberty of the party is not injuriously or unwarrantably infringed . . . the child [is] at liberty to remain in the charge of the respondent, or to go at large, as she may elect" (275). She elected to stay with Hammond. But what about the rights of the legally appointed guardian? In this case, they were non-existent, even though a judge had appointed Tufts as guardian. What was the status of "the letters of guardianship [which] were granted to Tufts" in relation to the "verbal contract" made between Hammond and the child's mother? Again, non-existent. Indeed, the most important element in the case was not "the relative rights of the mother and the guardian" but the child's desire to "remain with the respondent" (274). That an eleven-year-old "may elect" to remain "or to go at large" demonstrates the degree to which courts were invested in establishing and protecting a child's right to choose her family.

This choice, to which I shall return, was predicated upon two related and contentious developments in the antebellum family and in the legal scene – the dimunition of paternal rights and the expansion of maternal ones. The cases of *Mercein* v. *the People ex. Rel. Barry* (1840) and *Commonwealth* v. *Maxwell* (1843) exemplify these shifts. In the infamous *Mercein* v. *the People ex. Rel. Barry,* John Barry was granted four writs of *habeas corpus* against his wife and father-in-law, Eliza Anna and Thomas Mercein. Barry accused them of improperly restraining, which meant the "imprisonment or restraint or unlawful withholding of the infant child," their nineteenth-month infant daughter Mary. Justice Bronson of the New York Supreme Court (not the highest court in the state, as one might expect) held that common law "emphatically establish[ed] a paramount right of the father to the custody of the children."[14] Bronson's ruling, a throwback to English common law, clearly goes against the growing judicial consensus in America in favor of children's rights. It suggests that paternal authority, as the organizational principle of the family, was not easily dismantled. He continued, "in these unhappy controversies between husband and wife, the former, if he chooses to assert his right, has the better title to the custody of the minor children. The law regards him as the head of the family; obliges him to provide of its wants; and commits the children to his charge, in preference to the claims of the mother or any other person." Bronson's decision in favor of the father's right to the child reversed earlier lower court decisions that had granted Eliza Anna maternal custody, but his decision was itself reversed by the New York Court for the Correction of Errors, which held that "the father's right to his child is not absolute and inalienable . . . [and] it may be lost by his ill usage, immoral principles or habits, or by his inability to provide for his children." In a creative close reading of an earlier ruling in favor of the mother in the second writ of *habeas corpus*, Bronson argued that saying that the child was "not *improperly* restrained," was not equivalent to "decid[ing] that there was *no* restraint." Bronson then suggested that even if the child were not improperly restrained at the time of the second writ, improper restraint did take place during the period in which Mr. Barry petitioned for the additional writs of *habeas corpus*. The Court for the Correction of Errors, however, would have nothing to do with Bronson's interpretation of events: "*maternal restraint is no illegal restraint*, that if the child is of age to exercise its own judgment, the court allows it *to go where it will* – if not, the court may go farther, (but is *not bound* to go farther,) and *in its own discretion* may exercise its judgment for the child, having regard to its *health, comfort, and welfare*." Bronson's dogged and soon to be outmoded insistence on the preservation of the father's custodial rights, at the expense of all other considerations, was becoming less defensible as courts increasingly came to see their primary responsibility as determining "the best interests of the child."[15] Children had rights too, which could and would be protected by the court, at the court's discretion.

In a less legalistic but no less vitriolic case, Ivory Maxwell claimed that his wife, Elizabeth Maxwell, was illegally detaining their two young children (ages one and four) in the Boston home of Elizabeth's brother, and Ivory wanted them back. After hearing both sides of the case, her version detailing neglect and poor treatment on the part of the husband, and his version blaming the uncle for intruding on domestic affairs, Massachusetts

Supreme Court Justice Wilde stated that "the right of the father is not entirely absolute; the children are not his property, and their good is to be regarded as the predominant consideration." Wilde's circumscription of paternal rights went even further: "if the father could and would supply his children with suitable food and clothing, and a shelter from the inclemency of the weather, there are other wants which, during their tender years, no one can so well supply as their mother . . . To allow these children, during their tender years, to be torn from their mother, would seem to be inconsistent with the laws of nature and the comfort and the well-being of the children."[16] The recognition of a mother's right to care for her children, especially young children in their "tender years," dovetailed with the mounting importance of the "best interests of the child." The maternal dispensation for affection rather than the paternal transmission of property was coming to be understood by the courts as one of the truest measures of the best interests of the child.

What were these best interests? *State* v. *Smith* (1830) was, according to legal historian Jamil Zanaildan, "one of the most important disputes of the period" in its assertion of the child's best interests.[17] A father of four, Jonathan Hall, had voluntarily "relinquish[ed] to the mother the right of custody and control of her children." Hall had forfeited his rights, thereby establishing Mrs. Hall's right to the children. But Justice Parris of the Maine Supreme Court went a step further and outlined the rights of their children. They were to be "maintain[ed], protect[ed] and educate[d]." The delineation of the parents' responsibilities and the child's rights is important not only because it clarifies one party's obligation to the other, but because it transforms their relationship into a contractual one. And once the parent/child bond becomes a contract, it can be broken. Even by a mother. If "by immoral or profligate habits, the parent has become unfit to have the management and instruction of children . . . the courts have not hesitated to interfere to restrain the abuse, or remove the subject of such abuse from the custody of the offending parent."[18] Clearly, courts began to conceive of children less as the "inalienable" property of their parents and more as the inalienable property of themselves. For example, the fact that eleven-year-old Margaret Holst had the power to decide her whereabouts went against the common law which stated that "a child could not exercise such a choice until the years of discretion (generally twelve for girls and fourteen for boys). The courts [however] often relaxed the rule and allowed younger but more mature children to have a voice in custody proceedings."[19] It is important to note that the category of affection is not obliterated by virtue of contract's ascendance; rather, the degree to which parents (or guardians, or foster-mothers) fulfilled their contract was now to be measured by the child's affection. Once children were no longer the inalienable property of their parents, according to the law, their affections were free to circulate. This freedom, in turn, had to be protected. In allowing children "to have a voice," the courts bestowed upon the child the fundamental right to possess and bestow her affections.

The idea that family relationships could be as much about contractual obligations as blood relations was a key innovation of antebellum law. "The development of separate legal identities within the republican family," writes Grossberg, was accompanied by attempts to establish the rights and obligations of individual members, and to write into the law the consequences of improper behavior, or of breaking the contract."[20] The court's self-appointed obligation to protect children's rights, to serve their best interests, radically redrew the parameters constituting the family. If affection based on contract rather than biology were to organize domestic life, judges needed to imagine individual members in terms of whose rights and what rights were protected and relinquished in the contract. If parents could make contracts "*relinquish*[ing] custody of the child . . . by agreement of transfer or by abandonment or other course of conduct," to quote Hochheimer, then a contract, say adoption, protecting the child both from future transfers and from possible repossession had to be established.[21] Indeed, the same year that saw the passage of the Massachusetts adoption law witnessed two cases in which the court decided that the child belonged with (and belonged to) someone other than the biological parent. In neither of these cases was consanguinity deemed irrelevant, but a legal wedge between parent and child was being established in the name of the child's best interests.

In *Gilkeson* v. *Gilkeson* (1851), custody was granted to the child's aunt rather than to the father, and in *Pool* v. *Gott* (1851), the child's grandparents, not the father, were awarded custody. It was in these cases, according to Zanaildan, that "the words 'adopt' and 'adoption' make their common law debut."[22] In the first case, the parents of Mary Gilkeson, "by contract under seal transferred the custody of her to her uncle and aunt, who, by the same writing agreed to adopt her as their child."[23] Exactly what "adopt[ing]" meant to the parties concerned is unclear. But if the father imagined that the contract could be broken, the court vehemently disagreed. After a period of six years, during which Mary's mother and uncle died, her father "obtained possession of her, and insist[ed] on retaining the custody of her, though she prefer[red] remaining with her aunt." The child's preference was sustained, and Judge Lowrie of the Philadelphia District Court argued that "parental authority has been solemnly renounced for six years, and the child had grown to the age of fifteen years. She has been estranged from the customs and government of her father's house. She has formed new habits and views, and become accustomed to different associations and modes of living." The ultimate effect of the first contract was a transfer of affection, and a new contract, based on feeling rather than parental relation, was established. Interestingly, the court held out the possibility that this affection could be transferred back through "the influence of parental kindness, and consistently with honesty . . . but it cannot be well done by the enforcement of it as a legal right."[24] Influence and kindness, not parental rights, might reunite father and child. More important, though, is the validation of the child's right to make affection the basis of a new contract and a new family, and the judicial decision to make that contract stick.

Such a transformation in affection is also the subject of *Pool* v. *Gott*, a Massachusetts case decided by Chief Justice Lemuel Shaw, in which the father of Lydia Gott Pool attempted to regain custody after she had lived with her grandfather for fourteen years "with the father's consent." Unlike *Gilkeson* v. *Gilkeson* where a contract was used as evidence against the father's custody claim, Shaw conceded that "there is no evidence as to the nature of the agreement made, if indeed there was any agreement at that time." He nevertheless maintained that, "I have no doubt that it was understood on all sides that the child was to remain under the respondents' charge, and that they were to stand *in loco parentis*." Pool had, in effect, relinquished through contract his biological paternity and now wanted it back. Given the fact that the father showed relatively little interest in his child (three years in which there was no contact, and annual visits thereafter), Shaw argued that Pool had "allowed the parties to go on for years in the belief that his legal rights were waived, and this relation of adoption sanctioned and approved by him." *Pool* v. *Gott* transformed "a tacit understanding," if not an "express agreement," into "this relation of adoption." Shaw named adoption as that process by which the father "by his own acquiescence has allowed the affections on both sides to become engaged in a manner he could not but have anticipated, and permitted a state of things to arise, which cannot be altered without risking the happiness and interest of his child." His contract, whether tacit or expressed, enabled another contract by which affective ties replaced the more direct consanguineous ties of biological paternity as the organizing principle of the family.[25]

Pool v. *Gott* is especially interesting for our inquiry into antebellum deployments of sympathy because Shaw's decision vigorously acknowledges the important of feelings and, quite literally, judicial/judicious sympathy. The fact that Shaw was also Melville's father-in-law makes the Chief Justice's decisions even more intriguing, especially if we think of Pierre being surrounded by familial sympathizers and only a few steps away from committing murder. That said, in stark contrast to Justice Bronson who dispenses with sympathy early on in his decision ("whatever sympathy we may feel for this lady . . . we have no choice but to administer the law as we find it"), Shaw is quite willing to acknowledge the power of sympathy to influence his dispensation of justice.[26] First, Shaw anticipates the "pain and disappointment" that will follow his ruling. Second, his attention to the sentimental details of the case, by which I mean the powerful feelings evoked by the situation, is unusual. He considers the fact that Mrs. Pool, the only child of Mr. and Mrs. Gott, died in childbirth, and the certainty that "under such circumstances, the attachment of the grandparents was naturally strong." This circumstance leads Shaw to conclude that "a failure to secure the custody of the child would [not] be of as much consequence" to the father as compared to the "great suffering" that would result from separating Lydia from her grandparents. When "the right of the parent is not clear, the interest of the child will govern the decision of the Court," and here Shaw uses comparative suffering rather than comparative rights as the criterion for determining custody. Everyone in this case has rights, which are fairly commensurate. Everyone, however, does not have equivalent feelings, and it is feelings which finally tip the scales in favor of the child/grandparent relation. Indeed, Shaw self-consciously calls attention to his task as one which must balance rights and feelings from the start: "this case presents circumstances of interest and delicacy, involving both legal rights, and the dearest feelings of parties. On the one hand, is the legal right of the only parent, and on the other, the feelings of the child, and the feelings and rights, such as those rights may be, of the grandparents." It is interesting to note that the feelings of the only parent, as well as the rights of the child are missing in Shaw's formulation. These absent terms, however, are crucial to his decision because it is precisely the absent feelings of the parent which enable Shaw to deduce the best interests of the child, or the child's rights. Knowing that his decision will produce pain produces a kind of anxiety on his part ("it is to be regretted that the law leaves cases of this description with so few rules for the government of the Courts"). His decision is designed to cause the least pain, as is evidenced by the concluding remarks which offer a solution to Mr. Pool's pain in the form of "some agreement [which] might be made by which the child should spend part of her time with her father, to allow opportunities for mutual affections and interests to grow up between herself and her paternal relations." Shaw's sympathy extends itself in all directions, and that is part of his difficulty. He arrives, quite self-consciously, at a judicious dispensation of sympathy which, even as it causes pain, holds out the possibility for future redemption and reunion. *Gott* v. *Pool* made legal and authoritative the custodial transfer of Lydia Gott Pool to her grandparents, but as Shaw's last words suggest, a transfer back of sorts via agreement of contract might be effected should the parties be so inclined.[27]

III JUDICIOUS SYMPATHY

The Lamplighter imagines what it would look like for a child's affections to be continually transferred back and forth, and the picture is surprisingly hopeful. The novel invests Gerty, the child and the woman, with a tremendous amount of power by virtue of her limitless capacity for affection. But loving everyone, for Gerty, doesn't mean loving anyone less. It just means that sometimes people need to wait their turn to experience her affection. Like so many of the sentimental fictions of this period, *The Lamplighter* imagines a world of multiple guardianships, numerous adoptions, where no one loses the child, but no one possesses the child either – except the child herself. It is the story of Gerty's transformation from "the city's property" (12) to the object of everyone's affection, a transformation accomplished through Gerty's mastery of sympathy. This education in sympathy, however, is not just a matter of learning how to feel other people's pain, although that is the first step. The second, and more difficult, is the prioritization of that sympathy, the ability to exercise what I am calling judicious sympathy. Finally, Gerty's story is the discovery of her rights as a child and her growing self-knowledge about her own "best interests." Unlike Lydia Gott Pool, whom Shaw "examine[d] in private" so as to learn where her true affections lay and protect them, Gerty learns how to protect those affections herself.[28] No one has "unlimited or unalienable" rights over her, to use the language of *State* v. *Smith*, except herself. She is both child and judge. No longer does she belong to the city, she belongs to herself.

Like Shaw's, Gerty's sympathy extends in several directions at once, and much of the novel is concerned with the proper dispensation of that sympathy. Thus, for example, when the Grahams are planning a southern tour and the "tyrannical" (144) Mr. Graham, having assumed that Gerty would care for and entertain Emily, reproaches Gerty for deciding to nurse Willie's mother and grandfather, we are meant to condemn his unfair exercise of authority. He incorrectly assumes that just because Gerty lives in his home she belongs to him, and he has certain rights over her. He blusters, "You are under my care, child, and I have a right to say what you shall do" (139). As far as Gerty is concerned, however, he has no "rights," only certain "claim[s]'" (140) which she has the right to accept or reject. The narrator explains that "in the home of her kind foster father, she enjoyed a degree of paternal tenderness which rarely falls to the lot of an orphan" (141). She has, of course, enjoyed a "paternal tenderness" from others as well, which makes it wrong for Mr. Graham to assume that "nobody else had any claim upon her to compare with his" (142). Gerty then meditates on how Mr. Graham may have lost sight of the difference between a "foster father" and a father (an easy thing to do given the fact that the right of guardians were frustratingly vague, as Hochheimer points out): "He probably feels, too, as if I had been under his guardianship so long that he has almost a right to decide upon my conduct" (143–144). Although she acknowledges herself "a stranger, with no claims" (144), she nevertheless claims the right to act according to "what [her] duty is" (145) – a duty which she, herself, defines. Gerty imagines a gap between her understanding of guardianship, in which the rights of the guardian are ultimately circumscribed by the rights of the child, and Mr. Graham's.

When Gerty has responded to the claims of Willie's mother and grandfather, she is ready to entertain the claims which others are quick to make upon her, and once again it is Mr. Graham on behalf of Emily. He writes Gerty and invites her to accompany them, along with his new wife and her nieces, to Europe. Gerty's friends, Dr. and Mrs. Jeremy, point out how unfairly Mr. Graham has treated her and question her willingness to give up her teaching position and the economic independence that goes with it: "it does seem a sacrifice for you to leave your beautiful room, and all your comforts," to which Gerty replies, "nothing that I do for *Emily's* sake can be called a sacrifice; it is my greatest pleasure" (184–185). That this is a pleasure and not an obligation, that Gerty is in charge and not Mr. Graham is suggested in his letter, which acknowledges the possibility that Gerty may "have contracted debts," and if so, he "will see that all is made right" (183). We learn, however, that Gerty has no need of his "friendly interest" (183), given that she earns a sizeable "three hundred and fifty dollars a year" (184). Furthermore, Gerty's decision to accept Mr. Graham's invitation is in part based on the fact that "Emily was dependent upon a stranger" (185), rather than upon the beloved Gerty. Her decision to care for Emily underscores her self-confidence, not her self-abasement. Therefore, Dr. Jeremy's sense that Gerty will be "relinquishing all the independence that she has been striving after" (184) radically differs from Gerty's understanding of her independence. Independence, for Gerty, means the ability to decide for oneself when and for whom sacrifice (which, in this case, equals pleasure) is appropriate and necessary. Financial and biological independence are what allow her to determine which competing claims are most urgent, and Gerty is now ready to respond to Emily's "claim" (185). Thus, far from signifying her dependent or subservient status, Gerty's sympathetic and reasoned responses to the claims made upon her indicate the extent of her power. To be sure, she takes care of virtually everyone in the novel, but this is because she chooses to rather than has to. Her choices, furthermore, confirm her power. They are, as the narrator reminds us, a function of Emily's careful teachings in Christian duty which have made Gerty "powerful to do and to suffer, to bear and to forbear, when, depending on herself, she should be left to her own guidance alone" (73).

Gerty's independence and power are, I am arguing, made possible because of her ambiguous family relations. Everyone wants her to be part of their family, and yet no one knows exactly what "rights" or "claims" (to invoke two well-used but ultimately indefinable terms of the novel) they have toward Gerty or vice-versa. Perhaps, what they have is a right to make a claim, which Gerty then has the right to accept or reject. Furthermore, everyone wants her to be part of their family, but exactly what would she be (an adopted daughter, a daughter, a ward) and what would they be (a guardian, a father, a step-mother)? She chooses to be a member of everyone's family and yet no one's exclusively. At one point in the novel, Gerty is referred to as "a sort of adopted daughter" (198). Indeed, one can say with absolute assuredness that Gerty has no sure place, whether spatial, familial, or legal. She defies categorization. Is she adopted or is she "sort of adopted"?

As annoying as this categorical instability was for many commentators on adoption law and the children whose lives were affected by it, Gerty's narrative of spiritual empowerment depends upon the fact that her identity eludes any formal categorization. Because everyone and no one has claims upon her (legally, she belongs to no one), she enjoys a freedom that derives from the fact that in not knowing her true origins, she is free to choose them. That the "absurd" conclusion, to borrow Nina Baym's apt term, eventually provides her with the story of her origins, indeed legally effects her transformation into Philip Amory's daughter, points to the central tension within the novel: on the one hand, Gerty's unfettered, unstable identity is what permits her development and is therefore desirable, and on the other, the novel works toward a resolution of that instability, which is equally desirable.[29] Like its legal counterpart, *The Lamplighter* is torn between championing a contractual paradigm of family that was being developed in domestic relations law based, as we have seen, on affective rather than proprietary considerations and the independent needs of individual members of the family unit, and a more patriarchal model of family based on status, property, and blood.

When Gerty finally learns the mystery of her origins through a dizzying array of plot complications, she writes her "dear, dear father" (337) the following:

> When you took me in your arms and called me your child, your darling child, I fancied that the excitement of that dreadful scene had for the moment disturbed your mind and brain so far as to invest me with a false identity . . . I now believe that it was no sudden madness, but rather that I have been all along mistaken for another, whose glad office it may perhaps be to cheer a father's saddened life, while I remain unrecognized, unsought, – the fatherless, motherless one I am accustomed to consider myself. (337)

It is important to remember that this anxiety about "false identity" is relatively new to the novel. Up until this point, she has thrived on it. Earlier, however, the narrator does tell us that Gerty "was a little sensitive about her name, and, though she always went by that of Flint, and did not, on ordinary occasions, think much about it, she could not fail to remember, when the question was put to her point blank, that she had, in reality, no surname of her own" (127). Her letter suggests either that she was more than "a little sensitive" about not having "in reality" a "surname of her own," or that the prospect of finally having a surname makes her realize how much she has desired one all along. Even as Gerty indulges the possibility of having her true identity revealed, she imagines how to arrange things so that affection based on contract may prevail if consanguinity doesn't: "If you have lost a daughter, God grant she may be restored to you, to love you as I would do, were I so blessed as to be that daughter . . . let me be your child in heart" (337). No longer, though, will Gerty or, for that matter, Mr. Amory, be "mistaken for another." In fact, their consanguinity must be disclosed in order to a put a stop to the titillating and threatening incestuous overtones that have characterized their relationship from the start. It is not enough, indeed it is not permissible, that Gerty be either Mr. Amory's biological daughter or his "child in heart." Her position must be decided, as sentimental convention requires, but that's not to say that *The Lamplighter* simply reinstates the power of consanguinity to define the family.[30]

Knowing the identity of her father, then, puts an end to this endless round of substitutions, both for Gerty and the narrator, who hastens to add, "Mr. Phillips – or rather Mr. Amory, for we will call him by his true name – had either forgotten or neglected to mention his address" (338).[31] Justice Bronson's advocacy of paternal status would seem to have won the day. But not quite, because precisely at the moment that Philip identifies himself as father and Gerty as daughter, that language and his status are seen to be insufficient. He writes, "your grief unites the tie between us closer than that of kindred, and makes you a thousand times my daughter" (335). What does it mean to be "closer than that of kindred" and what would it mean for Gerty to be "a thousand times [Philip's] daughter?" The first part of Philip's statement would seem to suggest that the affections which developed between Gerty and her father, the grief that unites them before she knew his identity, signify the fact that their love is chosen rather than required by biological mandate, thus validating love as a form of contract. The second part also suggests the insufficiency of Philip's paternal claim – Gerty is not just his daughter once, but "a thousand times" – as if to make up for the thousand times she has become someone else's daughter in the text. Identities still seem unstable, even as they are incorporated into biologically identifiable and presumably fixed categories.

Furthermore, Philip's reappearance in Gerty's life signifies little, at least from a legal point of view. Clearly, Gerty's age (at this point, she is probably in her late teens) and her "sufficient discretion" would mean that most judges would second her parental preference. He is undoubtedly her biological father, but the fact that he has not been a part of her life for so much of it (a very long and complicated story allegedly explaining their separation comprises part of the "absurd" ending to which Baym refers), means, again from a legal point of view, that intentionally or not, he "waive[d] his parental rights" (465). The case of *Gilkeson* v. *Gilkeson* is a particularly useful gloss: "authority has been so long disclaimed and so solemnly transferred to another" that the "filial relation cannot be mended by "the enforcement of it as a legal right."[32] It is up to Gerty to decide whether or not to transfer back that affection, and it is up to Philip to "effect it by the influence of parental kindness" (197). Philip can be Gerty's "father," but at this point that biological designation is underwritten by a contract or, as Shaw had put it in *Gott* v. *Pool,* an "arrangement," making him a father. Parenthood is here translated into *in loco parentis.*[33]

The return of Philip and the disclosure of his paternal identity are not the only means by which the novel tries to negotiate the tension between contract and consanguinity. The topic comes up once more, and this time quite explicitly in the comical figure of Miss Patty Pace, a Dickensian character who first appears dressed in "a gray cloak, of some sort of silk material, that you certainly would have said came out of the ark, if it hadn't been for a little cape, of a different color, that she wore outside of it, and which must have dated a generation further back" (75). The wizened bachelorette Miss Patty, about whom Willie "wonder[s] who she belongs to" (76), the same question, we recall, asked of Gerty early in the novel, turns out to be as modern as she is ancient. When it comes to writing her will, she has little sympathy for her rightful heirs. Instead, Miss Patty solicits Gerty's help in composing "the last will and testament of Miss Patty Pace" (363). Before the women get down to the actual writing of the will, Miss Patty confesses her desire to "flee away from my kindred" who, like "vultures," have recently visited "for the sole purpose of taking an inventory of my possessions, and measuring the length of my days" (362). The conversation then takes a familiar turn:

> "I was not aware that you had any relations," said Gertrude; "and it seems they are such only in name."
>
> "Name!" said Miss Pace, emphatically. "I am animated with gladness at the thought that they are not honored with a cognomen which not one of them is worthy to bear. No, they pass by a different name; a name as plebeian as their own coarse souls. There are three of them, who stand to each other in a fraternal relation, and all are alike hateful to me. One . . . calls me aunt – aunt; thus testifying by his speech to a consanguinity which he blindly fancies makes him nearer akin to my property." (362)

Once again, names play a crucial role in both identifying and destabilizing family relations. Whereas the term "uncle" when applied to Uncle True signifies love freely given, "aunt" when used by Miss Patty's blood relations signifies specious affection. Gerty's love for her chosen uncle is indeed truer than anything Miss Patty's relations feel for her. Miss Patty fully intends to undermine through her will the blood relation established by the very term "aunt." By naming Willie the heir to her fortune (as a young boy, he had gallantly escorted Miss Patty through inclement weather, and had thus earned her ever-loving devotion), Miss Patty's will breaks the equation of consanguinity and property. In fact, Miss Patty's "own perfect acquaintance with all the legal knowledge which the case demanded," including the necessity of getting the document "witnessed, signed and sealed . . . prove[s] a satisfactory direction for the disposal of the inheritance" (363). It is no coincidence that Gerty is appointed "to gather and transfix in writing the exact idea which the woman's rambling dictation was intended to convey" (364). Miss Patty's "exact idea" accomplishes two things: it formalizes, through her will, the contractual paradigm of family that Gerty, interestingly called "Gertrude" in this scene of legal formality, has lived, and it validates, through the older woman's relation with Willie, the primacy of affection. As "the patient and diligent scribe" (364), Gerty herself gets to produce the legal text that both vindicates her rights as someone heretofore unprotected by the law and begins the process of producing her legal identity. Gerty, in other words, has any number of "parents," whose last name she doesn't legally share, and belonging to so many people could mean, from a legal point of view, that none of their belongings rightfully belong to her. Miss Patty's will is the kind of legal document that begins the process of transforming "a sort of adopted daughter" into an adopted daughter. Moreover, Miss Patty views the inheritance of property the way Gerty views the construction of family – not as biologically determined but as freely and contractually transmitted. That Willie "never availed himself of the bequest, otherwise than to make a careful bestowal of it among the most needy and worthy of her relatives "(363) doesn't take away from the importance of the act, an act made even more significant by the fact that it is motivated by something as seemingly insignificant as helping an old woman safely navigate a patch of ice. Consanguinity, one might conclude from this episode, is as changeable and unpredictable as the weather.

The embrace of the family in *The Lamplighter* is unlimited by virtue of adoption's productive ambiguity. The novel is part of a cultural moment in which the language, procedures, and meanings of adoption are being negotiated, in which the outlines of the family are being questioned and reestablished. That Cummins's novel, like so many other sentimental texts, doesn't know what either adoption or guardianship means, that the narrator and her characters don't know what to call one another, signifies the indefinability of these terms and the narrative difficulties (and opportunities) produced by such discursive chaos. Nevertheless, the fact that they are repeatedly used, qualified, and redefined points to the fact that *The Lamplighter*, like the law, is at once elaborating this phenomenon and trying to resolve its potential problems while exploring its possible advantages. Gerty looks forward to the resolution of these terms, while at the same time appropriates their instability as a means of becoming a stronger, self-possessed, and more sympathetic person. Meanwhile, she feels "a sense of relief in the adoption of a course which would satisfy all parties" (252).

CHAPTER 3

Thinking through sympathy: Kemble, Hentz, and Stowe

When Harriet Beecher Stowe asked her readers to "feel right" at the conclusion of *Uncle Tom's Cabin*, she most certainly didn't anticipate the many supporters of slavery who, in their reviews of her novel and in their own fictional rebuttals to it, claimed that they did indeed "feel right," and the benevolent institution of slavery was the result of their sympathies. But this is precisely what did happen, and in the months following the publication of *Uncle Tom's Cabin*, she prepared *A Key to Uncle Tom's Cabin* with the intentions of not only defending the authenticity of her novel and denouncing her critics, but reclaiming sympathy for the anti-slavery cause. Tears, the traditional evidence for sympathetic feeling and the primary mode of eliciting sympathy in Stowe's novel, registered one's feeling but not one's politics.[1] In fact, not only did those in favor of slavery insist that their sympathy for slaves surpassed that of northern anti-slavery aggressors, but slaveholders often made the case that they were more deserving candidates for sympathy than their slaves.

In response to pro-slavery appropriations of sympathy, anti-slavery advocates, including Stowe, Lydia Maria Child, Theodore Weld, and others, developed an expanded arsenal of sympathetic expression that would enable readers to see through the meretricious claims of their antagonists and convince them of the truthfulness of the anti-slavery position. Thus, evidence of Stowe's sympathy in *A Key* is not limited to traditional appeals to the "human heart" (104) but includes less conventional, less obviously emotional demonstrations such as irony and citationality – narrative strategies of sympathy that I will explore throughout this chapter. Furthermore, because the debate about sympathy became a debate about the reliability of the evidence upon which one's sympathy was based, *A Key* turns to the authority of facts in order to make its anti-slavery case: "Let us show the facts" (144); we must "[present] facts in detail, each fact being a specimen of a class of facts" (152); "the following facts" (61); "it is a well-known fact" (193). To prove the reliability of the "glaring facts" (133) of slavery, she cites southern laws, advertisements promoting the slave trade, and church resolutions designed to protect slaveowners. And, of course, the separation of families remains a key fact in *A Key*'s attack on slavery. These "facts" help her to demonstrate the implausibility of the pro-slavery contention that theirs was a society that not only liberally dispensed but truly deserved sympathy. Stowe savages such pro-slavery positions with ruthless irony, arguing that they can only be maintained at the expense of the facts, and getting the facts wrong is an expression of one's lack of sympathy. "Feeling right" is still Stowe's goal, but the reception of *Uncle Tom's Cabin* had undoubtedly convinced her that sympathy was as much a matter of fact as of feeling. Consequently, *A Key* endeavors to make the case that anti-slavery feelings are right because the facts upon which those feelings are derived are true.[2]

Through an analysis of texts by Fanny Kemble, Caroline Lee Hentz, and Stowe, I shall demonstrate and explicate the ideological complexities of sympathy as it is deployed in the antebellum debate about slavery. "Feeling right" produces dramatically different political allegiances, as sympathy motivates both Kemble's anti-slavery work, *Journal of a Residence on a Georgian Plantation in* 1838–1839 (1863), and Hentz's pro-slavery response to *Uncle Tom's Cabin*, *The Planter's Northern Bride* (1854). At first glance, one might suspect that such a grouping – white, relatively well-to-do-women – would produce a narrow account of the place of sympathy in debates about slavery, but just the opposite turns out to be true. Furthermore, because texts written by white middle-class women have borne the brunt of contemporary critiques of sympathy, I use that same group to argue against the homogenization of their cultural work. I do so, in part, by expanding the archive to include someone like Hentz, whose racist withholding of sympathy establishes a crucial, though often marginalized, context through which to consider anti-slavery dispensations of sympathy. Her pro-slavery appeal allows us to recognize, once again, the progressive force of Stowe's call to "feel right," which has been undermined so thoroughly that it has become increasingly difficult, but all the more important, to make distinctions between her version of sympathy, with its commitment to a progressive politics of abolitionism, and others such as Hentz's (and Adams's), which reveal the conjoining of sympathy and racism. What is so wickedly clever about Hentz's revision of Stowe is that in response to the claim that slavery destroys the biological family, Hentz makes the argument that the biological family isn't all it's cracked up to be – a theme we have repeatedly seen in sentimental fictions, but this time deployed in the service of an explicitly pro-slavery text. Hentz's attack on the biological family, in other words, grounds her defense of slavery.[3]

This chapter also makes the case that Stowe's *A Key* is essential to our understanding of her appeal to sympathy, which has been held, as I discussed in my introduction, in much disrepute. In revisiting the question of sympathy's effects, post *Uncle Tom's Cabin*, Stowe produces a model of sympathy not unlike the "judicious sympathy" of *The Lamplighter*, but with the explicit intention of making the case against slavery. Thus, Stowe aligns her sympathy as much with fact as with feeling, as much with irony as with sentiment, and in the process proves to her audience that because defenders of slavery are incapable or unwilling to distinguish between fact and truth, they are incapable of "feeling right."[4]

I THE SOUTH READS STOWE

The discursive battle over sympathy – who gets it, who gives it, who defines it – is a dominant feature in the antebellum debate about slavery, and Stowe's interventions are crucial. The controversy about sympathy has, as I have already discussed, been reduplicated in our own critical moment, with Stowe still at its center. Only now instead of standing for the promise (or threat, depending upon one's point of view) of anti-slavery ideology, Stowe's sympathy often exemplifies the dead-end of liberal politics. Lauren Berlant, for example, charges Stowe, specifically *Uncle Tom's Cabin*, with helping to create "a diacritics of congealed feeling" in which the imperative to act on behalf of those in pain (slaves, children, women) is blunted by the sentimental novels' even more strenuous injunction to end that pain through acts of imaginative reconciliation. But if Stowe comes to embody racist ideology, what are we to make of someone like Louise S. McCord, pro-slavery advocate and reviewer of *Uncle Tom's Cabin*, who writes in the January 1853 issue of *The Southern Quarterly Review*, "the negro has hitherto appeared simply as a blot upon creation?"[5]

The anti-slavery writings of Stowe, Kemble, and many others not only anticipate Berlant's critique of the "semiotic substance of sympathy," but also illustrate how feelings can eventuate in palpable acts of ameliorating other people's pain, whether those acts take the form of making garments for otherwise unclothed children or exposing their plight through the publication of a journal like Kemble's or a document like Weld's *Slavery*

As It Is (1839) or Child's *An Appeal in Favor of that Class of Americans Called Africans* (1833), the last two of which provided Stowe with a trove of information that found its way into *A Key*. Furthermore, Berlant's assumption that the structure of sympathy automatically establishes that "the sentimental subject is connected to others who share the same feeling" (646) has to be reexamined in the context of defenses of slavery, like McCord's, which hold precisely the opposite; her sympathy for slaves is established on her utter difference from them. She writes that while "Southern hearts and Southern souls can beat high," those very hearts maintain that "similar aims, similar hazards, similar hopes, and similar jealousies [are] in the ordinary relations of master and slave, feelings which are not only impossible . . . but ludicrous." Bizarre as it may seem, the case for southern sympathy is based on a disavowal of similarity, and slavery, with its racist hierarchization of difference, becomes the deepest expression of McCord's sympathy. Thus, she argues for the painlessness of being a slave, the only pain being that of a "homeless, houseless, useless negro," a condition which slavery mitigates by "providing the path marked out for him by Omniscience." My point is that if Stowe's sympathy is "congealed," what are we left to say about McCord's? Moreover, to lose sight of the differences between a McCord and a Stowe is not only to mistake the ideological intervention of their work, but it is also to repeat, without intending to, one of the major strategies of pro-southern writers, which was, as we shall see in the case of Hentz, to undermine altogether the differences between slavery and freedom.

Such a decontextualized deployment of Stowe, which doesn't take into account the pro-slavery position against which she is arguing, results in a misreading of Stowe's intervention in the slavery debate and disregards what many antebellum readers felt to be her devastating critique, which is, of course, precisely what pro-slavery advocates had in mind. In fact, McCord begins her review with an appeal to sympathize with the plight of slaveowners: "Truly it would seem that the labour of Sisyphus is laid upon us, the slaveholders of these southern United States" (81). Clearly, Stowe's appeal to feeling for slaves was being perverted by pro-slavery opponents who made the case for sympathy on behalf of themselves. Stowe's ideal of "feeling right" was vulnerable to such abuses, not because sympathy is categorically pernicious, but because it can be deployed in any number of different, indeed politically antithetical, contexts. As Stowe witnesses the appropriation of sympathy by southern racists, she realizes the necessity of thinking through sympathy yet again.

11 "I COULD HARDLY RESTRAIN MY FEELINGS": KEMBLE'S JOURNAL [6]

Kemble's *Journal* is a profound meditation on the value of sympathy which, while validating the necessity of "gentle sympathizing" (135), nevertheless questions the accuracy with which her sympathetic responses convey the horrors of slave life, and thus the effectiveness of any anti-slavery position that fails to defend its sympathies on the basis of fact. Although Kemble never relinquishes her belief in sympathy as the origin of all of her acts of kindness toward the slaves, she does worry about the extent to which her sympathy provides evidence in the case against slavery. The power of her sympathy – its power to move, to help, to instigate – is based on the extent to which her sympathy proves to be adequate (or not). Hers is a complex search for the most truthful and the most compelling evidence of her anti-slavery sympathy, and her surprising discovery is that the best evidence may not be her expressions at all, but rather those of the slaves. This is not to say that she ultimately renounces as worthless or ineffective her sympathy, whether its expression takes the form of irony or tears (she does, for instance, acknowledge the "good effect" of her "unmeasured upbraidings" [140]). She refuses to surrender any element of her sympathetic artillery as long as it helps to ameliorate the slaves' condition. It is to say, however, that she interrogates her expressions of sympathy, such as in this passage where she asks her friend, Elizabeth Sedgwick (and herself), "I wonder if my mere narration can make your blood boil as the facts did mine?" (76).

Kemble's "mere narration" is far from straightforward, as we shall see, but the logic of her sympathy goes something like this: she consistently acknowledges and establishes the importance of "human sympathy" (211), primarily through her words and tears; she scrutinizes the legitimacy of those words and tears, making her dissatisfied with her demonstrations of sympathy, even as she continues "to weep, and entreat, and implore, and upbraid for [the slaves]" (140); and she arrives at an alternative representation of sympathy which requires that she become the background to the foreground of the slaves' own expressions of pain. Needless to say, this is an interesting discovery to make in a journal where one's feelings, if not the text's explicit subject matter, are presumably of paramount importance. But Kemble realizes that it is the experiences of the slaves themselves – as represented in their words and upon their bodies – that prove to be the most reliable indicators of their pain and her sympathy. In what follows, I explore how she comes to this realization, as well as the linguistic and narrative consequences that accompany Kemble's sense that her own "exhibition of feeling" (78) is not necessarily the only way, or the best way, to advance the anti-slavery cause.

Kemble's *Journal* was written four years after the famed British actress married Pierce Butler, Philadelphia resident and heir to a large Georgia plantation that contained seven hundred slaves. For two years, Butler managed to put off his wife's desire to see the operations of his plantation and, perhaps, "take that opportunity of at once placing our slaves upon a more humane and Christian footing" (xxxv). Kemble's wish was granted when the overseers resigned and Butler had to journey south to find new ones. Husband and wife spent almost four months in Georgia, and the *Journal* powerfully records Kemble's experiences in a series of alternately humorous, informational, and devastating letters written, but not sent, to her close friend Mrs. Elizabeth Dwight Sedgwick, writer, educator, and sister-in-law of the popular New England author Catharine Maria Sedgwick. Although composed well over a decade before *Uncle Tom's Cabin,* the *Journal* was published a decade after, and the two texts share an abiding commitment to what Kemble calls "the commonest expression of human sympathy" (78).[7] In short order, Kemble discovers that her sympathy has very little in common with that of the neighboring slave owners, and this lack of agreement about what constitutes what is supposed to be "common" has important effects upon the narrative. Because southerners or, more precisely, pro-slavery southerners, deploy a radically different vocabulary from Kemble's in their descriptions of slavery, many passages of the *Journal* are taken up with defining and defending the correctness of her definitions against what she argues are their euphemisms. Thus, even as she confidently asserts that "slavery is answerable for all the evils that exhibit themselves where it exists" (62), at times, she finds herself less confident about how best to exhibit them.

Without a doubt, the complexities of Kemble's text are generated by her keen awareness of how language works, or how the same words can mean different things depending upon one's point of view.[8] En route to the plantation, for example, she and her two children, and their nursemaid Margery, spend the night in Weldon, North Carolina, about which Kemble scathingly observes: "although christened Weldon, and therefore pretending to be a place, [it] was rather the place where a place was intended to be" (19). The *Journal* is also filled with pointed references to the ways in which the moment she attempts to narrate her perceptions of slavery, the terms of that narration (and their significations) become subject to debate. The "fortunate dependence of the slave," for instance, is introduced and handily undermined by the phrase, "as it is called" (4). Elsewhere she comments on the fact that slaves are usually (and invidiously) referred to as "involuntary servants" and "seldom call[ed] slaves" (126). The clearest example of Kemble's terminological dilemma is found in the following description of the living spaces of the slaves:

> In the next cabin, which consisted of an enclosure called by courtesy a room, certainly not ten feet square, and owned by a woman called Dice – that is, not owned, of course, but inhabited by her – three grown-up human beings and eight children stow themselves by day and night, which may be called close packing, I think. (268–269)

The enormous gap between what things are called – enclosures or rooms, one's birth name or one's slave name, ownership or habitation – and what they are or "may be" produces a halting narrative that imagines at every turn in the argument an alternative to the one being produced. There are, in other words, two simultaneous and mutually exclusive readings and writings at play in this description of slave life. Thus, Kemble offers up and denounces a southern dictionary of sorts in which "being in despair at being torn from one's wife and children is called *kicking up a fuss*" (138), and "women in the family way" are called "lusty women, as the phrase is here" (179). Throughout her narrative, Kemble works to establish the correctness of her anti-slavery position by claiming that her words, unlike those of her pro-slavery antagonists, accurately signify the realities of slave life. Passages like this make the point that at the definitional heart of the pro-slavery meaning of words is the absence of sympathy. Kemble understands, moreover, that it is essential to expose these linguistic sleights of hand as strategies which not only misrepresent the reality of slave life but also muffle the absolute differences between being enslaved and being free.[9]

At certain points in the narrative, however, even Kemble's irony doesn't seem up to the task of demonstrating and dismantling the linguistic perversions that operate in defenses of slave culture. In this passage, for instance, her anti-slavery perspective needs to be supplemented by additional definition. She records "a visit that made me very sorrowful, if anything connected with these poor people can be called more especially sorrowful than their whole condition" (222). Her point, of course, is that the acknowledgment of any particular aspect of slavery as "very sorrowful" could be misconstrued to mean that other aspects are less sorrowful, or perhaps not sorrowful at all. Similarly, she concludes her detailed discussion of the particular sufferings of slave mothers with the following: "it seems to me marvelous with what desperate patience (I write it advisedly, patience of utter despair) they endure their sorrow-laden existence" (231). Again, she is acutely aware that she must write everything "advisedly," because her words and feelings are so vulnerable to misapplication. In a world where "nothing signifies except the cotton crop" (202), Kemble must work hard indeed to make her words signify what she wants them to as opposed to what the logic of slavery makes them mean.

The inability of language to convey Kemble's sorrows about the sorrows she witnesses, either because of potential misinterpretation or rhetorical insufficiency, forces her to seek alternative forms of expression. Her narrative seems to hold out the possibility that the frustrating opacity of her language can, perhaps, be circumvented by the transparency of her pained body responding to the pained bodies of the slaves who surround her. As a result, we find ourselves in the traditional realm of the sentimental protagonist – à la Charlotte Temple or Ellen Montgomery – where tears fall liberally and the female body speaks louder and clearer than her voice. Throughout the *Journal*, Kemble often finds herself "perfectly unable to speak, the tears pouring from my eyes" (70), or "breathless with surprise and dismay . . . with my heart and temples throbbing to such a degree that I could hardly support myself" (136). Similarly, images of howling (190) and choking (170, 179, 222, 241, 256) pervade the narrative. Like the archetypal sentimental heroine, Kemble's sympathetic (white) body continually registers the pain experienced by the (black) slaves: "I sat as usual at the receipt of custom, hearing of aches and pains till I ached myself sympathetically from head to foot" (267). What I find particularly compelling about Kemble's "exhibition of feeling" is her skepticism about feeling as an "exhibition" which can amount to nothing more than "impotent indignation and unavailing pity" (133). In an especially desperate moment, she laments, "poor people! How little I have done, how little I can do for them" (193). But even when she is most critical of her sympathy, never does she suggest that an absence of sympathy in the face of the slaves' condition is preferable or, in any way, defensible. That would be the start of an argument in favor of slavery. Sympathy for the slaves is the necessary foundation for any of her acts, whether it is making clothes for the children, sanitizing their living spaces and hospitals, or teaching them how to read.[10]

To be sure, as a world-famous actress, Kemble is accustomed to having her feelings exhibited on the stage, but the theatre of slavery in Georgia and her dramatic role in it are radically different. Her reactions are crucial as signs of sympathy, yet they aren't necessarily the subject that matters most. Rather, it is the pain of the slaves themselves. On the one hand, she believes that her sympathy guarantees her accuracy as a recorder of the slaves' experiences, and yet on the other hand, she worries that her sympathy, as a form of mediation, obscures the record. Thus, we find Kemble searching for a way to write a narrative that at once reveals her own pain upon witnessing the suffering of the slaves, but then works to foreground the pain of the slaves themselves by concentrating on their expressions. She often remarks, for example, upon the quality of the slaves' narrative voices, with comments such as, "she told it very simply, and it was most pathetic" (215), or "I wish I could write down the voice and look of abject misery with which [the woman's] words were spoken" (270). Elsewhere she ponders, "I am very much struck with the vein of melancholy which assumes almost a poetical tone in some of the things they say" (306). She now self-consciously occupies the position of the audience – forcing herself to listen, to witness, and to respond as effectively and practically as possible to the relentless and real scenes of horror playing out before her. Indeed, the *Journal* makes the very act of listening to the slaves' words a moral imperative. Unlike the overseer and Butler himself, both of whom assure her that "it was impossible to believe a single word any of these people said" (85), Kemble not only grants the truthfulness of the slaves' words but insists upon the impossibility of believing the words of the overseer and her husband. Against the wishes of her husband, then, and even though she sometimes "long[s] to stop [her] ears" (222), Kemble defiantly states, "I cannot and will not refuse to hear any and every tale of suffering which these unfortunates bring to me" (133). There can be no action on behalf of the slaves without the sympathy that can come only from hearing their words.

As much as Kemble's is an account of her own responses to the slaves' experiences of sexual abuse, violent punishment, and family separation, there is also a sense that the *Journal* ought to be something more or, as she suggests in this passage, something less: "I do not wish to add to, or perhaps I ought to say take away from, the effect of such narrations by amplifying the simple horror and misery of their bare details" (239). Kemble understands that such amplifications, which nonetheless make up much of her own text and help to register her anti-slavery sympathy, can detract from the representation of the slave experience itself and, perhaps, mitigate her potential to act effectively out of sympathy. An ideal of "bare detail" is held up but never completely actualized, such as in this passage: "I make no comment; what need, or can I add, to such stories? But how is such a state of things to endure? And again, how is it to end?" (270). Toward the end of the *Journal* she eagerly anticipates her family's return to the north when "we shall soon be free again," but sentences later she remarks, "I have let my letter lie ... but as mine is a story without beginning, middle, or end, it matters extremely little where I leave it off or where I take it up" (287). Although Kemble's own personal narrative *will* progress beyond the bounds of the plantation – she journeys to Georgia, lives there for four months, and then leaves – her *Journal* signals her belief that existence under the sign of slavery stops narrative in its tracks, in part because the words which comprise her narrative must continually be defined and defended against baleful appropriations and in part because the institution of slavery prospers by producing lives without progression. She laments, "what a curse of utter stagnation this slavery produces" (167). Such narrative and personal blockage is, for instance, powerfully exemplified by Kemble's recurrence to a flogging inflicted upon "the poor woman Harriet" (74) as a punishment for having told Kemble that slave women did not have time to keep their children clean. Kemble writes, "I again and again made her repeat her story, and she again and again affirmed that she had been flogged for what she told me" (74). It is as if Kemble and her narrative simply cannot absorb the shock of first, a system that doesn't permit mothers to care for their children and that doesn't allow them to speak about such trials, and second, of her own unwitting participation, simply by allowing Harriet to speak, in the slave's punishment.[11]

Kemble's *Journal* struggles to produce a narrative out of the experiences of slaves, experiences which she believes refute the very logic of narrative progression. Thus, the plot of the *Journal* is the plot of her sympathy – the actions which follow from it and her doubts about it – which provides her with a way of including, though subordinating, the slaves' experiences into a narrative of her responses to them. Her skepticism about her sympathy, however, leaves Kemble dissatisfied with this solution. Throughout, she wonders and worries "whether anyone who feels so many things can really be said to feel anything" (224), and there are places in the text that assume a different narrative form, as if she is struggling to get the content of her feelings out of the way in order to show just how very much she does feel. The best example of her attempted self-erasure can be found in the section about slave mothers where, after narrating the brutality of their lives and her reactions to it, she inserts a list of the names of these women and their reproductive histories. The entries are simple, unusual for Kemble in their absence of irony and linguistic complication, and gruesome:

Fanny has had six children; all dead but one. She came to beg to have her work in the field lightened.

Nanny has had three children; two of them are dead. She came to implore that the
  rule of sending them into the field three weeks after their confinement might be
  altered.
Leah, Caesar's wife, has had six children; three are dead . . .
Sophy, Lewis's wife, came to beg for some old linen. She is suffering fearfully; has
  had ten children; five of them are dead. The principal favor she asked was a piece
  of meat, which I gave her. (229)

This devastating list, in which Kemble's presence is powerfully superseded
by the slaves', presents a different demonstration of her sympathies, in
which her words needn't be defined and her tears needn't be scrutinized
because, quite simply, they aren't hers. In passages like this or elsewhere
when she writes, "I give you the woman's words" (241), or "I have written
down the woman's words" (270), Kemble's *Journal* points us in the direction of texts, such as Weld's, Child's, or Stowe's *A Key*, which, in their
documentary records of slave suffering, aim to promote the anti-slavery
appeal more on the foundation of what they believed were the unambiguous
facts of slavery and less on the basis of the unpredictable affiliations unleashed
by feelings. Here, Kemble's text materializes her sense of the incompatibility
of the slaves' experiences and narrative, as if the relentless births and deaths of
the slave women's children is not the stuff of narrative, but lists.

Kemble, though, never does efface completely her own feelings about
"these melancholy words" (127) from the pages of her *Journal*; after all, it is a
journal written with the explicit intention of recording her feelings. Thus,
even in the list of names from which I have just quoted, Kemble's more
conventional expression of sympathy presents itself: "*Charlotte*, Renty's wife,
had two miscarriages, and was with child again. She was almost crippled with
rheumatism, and showed me a pair of poor swollen knees that made my
heart ache" (230). These are the "bare detail[s]," the facts, that make
Kemble's "heart ache," that induce her to sew "little baby clothes" for
"children otherwise unclothed" (194), to give slaves more food, to "break
the laws of the government under which I am living" (271) by teaching them
how to read, to beseech and convince her husband not to separate families, to
pay them wages for their labor (217); they are, in other words, the facts
underwriting her sympathy, which then compel her to act.

III THE SOUTHERN HEART; OR, *THE PLANTER'S NORTHERN BRIDE*

Of the many pro-slavery novels written in response to *Uncle Tom's Cabin*,
Hentz's *The Planter's Northern Bride* stands out. Whereas much

"anti-Uncle Tom" literature, to use Thomas Gossett's phrase, folds a clumsy plot into a rabid pro-slavery diatribe, Hentz produces a novel whose central concern is sympathy or, as she states in her preface, the wish to find a "Northern heart [which will] respond to our earnest appeal"(10). To find this "Northern heart," she acknowledges that she must first repair the "Southern heart" that Stowe had so convincingly eviscerated. Hentz does this by presenting us with a carefully articulated defense of slavery, which is predicated upon the south's prolific capacities for sympathy (as giver *and* receiver), and the allegedly satisfying arrange-ments of the slave family. She upholds the integrity of slave families, first by not acknowledging and therefore not representing their separations, and second, by making the case that children don't necessarily love most their biological family, especially their birth mothers. This, of course, could not be more different from Stowe.[12]

In Hentz's fictional world, it is the master's white family, not the slaves', that is victimized by the agonizing separations so fully delineated and denounced in Kemble's *Journal* and *Uncle Tom's Cabin*. Hentz's is a world where slaveowners evince the spirit of sympathy, both in their everyday kindnesses to slaves and in their benevolent decision to maintain the responsibilities of owning them; abolitionists, by contrast, have "no compassion" (280). Hers is a world where every black person wishes to be a slave because one glimpse of freedom convinces him/her that, "if this is freedom, give us bondage and chains instead" (240). But bondage and chains turn out not to be real, as we learn that "the bondage of the slave" is dismissed as "nominal" (27), and the chains are "mere figures of speech" (51). Hentz's strategy throughout is to expose what she sees as the termino-logical chicanery of anti-slavery advocates whose demands for sympathy on behalf of slaves are precariously founded on "mere figures" rather than facts. She doesn't deny that slavery exists but claims that its "facts [have been] so distorted, so wrenched from their connexion with other extenuat-ing facts, that they present a mangled and bleeding mass of fragments, instead of a solid body of truth" (78). This passage is interesting (and typical of Hentz's subversive deployment of abolitionist discourse) in that it is not the slave body that is mangled and bleeding, but rather the body of facts about slavery. These facts, Hentz insists, are that slave families do not live in fear of separation, that white workers in the free north, not slaves, lead lives of real desperation, and that the evidence of the anti-slavery case consists of "awful tales" (237) and "horrible stories" (331), which simply aren't true. To present the accurate facts is, then, to repair the sullied reputation of "true-hearted Southerners" (302) – to recognize them as legitimate benefactors and deserving recipients of sympathy. Hentz's truth thus begins with the assertion of Stowe's (and others) lack of it, and she establishes this point, like Kemble, by critiquing the very words deployed by the opposing camp. Whereas Kemble works hard to maintain the linguistic and ideological differences between slavery and freedom, Hentz works equally hard to undermine them. She writes, "Free! I wonder who is free? Exclaimed the Northern Betsy. We repeat the exclamation. We wonder who is really free in this great prison-house" (338). To make freedom meaningless is to begin both the critique of Stowe and the reclamation of southern sympathy.

"I grant that some of these tales of cruelty are true; for, that man is sometimes a deadly tyrant, the annals of history too darkly prove. But, generally speaking, they are nothing but gross fabrications, invented to enlist the sympathies of credulous fanatics" (195). So declares Russell Moreland, hero of *The Planter's Northern Bride*, after having read a series of abolitionist tracts meant to "enlist the sympathies" of readers. Because these "tales of cruelty" can take place anywhere, anytime, the southerner Moreland believes that it would be a mistake to assign them a particular cause, like slavery, especially when the instances of their occurrence in the south are relatively few and primarily fictitious. They are, after all, "tales," "fabrications" designed to elicit a sympathetic response from readers who will then, if the tale works properly, adopt a critical stance toward slavery. Sympathy, in the hands of "credulous fanatics," will prove extremely dangerous in the novel, as we witness several abolitionists who have mistaken these "gross fabrications" for the truth and, as a consequence, destroy southern families and the lives of black slaves, and, as if that weren't bad enough, threaten the safety of the national body politic. Moreland does not wish to eradicate sympathy, but to direct it to the proper targets, and these include white slaveowners who must bear the burden of caring for the slaves, white working women of the north whose labor is unrelenting, blacks who have been duped into thinking they want freedom, and most importantly, the south, which has been unfairly persecuted by "the thorns of prejudice" (31).

For Hentz, a transplanted northerner who followed her husband from one academic job to another through the south, *Uncle Tom's Cabin* was the most potent of these "fabrications," and she published her novel within two years of Stowe's. Hentz claims in the preface that during her entire residence in the south, she "never *witnessed* one scene of cruelty or oppression, never beheld a chain or a manacle, or the infliction of a punishment more severe than parental authority would be justified in applying to filial disobedience or transgression" (5). To authenticate her statements, she refers to her studies of plantation life in North Carolina, Alabama, Georgia, and Florida, where she has "almost invariably been delighted and affected by their [the slaves'] humble devotion to their master's family, their child-like, affectionate reliance on their care and protection, and above all, with their genuine cheerfulness and contentment" (6–7). Hentz's novel tries to convince its readers that slaves do not require sympathy because their economic, spiritual, and affective needs are wholly cared for by their masters. Because they are free of needs, they don't require sympathy. Sympathy is a required emotion only when there is a material lack, and it turns out that those most lacking are white working women of the north and white people of the south. It is their experience of economic and national alienation that warrants a sympathetic response. Interestingly, the economic transactions at the heart of slavery, the buying and selling of persons, are minimized to the point of erasure. Economic considerations are shown to be far more pervasive and problematic within the spousal and parental relations of the novel's white families than between masters and slaves or within slave families.

The Planter's Northern Bride has as its overarching frame the love story between Moreland and Eulalia, who, though a northerner by birth, is "a tropic flower, born to be nurtured beneath milder skies" (148). Moreland has journeyed to the north to eradicate painful memories of a first marriage gone bad, when he first encounters Eula singing in the church choir. A brief courtship ensues, followed by a proposal of marriage. To counter the objections of Eula's father, Hastings, a staunch abolitionist who vehemently opposes his daughter's marriage to a slaveholder, Moreland convinces him of the national and providential consequences of this union between north and south. When Eula departs for the south, where the rest of the novel takes place, her father explains the reason for his change of mind: "I believe Providence has a mission for you to perform . . . you will be a golden link of union between the divided interests of humanity" (136). Clearly, their marriage is meant to function as an allegory of the conflict and hopeful resolution between north and south.

This resolution will first and foremost be accomplished by eradicating the prejudices of the north, and this is why Eula must venture southward to see that "there is no such thing as irresponsible power at the south" (204). Eula's encounter with plantation life allows Hentz to present a series of northern stereotypes about the south and slavery which are then dismissed as incorrect. Thus, the claim that slavery breeds an unregulated system of labor, which we find in everything from Stowe to Frederick Douglass's *Narrative of the Life of Frederick Douglass*, is countered by this description: "Eula admired the systematic arrangement of everything. The hours of labour were all regulated – the tasks for those hours appointed" (341). In answering the abolitionist charge that slavery meant a life of unending labor, the narrator asserts that the slaves "did not do as much work in one week as a white servant will accomplish in one day" (184). Here, Hentz invokes the familiar analogy between white workers and black slaves, to which we shall return, in order to argue that the lot of the former is far worse than the latter's. Lastly, the belief that slavery promotes unregulated passions within slaveholders, who are legally permitted to act violently upon those passions, is offset by Moreland's statement, "I would sooner give my right hand to the flames than make it the instrument of cruelty and oppression to them [the slaves]" (304). This passage strategically calls attention to the perils of the master's white body rather than the injuries sustained by black bodies under the system of slavery.

But the most pernicious northern prejudice is the fiction of southern prejudice toward slaves. Hentz takes great pains to explain that slavery is not based on prejudice, but is a system put in place long before her cast of characters entered the scene: "we had no more to do with its existence than our own. We are not responsible for it, though we are for the duties it involves, the heaviest perhaps ever imposed upon man" (82). In fact, Eulalia (whose name suggestively resonates with Stowe's Ophelia) has to enter the world of slavery to be cured of her own prejudice toward blacks. Her abolitionist household, which assumes the equality between black and white, has transformed Eula's instinctive (her disposition is, after all, more southern than not) understanding of the difference and superiority of white over black into an unnatural fear and loathing of blacks. Moreland admonishes her about this troublesome "repugnance to the African race. You must struggle with this from the first, and it will surely be overcome. It is of unnatural birth – born of prejudice and circumstance" (201). Only in the south, the sympathetic south, where this repugnance to the African race doesn't exist, can Eula be freed from her northern prejudice.

Eula's prejudice toward blacks is easily overcome once she realizes that the slaves of Moreland's plantation do not require the sympathy she thought they needed. Her conversion is quick and complete, as she contentedly tells her husband, "I never dreamed that slavery could present an aspect so tender and affectionate" (333). But there is one resident in particular who does need her sympathy, and that is Effie, the child of Moreland's first marriage to the monstrous and ultimately pitiable

Claudia. Effie is the Topsy-figure in *The Planter's Northern Bride*, unloved by her father because she reminds him of his awful first wife and heretofore undisciplined by a stable mother figure. Eula's task, according to Moreland, is to "make her like yourself, Eula, all that is lovely and good, and I will forget she ever had another mother" (217). Effie responds immediately and fully to the love and sympathy of her stepmother. So fully, in fact, that when Claudia takes her daughter from Eula and Moreland, claiming, "she is mine! I will not give her up! Has not the mother a right to her own child?" (368), Effie pleads with her biological mother, "take me to my dear, sweet, other mamma!" and asks her, "how come I have two mammas?" (466). Eula eventually gets Effie back, but the ideological complexities of this narrative strand are multiple. For example, when Claudia takes Effie away, she exclaims, "I will have the child, snatching Effie with frantic violence from her arms and rushing to the door" (370). She is virtually kidnapped by her biological mother. When the narrator ponders, "had not the mother purchased her child by the pains and sorrows of maternity, and could any legal decision annul the great law of God, which makes the child a mother's almost life-bought property?" (369), the answers are no and yes. The mother has not purchased her child through the pain of labor (such pain was no guarantee for slave mothers), and legal decisions can annul the great law of God (to wit, the slave code). A child, in other words, is not a mother's almost life-bought property.[13]

That the narrator even imagines the mother/child relationship economically, figuring the child in terms of property and inquiring about its/her purchase price, is in itself revealing. Indeed, Effie occupies the position of a slave with her mothers, Claudia and Eula, arguing over the right of ownership. In response to Claudia's, "she is mine," Eula decries, "this child is *mine* – committed to my guardianship by the father, who has abjured your maternal right!" (370). Biological attachments are not necessarily as powerful as cultural ones and, in this case, they most certainly are not. Effie easily shifts her attachments from birth mother to stepmother as she says to Eula, "she isn't my mamma, is she? . . . Make her go away – I don't love her" (369), surely a model for a slave child who is torn away from her biological mother and is forced to establish an alternative maternal bond. Effie's family drama, therefore, functions to validate slavery's creation of new parental relations at the same time as her tale displaces (and effaces) that very drama taking place in the slave family.

We need only think of Stowe's glorification of the mother/child relationship, Eliza and Henry immediately come to mind, to understand the radical difference between hers and Hentz's model of family. From Stowe's perspective, a reunion with the biological mother is every child's, particularly every slave child's, dream come true. In Hentz, this dream is inverted so as to become Effie's worst nightmare. Effie, in fact, *becomes* a slave once Claudia gets her back as "advertisement[s] are inserted in every paper, with offers of munificent reward" (432). Whereas the sanctity of the mother/child bond is precisely what should prevent the practice of slavery in *Uncle Tom's Cabin*, the flexibility of this relationship (children can have deeper attachments to second mammas; an idea that Hentz takes up in *Ernest Linwood*, as well, but not as part of an explicit defense of slavery) undergirds the structure of slavery and provides a defense for it. Effie, prototype for the slave, is most free when she is with her newly constructed family.

Effie's kidnapping, I have been arguing, mimics the structural logic of slavery whereby children are taken from their mothers, but inverts that logic by suggesting that the separation between children and biological mothers is a salvific one. Hentz's fondness for strategic appropriations of this kind pervades her text, but none is more striking, indeed perverse, than the representation of Crissy's flight from slavery. Crissy, to provide the necessary background, is the slave of Ildegarte, the sister of Moreland with whom she lives. Ilde, as she is called, must travel west with her husband, Richard, in a last-ditch effort to cure him of consumption. Crissy accompanies them on their journey, but meets up with the evil abolitionists, Mr. and Mrs. Softly, who seduce her with thoughts of freedom and effect her escape at the very moment Ilde needs her most – during Richard's agonizing death. The unthinkable parallel is, of course, the possibility that Tom were to leave St. Clare during Eva's protracted illness and death.

As Hentz explains it, freedom is the furthest thing from Crissy's mind when her journey begins, except to be afraid of it: "she glanced from one side to the other, with a vague dread of being pounced upon and carried off [by abolitionists]" (250). Indeed, when the Softlys finally do "exert [their] influence upon her, and not suffer her to remain in bondage and degradation" (270), her escape is described as a kidnapping, as "the abduction of Crissy" (357–358). The abolitionists in Hentz's world act very much like the slaveowners in Stowe's and, as these quotations suggest, the language of freedom is indistinguishable from the language of slavery. Questioning the ethics of the Softlys' commitment to abolitionism, the narrator asks, "what, but the carrying out of a fixed, inflexible purpose, at any cost, at any sacrifice; the triumph of an indomitable will?" (281) Their willfulness that she be free, regardless of Crissy's contentment with her position, all but cancels out Crissy's will to be a slave. It is the abolitionists, not the slaveholders, who undermine Crissy's agency: "thus beset, day after day, poor Crissy grew weak and impotent, till she became a passive tool in their soft, insinuating hands" (271). Crissy's escape sounds suspiciously like the kidnapping of a slave. Mr. Softly "had brought [Crissy] by water, so that she could not trace her path backward" (380). Unsurprisingly, the consequence of Crissy's freedom is an enslavement greater than any she has ever known. Her accommodations in the fugitive slave house can't help reminding the reader of Harriet Jacobs's sequestration: "The room was unplastered, not even lathed, and when she looked up she knew by the slanting rafters overhead that she had been sleeping in a garret . . . She began to feel deadly cold. Chill, shivering sensations went creeping up and down her back, while hot water seemed splashing on her face" (378–379). Instead of yearning for freedom, though, Crissy fondly remembers the suffering mistress she has abandoned: "how kind and sympathizing she was in sickness! How often her soft, white hand, had bathed the negro's aching brow" (379).

Because freedom, not slavery, produces suffering, sympathy for Crissy can be articulated only at the moment of her liberation. From Hentz's perspective, we are meant to sympathize with Crissy's plight as a slave on the brink of becoming free because she has been grossly misled into thinking that freedom would be a positive experience. Instead, "however glorious freedom was in itself, it had proved to her the only slavery she had ever known" (392). We should thus rejoice when Crissy "come[s] back," like a wandering sheep to "the fold" (399) of Moreland's plantation. Crissy's situation as a potentially free person is dire, indeed, but even worse off is Ilde, from whom the Softlys have stolen "a *friend*, in the hour of extremest need" (359). Ilde's need for sympathy at the moment of Richard's death supersedes Crissy's need for freedom, which according to Hentz is no need at all, but one manufactured by the Softlys for the "gratification of prejudice and intolerance" (281). The Softlys' sympathy is not only grossly misplaced but quite dangerous in its "fiery fanaticism [and] frantic zeal, which, reckless of all consequences, was spreading through the land" (272). It is not southern prejudice against blacks that threatens to destroy the union, but rather northern prejudice, which is expressed through abolitionism, against the south. Abolitionism, not slavery, is the "dark spot" (459) which endeavors "to destroy our liberties and rights" (407) and ends up enslaving the south.

Just as to be an abolitionist in *The Planter's Northern Bride* is to be as heartless as any slaveholder in an anti-slavery text (think of Covey, Flint, or Legree), so too a slave's acquisition of freedom condemns him/her to the worst slavery imaginable. This is why so many slaves in the novel who become free through manumission or escape end up begging to be returned to slavery. Crissy's friend Judy, for example, who has escaped one of the few slaveowners who physically abuses his slaves (and his wife as well), implores Eula and Moreland to buy her. Exhausted by her freedom and its concomitant responsibilities, Judy asserts, "I belongs to a mighty mean missus, just now, honey – dat's my own ugly, black self. I'm tired of being my own missus, dat I am" (290–291). It would seem that self-ownership is a version of slavery far worse than the one in the south, leaving freed slaves with the desire to return to their enslaved condition. Like Judy, Davy, the son of a slave freed by Moreland's father, requests that Moreland take back his family: "I give them to you, just as if they had never been free. I bequeath you all my property too, and wish it was more" (504). Hentz also tells the story of a free negro who had lost his boat-building business in a storm off the coast of St. Andrew's Bay. "He came to many gentlemen, entreating them to purchase himself and family, saying he was tired of the responsibility of their support. He had known what slavery and freedom were, and he preferred the first" (355). The only freedom these slaves seem to possess is the freedom to work for strangers for a minimum wage.

That northern workers had more difficult and impoverished lives when compared to slaves was an argument used time and again by pro-slavery advocates, and Hentz proves no exception.[14] Wounded workers, whether they are free blacks or northern women, as opposed to violated slaves, appear throughout Hentz's novel. And they all want to be slaves. When Moreland first journeys northward, he remarks upon the dolorous situation of its workers: "there was the bondage of poverty, whose iron chains are heard clanking in every region of God's earth, whose dark links are wrought in the forge of human suffering, eating slowly into the quivering flesh, til they reach and dry up the life-blood of the heart" (27). Nancy, a white worker at the inn where Moreland temporarily resides, is dying of consumption due to over-work. The solution? Slavery. "She thought of her days of servitude, her waning health, her anxious fears and torturing apprehensions of future want, and it seemed to her the mere exemption from such far-reaching solicitudes must be a blessing. She thought, too, of the soft, mild atmosphere that flowed around those children of toil, and wished she could breathe its balm" (52). Similarly, Betsy, who is the maid in the Hastings' household, tells Albert, Moreland's slave, "I'm ten times more of a slave, this minute, than you are, and have been all my life" (174). It turns out that the iron chains of poverty which destroy the lives of northern workers are far more palpable than any chains one might have read about in abolitionist descriptions of slavery. They are "mere figures of speech," not unlike the abolitionist words of Eula's father, which Moreland insists are "a figure of rhetoric" (105).

Hentz's novel works to make slavery "a figure of rhetoric" as she defends slavery against its conventional depictions in abolitionist literature in order to quash what she sees as the malicious and false distinctions made between freedom and slavery. Those distinctions don't hold, both because abolitionist texts are "fabrications" and hers is truthful, and because she has redefined freedom as slavery and slavery as freedom. She writes, "even *bondage*, which at a distance had seemed so dark and threatening, lightened up as they approached it, like the mist of their valley, and receded from their view" (576). The aim of her polemic is to make bondage recede from view so that it looks like something else, so that it can be called freedom. The chains, the family separations, the unrelenting labor, all of the alleged "facts" of slavery become merely discursive strategies in the abolitionist artillery against the south. She takes these supposed sectional and peculiar "facts" and argues for their applicability in the north. Thus, rather than standing for a commitment to abolitionism, as Senator William Seward intended in his "higher law" speech, Hentz's higher law means advocating the right of the south to preserve its own institutions. "The anathema of prejudice" (552) does not allude to black/white relations, but rather to the conflict between northern abolitionists and southern slaveowners. And finally, slavery is not slavery but freedom, and freedom is not freedom but slavery. In creating sectional differences where there need not be any, and in proposing the necessity for racial sympathy where none need exist (the slaves are loved, the south is not), Hentz argues that abolitionists like Stowe construct a south more enslaved by northern prejudice than any slave could ever be and a south more in need of sympathy than any slave could ever be. The work of sympathy, as it operates in Hentz's text, functions to erase the differences between north and south, between freedom and slavery. There is, however, one difference that Hentz's text will not challenge, because she believes that "inequality is one of Nature's laws" (305). For Hentz, black is black and white is white and it is, of course, the insistence upon and hierarchization of this difference that produces the real facts of slavery. And so, for Stowe, the need for sympathy.

IV READING THE *CODE NOIR*

Antebellum responses to *Uncle Tom's Cabin* reveal that the novel unleashed a furious debate not only about gender and race relations as they operated in both the north and the south, but about the very nature of evidence itself. In a vitriolic survey of what she takes to be the many flaws of the novel, McCord lambasts, in particular, Stowe's "remarkable facts" (83). Similarly, John R. Thompson, founder of the pro-slavery *Southern Literary Messenger* and reviewer of *Uncle Tom's Cabin*, intends his response to "expose the miserable misrepresentations of her story."[5] On the other side of the aisle, Kemble contends that "the evils of slavery" presented by Stowe were "not only possible, but probable, and not only probable, but a very faithful representation of the existing facts" (349). But Stowe's own *A Key* provides us with indisputable evidence that one of the most powerful effects of *Uncle Tom's Cabin* had been to conjoin the debate about slavery with epistemological questions about the nature of evidence, fact, and truth.

Stowe's documentary sequel to *Uncle Tom's Cabin* is an irate, ironic, and intellectual critique of critiques of the novel. *A Key* rigorously examines the evidence proffered by defenders of slavery, whether it be court cases, legal statutes, or newspaper articles, and argues for its utter unreliability (in more generous moments) or its shameful mendacity (in less patient ones). Such evidence, furthermore, confirms Stowe's sense that "the slave code of America... is a case of elegant surgical instruments for the work of dissecting the living human heart" (82). *A Key* aims to prove the absolute impossibility of being both pro-slavery and sympathetic by establishing their mutual exclusivity. What Hentz calls the "southern heart" doesn't exist as a functioning organ. And if hearts have been dissected, not only can they not feel, but they certainly cannot "feel right." "Feeling right," to invoke once more Stowe's famous injunction at the conclusion of *Uncle Tom's Cabin*, *has* to produce an anti-slavery stance because the facts of the pro-slavery position are predicated upon the absence of feelings.

A Key proceeds along the lines of an archeological discovery of facts because, as Stowe never tires of pointing out, defenders of slavery specialize in the art of euphemism or, as she puts it, their "endless variety of specifications and synonyms" (113). Stowe's task is to pierce through that endless variety in order to get to the facts of the brutality of southern slavery and, in the process, to claim and prove that their version of the facts is a lie. This means that Stowe, like Kemble, focuses much of her energy decrying the fraudulent language used to defend slavery. Stowe, however, transforms Kemble's terminological dilemma into an opportunity for, rather than an obstacle to, the production of narrative. The exposure of euphemism, which Stowe believes to be at the core of defenses of slavery, acts as the spur to her narrative. In fact, Stowe deploys pro-slavery euphemism and linguistic manipulation as evidence which begins to prove that the facts supporting the argument in favor of slavery are fallacious. And not for a moment does she doubt, as Kemble did, whether hers is a "mere narration."

Stowe is unapologetically ubiquitous in *A Key*, even inserting herself through punctuation, whether through capitalization, italics, or quotation marks, as a way to establish the insincerity of pro-slavery terminology. Although it is a compendium of citation, in other words, she has to call attention to the places where she is not: "the following is quoted without comment" (188), or "the Italics are the writers [*sic*]" (197). All of Stowe's interventions require the reader to wonder, if people like Hentz, McCord, and Thompson don't know the meaning of words, if they insist on obfuscating the differences between "nominal bondage" and "bondage," for example, how can one trust them, their facts, their feelings? Stowe thus understands and uses to her advantage the strategy of texts like *The Planter's Northern Bride* and other "anti-Uncle Tom novels" that attempt to extinguish the differences between freedom and slavery in order to defend the peculiar institution on both its evidentiary and sympathetic merits. She exposes this tactical maneuver as contingent upon a perversion of the facts of slavery, and she does so, I shall show, through her use of irony, citation, and hermeneutic expertise. Furthermore, to make implausible the pro-slavery counter-assertion that her version of the facts is fiction, she demonstrates how defenses of slavery – whether in the legal, religious, or novelistic domain – instantiate the "deadening of sensibility" (203), "the numbness of public sentiment" (83), the "gradual deterioration of the moral sense" (206). Such numbness has made it virtually impossible for defenders of slavery to recognize the difference between fact and fiction, truth and lies, freedom and slavery. And not to know or not to acknowledge these differences (Stowe alternates between these two readings of slaveholders' intentions) is the clearest sign of that "awful paralysis of the moral sense" (128). Stowe's sympathy, then, is validated precisely because she has the facts to prove such categorical distinctions, the most important fact being that a person is not a thing.[16]

Stowe quickly wrote *A Key* with the intention of defending herself from critics who questioned everything from her right as a woman to participate so publicly in the slavery debate to her first-hand knowledge of slavery itself. In the process, she took the opportunity of attacking them all over again. Although *A Key* has received scant critical attention, it is a fascinating text for several reasons, one of which is its status as Stowe's own rereading of *Uncle Tom's Cabin* in the context of responses to it.[17] Another is the text's insatiable appetite for (and amalgamation of) a variety of discourses, whether novels, poetry, newspapers, personal correspondence, the Bible, statistics, or the law. The text's generic hybridity formally makes the point that the ideology of slavery is not limited to a particular genre but rather inhabits discourse itself. To the extent that *A Key* is a "mosaic of facts" (5), as Stowe maintains in its opening chapters, its hybridity works to underscore and undermine the ubiquitous facts of pro-slavery discourse (most importantly, the notion that slavery is benign), which are, from Stowe's point of view, lies. Its opening chapter, for example, characterizes *Uncle Tom's Cabin* as an "arrangement of real incidents – of actions really performed, of words and expressions really uttered" (5). By way of contrast, Stowe quotes a passage from J. Thornton Randolph's *The Cabin and Parlor* in which the author suggests that the separation of slave families may happen in "'novels,'" but doesn't occur "'in real life, except in rare cases.'" She then asks the question that had been unceasingly asked of her book, "are these representations true?" (133). Stowe's answer is a resounding no, and her critique of Randolph tactically proceeds by reproducing advertisements with headings such as "NEGROES WANTED" and "NEGROES FOR SALE" from two South Carolina newspapers. Stowe's rage at such mendacity is evident throughout, as she juxtaposes expressions of southern benevolence toward slaves with advertisements describing slaves with missing teeth or toes, or she lists instruments used in torturing slaves, such as "gags, thumb-screws, cowhides" to which masters resort when "gentle force will not do" (220). In addition, Stowe intersperses searing close readings of the pervasive and perfidious language of the "indefinite terms" (142) used to describe slaves for sale, such as "'*selected*'"(140), "'assortments'"(142), and "'lots'"(142), all of which help Stowe make the argument that *Uncle Tom's Cabin* is true and *The Cabin and Parlor* is false.[18]

Although *A Key* concerns itself with a variety of texts, both fictional and non-fictional, written in response to *Uncle Tom's Cabin*, Stowe turns to slave law for evidence of many of the institution's most "glaring facts"(133). She launches her devastating explication of the barbarity of slave law by quoting Thompson's excoriating review, in which he writes, "she has shockingly traduced the slaveholding society of the United States, and we desire to be understood as acting entirely on the defensive" (631). His primary method of defense is the citation of slave law which, according to Thompson, definitively proves that the scenes describing Eliza's escape with Henry could never have taken place because Louisiana law prohibited the separation of children under the age of ten from their mothers. He also quotes a portion of the Crimes and Offenses section of Louisiana's *Code Noir*, a set of imported French laws considered by some to protect more adequately than most the rights of slaves, in order to demonstrate "the utter falsity" (635) of St. Clare's statement that "he who goes furthest and does the worst only uses within limits the power that the law gives him" (634).

Stowe warms up to Thompson's challenge by reproducing a barrage of citations from a variety of sources: court cases that document physical abuse endured by slaves such as *State* v. *Mann* (1829) and *Souther* v. *Commonwealth* (1851) (a case from which she borrows heavily for *Dred*); legal treatises on slave law such as Jacob D. Wheeler's *Law of Slavery* (1837) and George M. Stroud's *Sketch of Slavery* (1827); and Weld's *Slavery As It Is.* She then sets her critical sights on "the following most remarkable provision of the *Code Noir*": the offending person " 'shall be deemed responsible and guilty'" unless that person "'shall by means of good and sufficient evidence, or can clear himself by his own oath.'" Stowe responds with absolute disgust to this law, calling it a "specimen of utter legislative nonsense" (88). In answer to Thompson's contention that the Eliza/ Henry narrative is impossible because of the benevolence of Louisiana's protective statutes, Stowe quotes the section of the *Code Noir* that Thompson had quoted, and sarcastically comments, "what a charming freshness of nature is suggested by this assertion! A thing could not have happened in a certain state, because there is a law against it!" (92). Stowe sabotages Thompson's attempted use of law as evidence of slavery's humanity by her characteristic use of irony. Hardly a page of *A Key* goes by without Stowe italicizing, underlining, capitalizing, or putting in quotation marks words whose meanings she believes have been perverted in defense of slavery. The protective statutes, she argues, are fictions which Thompson, in his "amiable ignorance and unsophisticated innocence" (92), has mistaken for facts. Defenders of slavery are categorically incapable of producing reliable evidence because they either don't or won't know the difference between fiction and fact. Under the best of circumstances they are wrong; under the worst, they lie.

Of course, this mishandling of evidence is precisely what Stowe was accused of in reviews of *Uncle Tom's Cabin*. Her position is precarious, indeed. In order to defend her fiction in terms of the accuracy of its anti-slavery facts, she must prove that pro-slavery facts are lies, and anti-slavery fictions (that is, *Uncle Tom's Cabin*) are truths. She accomplishes this immensely difficult task by undermining the reliability of particular sites of fact and fiction (newspapers, the law, church resolutions being her especial targets), as they operate in defenses of slavery, not fact and fiction themselves, thereby maintaining the functionality of these categories for the anti-slavery appeal. Stowe's running commentary, which surrounds her citation of documents related to the slave trade, uses the language of literary analysis in order to illustrate the point that the facts of slavery as presented in pro-slavery sources must be interpreted because defenders of slavery know no "scorn of dissimulation, that straightforward determination not to call a bad thing by a good name" (79). In a lengthy section of *A Key*, for example, she quotes from newspapers advertising slaves wanted or rewards for captured fugitive slaves. Her reproduction of rewards offered for runaways begins with the words, "let us open the chapter" (176). Her characterization of the cruelties of Mississippi slave law begins with the claim, "they are a romance of themselves" (114). After quoting two advertisements from the *Wilmington Journal* of 1850, both of which call for the capture of an escaped slave Harry, Stowe remarks, "there is an inkling of history and romance about the description of this same Harry" (85). Similarly, she reproduces the following advertisement for a "negro woman and two children" who have run away from a Mr. Ricks of North Carolina: "I burnt her with a hot iron, on the left side of her face. I tried to make the letter M" (109). Stowe scathingly observes, "it is charming to notice the *naïf* betrayal of literary pride on the part of Mr. Ricks." Stowe also believes legal discourse to fall under the sign of the literary as exemplified in her prefatory remark that the case of the *State of Mississippi* v. *Jones*, in its reasoning "against very respectable legal authorities, that the slave *is* a person, . . . and is worthy of attention as a literary curiosity" (75). Stowe's application of the "literary" accomplishes two seemingly mutually exclusive *desiderata* at once: she sustains her defense of *Uncle Tom's Cabin* on the grounds that "under the advertisements, a hundred such scenes as those described in 'Uncle Tom' may have been acting in his very vicinity" (136), while at the same time the palpable irony with which she deploys those literary terms signals to the reader that she is in full control of the differences between fiction and fact. Thus, only sentences after implying an interpenetration of the vicinities of her novel and of slaves in South Carolina, she authoritatively states the difference between them, "this is not novel-writing – *this* is fact" (137).

But isn't Stowe doing precisely what she accuses her opponents of doing? Isn't she being "far from straightforward" and playing an anti-slavery version of Hentz's terminological game? After all, throughout her text, Stowe calls things and people what she clearly believes they are not, referring to slavery as "the good trade" (140) and "the blessed trade" (141), or describing one slave trader as "judicious" (140) and another as "a man of humanity" (142). What distinguishes Stowe from her antagonists is, of course, the irony which both exposes their necessary and insidious euphemisms, and guarantees the authenticity of her not-so-humble "humbl[e] inquir[ies]" (138) and words. Irony, a tonal feature interestingly absent from Hentz's texts and the countless pro-slavery documents Stowe assembles in *A Key*, becomes the unambiguous sign of Stowe's truthfulness. Unlike Kemble, for whom irony is an occasional and somewhat limited tactic in her rhetorical battle against her detractors, Stowe relentlessly deploys it. Not a page of *A Key* goes by that doesn't pit Stowe's irony against her opponent's reckless unconcern for the truth. For example, Stowe cites an advertisement for the purchase of 5,000 slaves which includes the words, "families never separated" to which she responds, "if a man offers him a wife without her husband, Mr. John Denning won't buy her. O, no! His five thousand are all unbroken families ... This is a comfort to reflect upon, certainly" (142). In another advertisement whose headline reads, "75 Negroes," Stowe "humbly inquires" what " *'assorted A No. 1 Negroes'* means" (138). The advertisements include no irony, just an intentionally bewildering mishmash of half-lies and half-truths designed to convey information to slave traders in such as away as to obfuscate the cruel family separations at the core of slavery, to make them "recede from their view" (576), to invoke Hentz. Stowe's irony, however, is present in her "respectful" (139) inquiries which are anything but, as well as her use of italics (nothing in the advertisement is italicized) which registers Stowe's suspicion, indeed certainty, that "assorted" means broken families. She wonders, "We hear a lot of field men and women. Where are their children?", and "what is the process by which a trader acquires a well-selected stock?" (139). Her ironic citation of their unironic words exposes the facticity of their facts – "families, of course, never separated!" (139) – and the authenticity of her own.

A Key, I am claiming, is a hermeneutic *tour de force* whose indictment of slavery begins and ends with recognizing the difference between fact and fiction and, by extension, between the true and false meaning of words. Thus, her commentary on the 1851 *Souther* v. *Commonwealth* case, in which a Virgina slave named Sam died after being brutally tortured by his master, centers on the language of the case: "any one who reads the indictment will certainly think that, if this be murder in the *second degree*, in Virginia, one might earnestly pray to be murdered in the first degree, to begin with," and "as he preferred to spend *twelve hours* in killing him by torture, under the name of '*chastisement*,' that, says the verdict, is murder in the second degree" (81). Similarly, her attack on pro-slavery ministers pivots on their corruption of language, specifically their understanding of the Greek word *doulos*, which they take to be a New Testament vindication of slaveholding.

Stowe contemptuously characterizes their reading as "dry, dull, hope-less ... [and] stupid" (232), explaining that while *doulos* "may mean a slave," it cannot possibly authorize slavery "in the sense of Roman and American law"; after all, "it was not the business of the apostles to make new dictionaries; they did not change words, – they changed things" (232). At another point in the text, Stowe quotes Christ's words, "'inasmuch as ye have done it unto *one of the least* of these, ye have done it unto me,'" reminding them of the second coming at which "every one of these words shall rise up, living and burning, as accusing angels to witness against thee" (170). Stowe's point is that the perversion of the meanings of words is the perversion of the Word or Christ himself. Irony aside, her faith in Christ, she believes, ultimately ensures the truthfulness of her words.

Thus, like *Uncle Tom's Cabin*, *A Key* demands religious renewal as an essential means of combating the linguistic, religious, and political corrup-tion wrought by slavery. And, like the novel, sympathy is key. Stowe writes, "a delicate and mysterious sympathy is supposed to pervade this church ... the meanest member cannot suffer without the whole body quivering in pain" (231). But what "is supposed to" happen clearly isn't, because defenders of slavery make their case through a perversion of fact and feeling. The result is "congealed mass feeling," to reinvoke Berlant's words, but that is not sympathy. Rather, it is that "deadness of public sentiment" (204) that calls itself sympathy. It is not an inevitable inad-equacy of sympathy, in other words, that produces a "passive ideal of empathy" (641), but people who have no real sympathy at all. At one point, for example, Stowe presents a detailed account of the Presbyterian church's complicity in banishing anti-slavery advocates from the fold. She imagines a scene in which pro-slavery ministers speciously deploy the rhetoric of sympathy in order to excuse their inaction: "Brethren, our hearts are with you. We are with you in faith, in charity, in prayer. We sympathized in the injury that had been done you by excision ... We have no sympathy with the party that have expelled you" (212). Here, Stowe envisions how the language of "feeling right" is being manipulated to validate feeling wrong.

Clearly, when Stowe asks in the concluding pages of *Uncle Tom's Cabin*, "what can any individual do?" (624), such passivity is not what she had in mind. *A Key* aims to correct the problem. Whereas earlier she answered this question with, "they can see to it that *they feel right*" (624), only a year later the question and the answer have changed. In *A Key*, she asks, "what is to be done?" and answers, "the whole American church, of all denominations, should unitedly come up, not *in form*, but *in fact* ... to seek the ENTIRE

ABOLITION OF SLAVERY" (250). Individuals and their feelings still matter; for example, she refers to the human heart as "that very dangerous and most illogical agitator" (104), and during an account of slaves being " 'assorted' for the Natchez market," she wonders in a passage reminiscent of *Uncle Tom's Cabin* whether "no sad natural tears stream[ed] down their dark cheeks" (139). Those feelings matter as one element, albeit a crucial one, in the anti-slavery movement, as Stowe begins to make the case for group action not in the form of church resolutions, but in fact, by which she means breaking the laws of slavery through the organized efforts of the American church. She concedes that "although the sentiment of honorable men and the voice of Christian charity does everywhere protest against what it *feels* to be inhumanity, yet the popular sentiment engendered by the system must *necessarily* fall deplorably short of giving anything like suffi-cient protection to the rights of the slave" (132). Elsewhere, she notes, "all the kindest feelings and intentions of the master" do nothing to obviate the "absolute despotism of the slave-law" (115). Throughout *A Key*, then, Stowe articulates an awareness that for some "feeling right" is not the equivalent of being anti-slavery and, as a consequence, she revises and reinforces the terms of her first call to action.

The revision looks like this – "to *mean* well is not enough" (217). This wonderfully rich statement expresses Stowe's sense that "meaning well" as in "feeling right" comprises just one part of the anti-slavery crusade. Her formulation, it should be noted, resonates with the imperative to "mean *well*" (my emphasis), especially since so much of *A Key* is about the distinctions between the truthful or Christian meaning of words as opposed to the perverse significations attributed to them through slavery, "or whatever the trade pleases to term them" (209). Let us recall that Stowe admonishes her readers to "feel right," and then repeats the message, "see, then, to your sympathies in this matter!" (624). Many people did just that, including southern sympathizers like McCord, Thompson, and Hentz, and armed with their own set of "remarkable facts," they found that their sympathies resided with white slave-owning southerners. Stowe's brilliant hermeneutic performance in *A Key* aims to make such a finding impossible.

As in *Uncle Tom's Cabin*, sympathy remains the originary condition for anti-slavery action just as the lack of sympathy is the condition for pro-slavery inaction. *A Key*, however, reclaims the radical powers of sympathy, not with the belief (and hope) that "an atmosphere of sympathetic influ-ence encircles every human being" (624) – defenders of slavery had proven incapable of registering that point – but on the basis of her presentation of "hard facts," such as judicial decisions, legislative actions, and the published activities of the slave trade. Realizing that seeing to one's sympathies is no easy task and unwilling to take a chance that her readers' sympathies will be led astray by "the shams and sophistry wherewith slavery has been defended" (36), Stowe shows her readers exactly what to see and, perhaps, more importantly, how to see it. She establishes the rightness of her sympathies by asserting their foundation in facts, facts which she proves by reading the evidence presented in defenses of slavery against itself. She, then, deploys those defenses as evidence of their own disingenuousness, which then become evidence of the unfeelingness at the core of pro-slavery belief.

Stowe's sophisticated recuperation of the progressive possibilities of sympathy provides us with an important model for reevaluating our understanding of sympathy to include kinds of affect and modes of expression not usually associated with sympathy, such as irony, citation, and facts. To read irony and fact as an expression of sympathy as deep as tears, to read Hentz's deconstruction of freedom and slavery as her most profound expression of a lack of sympathy, is to begin to use the expanded repertoire of sympathy that Stowe provides in *A Key*. These texts encourage, indeed require us to think through sympathy in the antebellum years as well as our own.

CHAPTER 4

Behind the scenes of sentimental novels: Ida May and Twelve Years a Slave

Behind the scenes of many sentimental texts lie the traces of slave narratives. Such a claim, I realize, requires this immediate counter-statement – that sentimental texts radically differ from slave narratives, even though both genres share a conceptual investment in the matter of eventual self-possession, a structural equivalence in their protagonists' journey from a state of bondage into one of freedom, and an affective contiguity in their concern for the condition of their readers' sympathies. The aim of this chapter is to provide a more nuanced reading than currently available of the uses to which the tropes, rhetoric, and goals of slave narratives are deployed within sentimental texts.[1] I also hope to make the rather simple point that sentimental texts, for all of their intersections with the slave narrative genre, register in a variety of ways the all-encompassing difference between a sentimental narrative and a slave narrative, which is to say that the texts under consideration recognize the difference between someone who is and is not a slave. A pro-slavery text like Hentz's not only does not acknowledge this decisive distinction but works to erode it.

In fact, this chapter continues where my reading of Effie's symbolic function in *The Planter's Northern Bride* left off. There, let us recall, Moreland's daughter is kidnapped by her biological mother and becomes, analogically speaking, a fugitive slave – advertisements are posted and her return to her father and Eula is eventually secured – whose return to the plantation guarantees her future happiness. Hentz's ideological point, of course, is that the happiness of the fugitive slave lies in her restoration to what Frederick Douglass had called "the arms of slavery."[2] Crissy's story, by virtue of its obvious differences from Effie's, confirms this pro-slavery logic. Crissy becomes a fugitive slave in spite of herself (and because of the Softlys' nefarious abolitionist agenda) and suffers greatly as a result. If only Crissy had been the subject of advertisements and rescued by her owners, then she, like Effie, would have a bright future, too. Hentz's subversive deployment of the structure of the slave narrative is wickedly clever.

Crissy's slave narrative is a downward spiral as she journeys away from the freedom of slavery toward the slavery of freedom. Effie, however, is mercifully spared that trajectory as she finds herself back in slavery's comforting environs. Her journey is what we might call an "anti-slave narrative," as the gravitational and ideological pull of the narrative is southward, toward slavery. The enslavement that Effie supposedly endures in the time spent with her mother, Claudia, serves to expose, if Hentz's novel works on the reader the way it's supposed to, the misguided notions of freedom and slavery which supply the slave narrative with its necessary foundations.

Those foundations are the subject of this chapter and the next. Of particular interest is how the analogy between sentimental protagonist and slave might operate. I focus on Mary Hayden Green Pike's *Ida May* (1854) because the heroine experiences both subject positions. She is black-faced and kidnapped into slavery, during which time she is physically beaten and "sort of" adopted by her mammy, only to be eventually rescued from slavery in order to go on to endure the trials and tribulations of sentimental heroines. Although Nina Baym describes Pike's fiction as "ideologically appalling," I shall argue that this text, which at times is indeed difficult to bear, is more complicated and interesting than this dismissal might suggest.[3] That Frederick Douglass's *Paper* heartily recommends Pike's novel because it presents "a careful argument against slavery" (December 15, 1854) and links the power of its anti-slavery message to *Uncle Tom's Cabin*, even going so far as to suggest a "happy contrast which, in some particulars, it affords to Mrs. Stowe's 'Uncle Tom's Cabin'" (December 22, 1854), indicates that from the perspective of at least one high profile antebellum anti-slavery activist (and there were more), *Ida May* was doing important cultural work. Similarly, *The National Era*, in which *Uncle Tom's Cabin* was serialized, applauds Pike's anti-slavery efforts in its advertisements for *Ida May*. It does so by quite cleverly comparing Pike's novel with its "reliable information as to the practical workings of a system" with pro-slavery titles, such as Nehemiah Adams's "*Southern Life as it is*" and J. Thornton Randolph's "the cabin and the parlor."[4] The comparisons between Pike and Stowe are significant because *Ida May* confronts twenty-first-century readers with some of the same ideological problems as *Uncle Tom's Cabin* in terms of racial stereotype, coincidences in plot, and the sentimental disposition toward tears. I would, however, like to take the cues provided by the favorable reviews in Douglass's *Paper* and *The National Era* in order to present a reading of the novel that tries to capture both the reasons why it would be welcomed by those on the anti-slavery side in the antebellum period and why it would be seen as "appalling" in our own day. Because Ida is both enslaved and free, Pike's novel offers us an excellent opportunity to analyze the dialectic relationship between Ida's two identities, as well as the two genres to which she belongs. *Ida May* is fundamentally about a sentimental heroine kidnapped into the genre of the slave narrative, and it is her experiences in both genres that enable us to understand better the conditions under which slave narratives and sentimental novels operate.[5] This chapter, furthermore, uses Solomon Northup's *Twelve Years a Slave* as the slave narrative against and through which I read *Ida May*. Northup's narrative is especially appropriate because he, like his fictional foil, is kidnapped into slavery. The fact that they – the real Northup and a little girl named Mary Mildred Botts, "a real 'Ida May' "– appear together in Douglass's *Paper* gives historical credence to the conjunctions and disjunctions that this chapter will pursue.[6] Despite their overlapping *données*, the narrative and material possibilities available to Northup could not be more radically dissimilar than those at Pike's disposal. By examining the differences between Ida's rescue from slavery into freedom and Northup's journey toward freedom, and his discursive relation to it, I demonstrate the generic ties that bind and break sentimental novels and slave narratives.

I KEMBLE'S HOUSE DIVIDED

My analysis of the relation between these two genres begins by returning to Kemble. The earlier reading of the *Journal* omitted an important component of her story – the narrative of her crumbling marriage to her husband. Unlike the horrific experiences of slaves which, I argued, forced Kemble to cede narrative authority to the spare, documentary voices of the slaves themselves, her dissolving relationship with Butler reveals the extent to which her marital status presupposes that she has ceded authority over herself and her narrative to him. In an acknowledgment of her invisibility before the law, she concedes, "I am *feme couverte*."[7] Not for a moment, though, does she confuse her legal and emotional disempowerment with the brutal outrages committed upon the slaves. Her subservient position *vis à vis* her husband, however, obfuscates her precise relation to the slaves. Do they belong to her? Does she belong to herself once she's married to Butler? If not, if she doesn't own herself, how can she own someone else? In her inimitable way, Kemble poses and pursues the logic of these questions, and ultimately imagines her escape from marital unhappiness and legal disenfranchisement through the liberation of her (or is it his?) slave, Aleck, to whom I shall return. Although Aleck's narrative from slavery to freedom is both preliminary and truncated, it nevertheless provides Kemble with the only available paradigm and strategy by which to imagine an alternative life for both of them, safely away from the bonds of marriage, in the one case, and the bonds of mastery, in the other, that tie them both to Butler and to each other.

Kemble doesn't often comment on her relationship with Butler, but the occasional glimpses we do get indicate that trouble lies ahead. Early in the *Journal*, after Kemble has seen the deplorable conditions of the slaves' infirmary, she remarks, "I was glad to return to the house, where I gave vent to my indignation and regret at the scene I had just witnessed to Mr. [Butler] and his overseer, who, here is a member of our family" (71). This last phrase is no endorsement of their domestic arrangement, especially given Kemble's open enmity toward Mr. King, the overseer. In this description of a funeral service held for one of the slaves, Shadrach, Kemble's emotional distance from her husband is also made painfully clear. Whereas the religious ceremony powerfully affects Kemble, who with the slaves "knelt down in the sand . . . [while Mr. Butler] alone remained standing" (147), Kemble voices her pain and disappointment at her husband's unwillingness "to have given his slaves some token of his belief that – at least in the sight of that Master to whom we were addressing our worship – all men are equal" (148). Having registered their antithetical reactions to this most solemn event, Kemble then suggests the even wider scope of their incompatibility: "I could not speak to [Mr. Butler]. . . and, whatever his cogitations were, they did not take the usual form with him of wordy demonstration" (149). Exchanges between husband and wife seem to fall into one of three categories – silence, condescension, and lies.

The discord within her marriage is, however, most compellingly exemplified by her meditations on her individual relationship with her slaves; that is, are they or aren't they hers? Upon first arriving at the plantation, she seems to understand what her relationship is to them. She records her initial encounter with the slaves in which she tells them, "I had no ownership over them, for that I held such ownership sinful, and that, though I was the wife of the man who pretends to own them, I was, in truth, no more their mistress than they were mine" (60). This statement is particularly striking because it illustrates the confidence with which Kemble distinguishes between her own convictions and her husband's, between truth and pretense. It is as if Kemble believes that even though she lives on a plantation and is married to a slaveowner, she can nevertheless, through the sheer force of her belief, carve out a space untouched by slavery in a world that is completely organized according to the logic of slavery. This confidence in her power to undermine the pretenses of slavery is soon deflated as she comes to realize that the awful pretenses of slavery are horribly real: "[the master] may, if he likes, flog a slave to death, for the laws which pretend that he may not are a mere pretense" (79). Butler's possession of slaves may, from Kemble's point of view, be "a mere pretense," but it is a pretense that allows him (and her as well) to kill them. Thus, knowing that she is "no more their mistress than they were mine" doesn't matter because it has no bearing on the fact that in the world she inhabits, she is their mistress and they are her slaves.

Being their mistress, however, seems to give her only the power to harm, to reproduce in her relationship with them the degradation they experience with her husband. How to get out of this dilemma is one of the central issues in her *Journal.* Kemble's ability to improve the lives of the slaves, it turns out, depends upon her possession of them. Thus, the importance of the question, does she or doesn't she own them? On the one hand, they belong to her by virtue of her being their mistress. On the other hand, she belongs to Butler as a *feme couverte,* which mitigates her ownership of them.[8] Kemble evinces little comfort in being partially absolved from the moral stain of slaveholding; in fact, the *Journal* is preoccupied with understanding an ambiguous relation to slaves that, at once, gives her absolute power over them and, yet, doesn't recognize her ownership of them. At one point, for example, when she is about to witness the punishment of a slave at the hands of a slave driver, Kemble contemplates taking the whip inside the house in order to protect the slave. She then remarks, "an instant's reflection, however, served to show me how useless such a proceeding would be. The people are not mine, nor their drivers, nor their whips" (110). During Shadrach's funeral, however, she assumes the opposite position and admits to "an indescribable sensation of wonder at finding myself on this slave soil, surrounded by *my* slaves" (emphasis Kemble, 148). Elsewhere, she imagines giving the slaves information that would hasten their flight to freedom but then questions whether she has "any right to tell them if they could find it [freedom], for the slaves are not mine, they are Mr. [Butler]'s" (233).

Kemble narrates her experience of powerless benevolence *vis à vis* the slaves through the language of possession or, more precisely, dispossession. Her inability to intervene on the slaves' behalf is the direct consequence of laws designed to ensure that she cannot possess them. But it is also the case that this narrative of disempowerment applies to her relationship with Butler. The laws guaranteeing that Butler's possessions remain his own during marriage require that Kemble relinquish all that is hers and become "a *feme couverte*," which, we recall, Blackstone had defined as that state in which "the very being or legal existence of the woman is suspended during the marriage, or at least is incorporated and consolidated into that of the husband."[9] She cannot, in other words, possess herself. Her struggle to unincorporate herself from her husband and regain self-possession is evident in this lamentation, "I listen – I, an Englishwoman, the wife of the man who owns these wretches, and I cannot say: that thing shall not be done again; that cruel shame and villainy shall never be known here again" (241). This passage reflects a profound change in Kemble's language. No longer is she the "wife of the man who pretends to own them," as she maintained in the earlier passage; now she is "the wife of the man who owns" them. The tone, as well, is markedly different as desperation replaces irony. Kemble's attempt to recapture herself and her worldview is acute as she strenuously repeats and refines the composition of the "I," only to find its negation in what she cannot say. It is important to note, however, that Kemble doesn't confuse her dispossession with the slaves' utter abjection. For example, she contrasts the slave's "deadly dread" of losing her family with her own "blessed security, safe from all separation but the one reserved in God's great providence" (135). She doesn't, in other words, discursively appropriate the pitiable condition of the slaves in order to make the case for her own degradation; rather, she chooses to do something far more daring and effective, which is to take possession of herself and the slaves by breaking the law.

At the very moment that Kemble seems least able to see herself as anything other than a hidden woman (*feme couverte*), she chances upon a loophole that promises some degree of freedom both for herself and for the slaves. The context is a discussion of a young waiter named Aleck who requests that Kemble teach him to read. She agrees to do it, knowing that she is "breaking the laws of the government," but then has second thoughts because "I am a woman, and Mr. [Butler] stands between me and the penalty" (271). The penalty, from Kemble's point of view is, in fact, a reward that recognizes her identity separate and apart from Butler. Such an unusual opportunity turns out to be crucial to her intentions as is evident from this passage, which I shall quote at length, in which Kemble penetratingly analyzes the obstacles and possibilities presented by this situation:

Teaching slaves to read is a finable offense, and I am *feme couverte*, and my fines must be paid by my legal owner, and the first offense of the sort is heavily fined, and the second more heavily fined, and for the third, one is sent to prison. What a pity it is I can't begin with Aleck's third lesson, because going to prison can't be done by proxy, and that penalty would light upon the right shoulders! I certainly intend to teach Aleck to read. I certainly won't tell Mr. [Butler] anything about it. I'll leave him to find it out, as slaves, and servants, and children, and all oppressed, and ignorant, and uneducated, and unprincipled people do; then, if he forbids me, I can stop – perhaps before then the lad may have learned his letters. I begin to perceive one most admirable circumstance in this slavery: you are absolute on your own plantation. No slaves' testimony avails against you, and no white testimony exists but such as you choose to admit. Some owners have a fancy for maiming their slaves, some brand them, some pull out their teeth, some shoot them a little here and there (all details gathered from advertisements of runaway slaves in Southern papers); now they do all this on their plantations, where nobody comes to see, and I'll teach Aleck to read, for nobody is here to see, at least nobody whose seeing I mind; and I'll teach every other creature that wants to learn. (272)

Here, Kemble's devastating attacks on both the laws of coverture and slavery go hand in hand as she illustrates how her determination to instruct Aleck in reading undoes both at once. She begins with the frustrating acknowledgment that being *feme couverte* means that Butler, "her legal owner," will be monetarily punished for her illicit actions. After two fines, however, her husband can no longer function as an obstacle between herself and the law, forcing Kemble and not her "proxy" to bear the responsibility of her actions. In breaking the law a third time, her agency will be legally recognized by her incarceration, which Kemble regards as a great victory over the institutions of slavery and marriage that systematically work to erase her personhood as well as the slaves'. That this revitalization of herself is accomplished by teaching Aleck to read (a revitalization of himself that Kemble hopes will eventuate in his self-possession through freedom) signifies a strategic union of their relative experiences of dispossession. Educating Aleck becomes a mechanism of "unincorporation" for both wife and slave as Kemble and Aleck incorporate themselves each to the other in order to break the bonds of husband and master Butler. Furthermore, their seemingly crippling invisibility ("no one is here to see") becomes the means to legal recognition and power. To be sure, Kemble also evinces an aggressive pleasure both in keeping her activity a secret from her husband and in imagining how that secret and its disclosure will relegate Butler to some less than desirable subject positions, including the "oppressed, and ignorant, and uneducated, and unprincipled." No wonder she is "delighted" (271) when Aleck makes his request.

Just as Aleck helps Kemble to challenge the structure of coverture, he also gives her a means to deploy the logic of slavery against itself. The passage demonstrates how teaching him to read provides her with a sense of heightened power with respect to Butler, which interestingly gets represented by Kemble's commitment to the radical possibilities of ownership – a commitment, we should recall, that she had firmly disavowed upon first coming to the plantation ("I had no ownership over them" [60]). The fact is that once Kemble is able to establish herself as a person legally separate from Butler, even if it means her incarceration, the plantation and its inhabitants are no longer only his: "You are absolute on your own plantation." This passage, then, registers her liberation from the status of *feme couverte*, even going so far as to envision a legal scenario in which she might prohibit unwelcome "white testimony" (perhaps Butler's?) from the courtroom. She becomes an owner with a fancy not to maim slaves but to teach them how to read. By positioning herself as their owner, she can free her slaves. In liberating them, she frees and repossesses herself.

The stories of Kemble and Aleck come together for a brief moment in the narrative. How might we understand that intersection? One reading holds that Kemble appropriates Aleck's subject position in order to use its affective powers for her own agenda, thereby erasing the specific and individual horrors of the slave experience in order to make the case for the allegedly equivalent oppressions of white, married women. Another reading, and the one I will pursue in this chapter, maintains that the structural analogies between Kemble and Aleck, and the uses to which they are deployed in the narrative, do not necessarily elide the differences between a married white woman (or a sentimental heroine) and an enslaved black man; rather, those analogies can provide the foundation for acts of sympathy which hold out the possibility of better lives for both. Kemble's recognition of herself as a *feme couverte* is essential to the development of her anti-slavery position, because it changes the terms of her sympathetic engagement with the slaves. Like the slaves, she too has a "legal owner," but unlike them, she is in a position to change both her own dispossession and the slaves' by breaking the law. Up until this point, that particular mode of combat had not occurred to her (although it clearly had to Aleck). The analogy, in other words, allows Kemble to imagine a way to effect her own deliverance as well as Aleck's, and the two are inseparable. That Kemble's dispossession is the epistemological foundation which spurs her to this particular action does not take away from its legitimacy. To be sure, Kemble's text does not sacrifice itself in order to become Aleck's slave narrative, but just because it doesn't does not mean that the *Journal* has failed in its anti-slavery intention.

II "AM *I* A SLAVE?"[10]

These words are uttered by Ida May, the young heroine of Mary Hayden Green Pike's (pseudonym for Mary Langdon) best-selling *Ida May*, who has just heard her "mauma" (82), Venus, recount the sufferings she has experienced as a slave. Until now, Ida has been happily unaware of the institution's horrors, but Venus's moving account of being separated from her family makes the child realize that this, perhaps, is the fate that awaits her. When Venus replies, "Yes . . . you are a *slave*," Ida "trembled all over, and looked around with a terrified expression, as if seeking a way of escape" (89). Ida does succeed in escaping, but it is not as a slave attempting to find safety from the brutalities of slavery; rather, she escapes or, more precisely, is released from her condition because she is *not* a slave. Her freedom, in other words, is not a consequence of challenging slavery *per se* but a process of discovering her true identity as a white, middle-class girl, whose rightful place is as the heroine not of a slave narrative but of a sentimental novel. She just needs to wait long enough until those around her can prove that she has been the victim of a crime perpetrated upon her during childhood (a crime, of course, that is being perpetrated upon all black children in the south).

This isn't very hard to do. After being kidnapped by evil slave traders in her home state of Pennsylvania, painted in blackface, sold to a Virginia slaveowner, Mr. Bell, and bereft of memory, Venus renames Ida after her dead daughter, the appropriately named Lizzy White. In addition, the capable Venus makes sure that the little roll of silk which Ida had worn at the time of her kidnapping and which, conveniently enough, has Ida May's name sewn into its interstices, is kept away from master Bell, and reappears just in the nick of time to save Ida from further cruelties. Now free, she is adopted by the man who initially had bought her and Venus, Charles Maynard, a kind-hearted uncle of the family. When he dies, Ida is the "ward" (340) of Mr. Wynn who becomes "her stern guardian" (318). Ida's outspoken anti-slavery opinions, however, make her realize "the breach is rapidly widening that sunders me from this family" (328). She claims her inheritance, which includes a plantation with a few dozen slaves, makes plans to free them, is reunited with her father, and claims Walter Varian's love.

Hokey and ideologically problematic as much of this sounds – and it is – the fact remains that the novel is, generically speaking, doing something quite interesting. *Ida May* sets itself the task of rescuing the sentimental heroine from the slave narrative into which she has been intentionally, but mistakenly, captured. Several questions seem worth asking: why has she been plunged into or, might we say, kidnapped by a slave narrative in the first place? What are the narrative and ideological effects of this generic hybridization? What resolutions, on the level of both plot and politics, are possible given the seemingly very different requirements of sentimental novels, on the one hand, and slave narratives, on the other? This section argues that Pike's novel epitomizes the analogical inescapability of conjoining the two genres at the same time as it asserts their fundamental incongruity. More specifically, *Ida May* permits us to see that the incongruity of the two genres is based on the fact that sentimental novels operate according to a logic of available contract whereas slave narratives reveal the extent to which contract, if not unattainable, is attained and sustained at the risk of one's life. It is possible, then, to understand the fundamental tension between the genres as the defining tension – contract v. slavery – within antebellum culture itself.[11]

Like many of its sentimental counterparts, *Ida May* features the genre's usual twists and turns: the tale begins with the death of Ida's mother and is followed by the disappearance and supposed death of her father; the middle narrates the trials, successes, and multiple adoptions of the orphaned Ida who, like Gerty, turns out not to be orphaned as her father reappears in the final scenes; and the conclusion rewards her with the affections of Walter, whom we have been led to believe may end up in a disastrous marriage with Ida's competitor/step-sister, Mabel Wynn, a beautiful, wealthy, but mean-spirited girl. What distinguishes Pike's novel from, say, *The Lamplighter* or *The Wide, Wide World*, is its explicit engagement with the slavery question. In other words, Ida's *Bildungsroman* is inextricably linked to her position *vis à vis* the peculiar institution, whether as a slave, as a freed slave, or as an anti-slavery advocate. The novel uses the master narrative of the sentimental novel – the development and the deployment of the heroine's sympathies – in order to make the case against slavery. Bizarre as it may seem, given the novel's propensity for racist depictions of black characters, *Ida May* thinks of itself as an anti-slavery text.[12] The narrator, as well as other characters in the novel, argues against slavery, using rhetorical strategies typically found in antebellum abolitionist texts. During his radical phase at college, for example, Walter lectures his pro-slavery family that, "a slave can never be a *man*" (139) to which his cousin Mabel scornfully replies, "they wouldn't be free if they could, – you may ask any of them." Walter shoots back that "there isn't a mother's son among them [the slaves] but has wit enough to know what answer to make to anybody his *master* allows to question him" (140). Later, when Walter's anti-slavery leanings have taken a back seat to his family obligations, Ida lectures him on the treacherous power of the slaveholder: "dare you trust yourself with the possession of absolute power over the lives, and persons, and destinies, of your fellow-men?" (281).

But clearly Pike's most creative and ideologically precarious way of making her anti-slavery point is the temporary transformation of her protagonist from a white girl into a black slave. Shortly after Ida is kidnapped, the perpetrators ready her for sale, changing her from white to black and girl to boy, presumably switching gender so as to make her discovery all the more difficult: "he stained her skin with a sponge, dipped in some dark liquid, until it was the color of a dark mulatto" (58). Interestingly, this process is accomplished during one of Ida's many periods of unconsciousness, which links her descent into slavery with the loss of mental clarity. Not only is she "senseless" (59), "insensible" and "oblivious" (61), but by the time Mr. Bell has purchased her, she has a bad case of amnesia, frequently replying to questions about her childhood with "I can't remember" (74, 78, 107, 108). Everyone remarks upon Ida's bizarre behavior, from Mrs. Bell who comments, "she don't seem like other children, and has a slow, dreamy manner, as if she were asleep" to the slaves who wonder whether "somebody done conjur de child" (80). The discovery of Ida's identity is represented as an awakening of her consciousness, as if the conjure is at last being broken: "something in that recital seemed to clear away the thick haze that clouded her mental vision ... as with a lightning glare, all the long hidden years were visible before her" (197). Ida begins to see the light again as evidence of her whiteness accumulates. Her past returns bringing with it the knowledge of her (temporarily) lost biological origins.

Ida's metamorphosis from white to black, albeit Lizzy White, to white again helps satisfy several conventions of sentimental fiction, not least of which is the breaking apart of the biological family. Like Gerty, Ellen Montgomery and a whole host of (seemingly) orphaned girls, Ida's kidnapping catapults her into a world of strangers who then become the means through which the heroine establishes a new set of family relations based on the paradigm of contract rather than consanguinity. Indeed, the fact that the past and any memory of her biological origins is unavailable to her, if only temporarily, guarantees that any new family structure in which she participates will have to incorporate her through the mechanism of a contract, in this case adoption. Thus, like her sentimental sisters, Ida is adopted or "sort of adopted," to invoke the relevant language of *The Lamplighter*, multiple times in the course of the novel: first by Venus who calls Lizzy/Ida "her adopted child" (125); second by Charles

Maynard (also Walter's adoptive father, whom he calls "uncle" [207]) who declares, "I should enjoy, amazingly, to adopt this child" (207); and third by Mr. Wynn who, upon Maynard's death, becomes her guardian. Because adoption is one of the novel's primary means of establishing family relations, it seems only natural that Ida becomes an adoptive mother herself at the conclusion of the novel, agreeing to raise the orphaned black grandchild of Maum Abby, whose son has committed suicide rather than accede to the cruel punishments of Mr. Wynn, and whose daughter-in-law's death soon follows. The fact is that the best, most virtuous, and most sympathetic characters in the novel are those persons willing to participate in an adoption, such as Mr. Maynard, "her kind guardian" (361) or Mrs. Wynn who "wants to adopt her [Ida]" (206), or Ida who assures Maum Abby, "I will certainly take him . . . I will always provide for the little one, and see that he is well cared for, and educated as he gets older" (422).

The importance of adoption in sentimental novels, both as an alternative to consanguinity as the defining paradigm of family *and* as the best expression of sympathy's potential, cannot be over-estimated. *Ida May* is no exception. But by taking this generic requirement a step further and using adoption as a trans-racial expansion of family, Pike's novel becomes more distinctive.[13] In order to show how distinctive, I want now to consider the differences between Venus's "adoption" of Ida and Mr. Maynard's adoption of Ida. Such a comparison will begin to crystallize the generic bind in which Pike finds herself as the conventions of the slave narrative demand one outcome (for Lizzy) and sentimental conventions demand another (for Ida).

Ida is purchased by Mr. Bell, but she soon becomes the responsibility of Aunt Venus. The two quickly form a loving attachment, the nature of which Ida seeks to define more clearly. Having no memory and, thus, no sense of her racial composition, Ida, whose "emaciated hands," the narrator reminds us, "were now returned to their original whiteness"(74), asks Venus, "Am I your child?" (77). Venus's first response is biologically based, "Don't ye see I'se an old black thing and you'se white?" (77). Such an explanation, though, is clearly insufficient for several reasons. On the one hand, Venus has already begun the psychic work of transforming Ida into her child by naming Lizzy White after her "own child . . . that was sold away from me when we was all toted off" (82). On the other hand, Ida (the name consistently used by the narrator even though the characters in the novel know her as Lizzy, a subject to which I shall return) has already started to transfer her affections from the biological parents she cannot remember to Venus, whom she soon will be calling "mauma" (82).

Furthermore, the fact that Ida's skin is white and Venus's black does nothing to cancel out the possibility that they may, indeed, be mother and daughter because, as Venus rightly notes, "some niggers *is* white" (78). The more accurate answer to Ida's question, then, is no, maybe, or yes, depending upon how the words, "your child," accommodate different kinds of possession, be they biologically or culturally determined. To be sure, Venus is convinced that the response is "no," disclosing her suspicions that Ida is the "child of wealthy parents" (79), wealthy white parents to be more precise, and has been kidnapped in order to be sold on the slave market. But her affective response to Ida indicates that the opposite might also hold true; that "yes," Ida is on her way toward becoming her child.[14] For example, about her life with Venus, the narrator comments, "[Ida] was almost as fondly cherished as if she had been in her own home" (100), "Aunt Venus welcomed this delicate and beautiful child who had been, in some degree, given to her as her own!" (101), and Ida is loved by Aunt Venus "as if she had been her own" (102). The persistent language of ownership is important in these passages because it leaves open the possibility that even though Venus may not be Ida's consanguineous mother ("your child," biologically speaking), Venus is "in some degree" ("your child," contextually speaking) Ida's mother. It should come as no surprise, then, that Ida and Venus's relationship is characterized as an adoptive one, with all of the ambiguity that that term implies (and more, as we shall see). Ida is alternately Venus's "little charge" (101) and "her adopted child" (125), and Venus is Ida's "mauma" (131, 163, 389), her "aunt" (106), her "nurse" (74, 101).

And eventually her slave, courtesy of Mr. Maynard who "had assured that his will was made, and, in case any fatal accident happened to him . . . [Venus] would become the property of Miss Ida" (224). Ownership is key, indeed. As long as Ida and Venus are both slaves, neither of them can claim ownership of the other because neither of them can own anything, including themselves. The narrator makes this point early in the text when she reflects upon the sufferings of the wretched slave Chloe and her family who are "sent away from the home where they had been so happy, to live as slaves in another family . . . In all other cases the sufferer has *himself* left, – the slave has not even *himself*" (35). Thus, another way to respond to Ida's question – "am I your child?" – is legalistically, which means no. Even if Ida is Venus's child, from a biological or affective point of view, she can't be her child because Ida (as well as Venus) is ultimately a legal possession of her master. Venus voices their utter dispossession in the following exchange with Ida, who inquires, "who is Mass' James?" to which

Venus replies, "Mass' James – why he our massa, your massa and mine. He bought us, so I s'pose we b'long to him" (78). In belonging to Master James, they do not necessarily belong to or with one another. Thus, when Master James decides to sell several of his slaves, and Ida is initially purchased without Venus, the slave driver reminds Ida's buyer, Walter, "She belongs to you, but Venus belongs to me" (165).[15]

Slavery trumps adoption when it comes to an absolute state of ownership, a point perfectly understood by Venus and reinforced by a bizarre sequence of events and coincidences typical of many sentimental texts. Walter, who had met Ida "a few weeks since" (193) and had promised to "do all I can to help you" (109), finds her again while walking with his uncle/guardian, Mr. Maynard, but this time she is being attacked by wild swine. Not only does Walter rescue her from this immediate peril, but he convinces Mr. Maynard to purchase Ida on his behalf with assurances to her that "you shan't be treated badly any more" (162). It is significant that Ida is first a slave in the Wynn household before she is adopted by Mr. Maynard. Although her progress from the one to the other is rapid indeed, Ida's hybrid status as slave and adoptee accomplishes several things, on the level of plot, politics, and genre. First, Ida's position as a slave grants her access to the other slaves (providing her with information about their families, their feelings), which she will later use to make the anti-slavery case against Mr. Wynn and the institution he so vigilantly and cruelly upholds. Second, Walter has never really believed that Ida is a slave, and when, during their first meeting, Ida tells him that she "belong[s] to Massa James Bell," he incredulously retorts, "*you* don't belong to him, do you?" (106). Purchasing Ida, upon their second encounter, gives Walter the opportunity to respond to that question in the negative because, as he tells her, "you belong to *me*, now, Lizzy" (162). Once she is Walter's, her whiteness will not be denied. Not only does Walter contend that he has "no doubt she is of white parentage"(192), but Venus also remarks, "'pears like you was n't a nigger, now!" (185). It is only a matter of time until her identity is revealed: Ida May's name is soon spoken, the recital of which "seemed to clear away the thick haze that clouded her mental vision" (197), and the "fragment of linen" which decoratively conceals her name is recovered. Third, the shift from slave to adoptee signifies the text's transition from slave narrative to sentimental novel, from Lizzy White to Ida May. With the disclosure of her real name, Ida sinks into a "long and death-like swoon...succeeded by a burst of weeping so violent and hysterical" (198). This sentimental swoon has effects quite different from those that accompanied her descent into slavery. "From that day Ida's memory was awakened, and her mind recovered its tone, there had been a change in her appearance" (213). We also learn that Walter, with proof positive of Ida's racial identity, has commenced instructions in reading. Now described as "the little orphan" (208) – how many slave narratives describe their protagonists in that way, accurate as the designation might be? – "alone in the world, with none to love her as they would love her," she is ready to remember and rejoin the genre to which she belongs: "[they] were anxious, from that moment, to adopt her as their own" (212).

Ida's new position as orphan resonates with her earlier translation into a slave. On the micro-level, both metamorphoses induce her to cry prolif-ically, lapse into unconsciousness, and undergo a significant change in appearance. More important, however, is the fact that because these transformations are the result of Ida's separation from family (both bio-logical and adoptive), both scenes must represent Ida's feelings of sadness and dispossession, and settle the question of to whom Ida belongs. In other words, the structure of domestic dissolution makes these moments analo-gous, leading Ida herself, at the conclusion of the novel, to say this about Walter: "he redeemed me from slavery, and now he has redeemed me from orphanhood, by bringing you [Mr. May] here" (389). But even as the novel links Ida's enslaved and orphaned conditions, it works even harder to maintain and highlight the absolute differences between the two. For example, although Ida cries in both scenes, her tears signify physical pain as she experiences her first whipping as a slave in contrast to the tears in the later scene which register the "disappointment of her hopes"(212) that her biological family would rescue her. Similarly, the two swoons are the result of incommensurable experiences. "So unused to suffering" (44), Ida faints from the application of the whip, whereas her "death-like swoon" (198) in the Wynn household is the result of the accumulated trauma of Ida's recovered memories. Lastly, Ida's alteration in appearance signifies her progression from beaten slave who "never once spoke, or manifested any consciousness of her surroundings" (62) to sentimental heroine: "instead of the slow, dreamy, and listless manner that had formerly marked her, her eyes now sparkled with life, and her step became quick and buoyant" (213). The absolute difference between being and not being a slave is, however, most fully evident by virtue of the fact that she is now ready to be adopted.[16]

True to the conventions of the sentimental genre, many people want to adopt Ida, including Mrs. Wynn (although Mr. Wynn forbids it), Bessy (Ida's former nurse in Pennsylvania), and Mr. Maynard. Not only does Ida reject Bessy's offer, "express[ing] no inclination to accept the invitation," but she explicitly chooses to accept Mr. Maynard's. "Ties later formed were stronger, and, placing her hand in Mr. Maynard's, she said, as she wiped away her tears, "I will stay here and be your little girl, Uncle Charles, – yours and Aunt Emma's," to which Walter adds, "And mine, too!" (212). This passage is significant for a number of reasons, not least of which is that in presenting the moment of adoption as a choice to be made by Ida, the unbridgeable gap between slavery and freedom is underscored. It is also worth pointing out that several people adopt Ida in this scene, calling attention to the exclusivity of ownership under slavery as opposed to the diversity of ownership within adoption. And last, slaves don't get to choose with whom they belong or, if they do, their choices don't necessarily have any relation to the outcome they desire. Venus and Ida belong to each other so long as their master says they don't. Mr. Maynard's adoption of Ida, however, sticks because it partakes of the nature of a contract. Mr. Maynard expresses his intention to enter into the contract – "I should enjoy, amazingly, to adopt this child" (207) – and Ida agrees. Ida can make a contract. Lizzy can't. Ida can free her slaves. Lizzy can't because she is one. Thus, no matter how melancholy Ida might become in the remaining three hundred pages of the novel – "I was doubly orphaned, and the world looked dark, indeed, when he [Mr. Maynard] died" (247), "she had been murmuring at the Providence which had ordered for her such a changeful and lonely life, and made her so early fatherless and motherless" (338), "a sense of her helplessness, of her loneliness, of her powerlessness . . . all this came over her in the moments that succeeded, and her courage died" (360-361) – no matter how painful her sentimental travails, the fact is that her experience as a slave, as Lizzy, has revealed those complaints to be of an order of suffering absolutely different from and incommensurate with her horrible experiences as a slave, regardless of how analogous their rhetoric and structure may be.

III "MY NARRATIVE IS AT AN END"[17]

Whereas adoption, as *The Lamplighter* and *Ida May* demonstrate, can flexibly accommodate multiple owners, slavery can't. It can't, because to acknowledge that a person might have more than one owner is to open up the possibility that one of those owners might be oneself. In belonging to her master, then, the slave can belong to no one else. The progress of adoption, by contrast, eventuates in what we might call one's self-adoption, which is to say that the lesson of communal ownership culminates in self-ownership. There is and can be no analogous narrative progression within slavery, because the master's exclusive ownership of the slave operates to eradicate any sense that she might belong to someone other than her master, whether to one's family, friends, or oneself. Slavery's dominant narrative, as Kemble's *Journal* illustrates, is an anti-narrative of repetition, circularity, and blockage. The slave narrative is thus aptly named because it is a text (and a genre) dedicated to making a narrative out of that which operates to stifle individual character development, communal progress, and lasting personal ties, whether consanguineous or contractual. As Lucius Matlack thoughtfully writes in his 1849 introduction to the *Narrative of the Life and Adventures of Henry Bibb*, "Naturally and necessarily, the enemy of literature, it [slavery] has become the prolific theme of much that is profound in argument, sublime in poetry, and thrilling in narrative."[18] The only story possible is one of escape, from slavery to freedom and into narrative.

The slave's narrative thus ends with escape from bondage into freedom and, hopefully, reunion with loved ones. The sentimental heroine's narrative ends with escape from a tyrannical authority figure, whose disciplinary practices and rhetorical styles come perilously close to the slave master's (think Mr. Lindsay of *The Wide, Wide World*, Mr. Graham, Mr. Wynn), and marriage. *Ida May* combines the two, concluding one narrative, which is her escape from slavery, only to begin the other, which is her journey toward marriage. But this combination is made possible because of a mistake; she doesn't really belong in the first narrative. She's been kidnapped into (or by) it, as have children whose condition follows that of the (black) mother, a point that Pike makes in the text.

Solomon Northup, a free black man living in New York with his wife and three children, is also kidnapped and forced to endure the horrors of bondage in the Red River region of Louisiana. Unlike the fictional Ida May, however, Northup's "candid and truthful statement of facts" (3) concludes with his redemption from slavery, bringing his "narrative [to] an end" (252). There is no more to be said, at least publicly, after such an experience, which is why Northup declines to describe in any detail his reunion with his family, other than to allude generally to embraces and tears, and then to "draw a veil over a scene which can better be imagined than described" (251). The image of a veil or some kind of facial covering is a feature of many slave narratives, including the veil that Harriet Jacobs purchases upon her arrival in the north or the "white handkerchief" that Ellen Craft wears "under the chin, up the cheeks and ... over the head" (289). There are no veils at the conclusion of Ida's story because she is completely free by virtue of her whiteness.

I introduce Northup's 1853 slave narrative, *Twelve Years a Slave*, into this discussion of *Ida May* because, even though the trajectories of both texts and their protagonists are similar (free, kidnapped, free), the differences between them are important and instructive. One can attribute these differences to a variety of factors, among them that Northup is writing autobiography and Pike fiction or that Northup is a black male adult and Ida a five-year-old white female child when she is first introduced to the reader. Although the sentimental heroine and the protagonist of the slave narrative are linked by virtue of the freedom with which their journeys conclude, it is equally true that their paths to freedom widely diverge. Yes, it is only a matter of time before both Ida and Northup get out of their predicaments (the surprise ending is *not* a convention of either genre), but the composition and representation of that time endured within the institution of slavery – of being a slave, reflecting upon being a slave, trying to escape being a slave – radically differ. To think about the divergences between these two texts from the point of view of genre helps to clarify the extent to which the slave's freedom in contrast to the sentimental protagonist's depends upon escape more than rescue, secrecy more than exposure, human acts of courage more than the divine interventions of a *deus ex machina*.

One of the first lessons Northup learns, as a kidnapped free man now slave, is the necessity of concealment. Upon awakening from an "insensible" (19) state, he finds himself in a slave pen, only steps away from the Capitol. He is greeted by James Burch, whom Northup "learned afterwards [was] a well-known slavedealer in Washington" (21), and informed that "[he] was his slave" (23). Northup responds to this outrageous claim, "assert[ing], aloud and boldly, that I was a free man," to which Burch replies that "I came from Georgia" (23). Northup's continued assertions of his true identity are not only met with "blasphemous oaths" (23) but eventually with the paddle and the cat-o'-ninetails. The more he insists upon his status as a free man, the crueler the punishment, until finally Northup is unable to speak. This scene is important because it helps to establish Northup's narrative as "a full and truthful statement" (29) in contrast to the claims made by supporters of slavery who have no respect for the truth.[19] This point is reinforced pages later when Northup, "forgetting [himself], for a moment" (37), discloses his New York residence to the owner of the slave pen. Burch, once again, threatens Northup with the consequences of his honesty, which is, of course, a remembering of himself not a forgetting: "if ever I hear you say a word about New-York, or about your freedom, I will be the death of you" (38). Northup's narrative signifies not only the antithesis of this enforced silence but a repossession of the truthful narrative of his life. Whereas Burch and company are "the authors of [his] imprisonment" (23), Northup will author his redemption. Northup is in the classic position of the slave narrator for whom honesty is at once tantamount to death and essential to the anti-slavery purpose of the text.[20]

Clearly, the most important thing that Northup conceals is his own identity. This fact comes up repeatedly in the narrative, for example, in this exchange with a fellow slave and friend, Harry, where Northup "in answer to his inquiries from whence I came, told him from Washington" (68). Elsewhere we learn that he has also deceived one of his mistresses into thinking that "Washington...was my native city," even though she believes that he had "seen more of the world that I admitted" (175). He also describes a brief conversation with a sea captain in whom Northup chooses to confide, at least partially: "I did not relate to him the particulars of my history, but only expressed an ardent desire to escape from slavery to a free State" (150). Northup understands that his path to freedom doesn't lie in the assertion of it, because such a direct contradiction of the slave-owner's words, as his experience with Burch teaches him, only guarantees continued and ever harsher enslavement. Northup also knows the obvious – that his freedom can only be attained through an initial assertion of it. To become free (again) means to risk death. In the face of such a dilemma, he "resolved to lock the secret closely in my heart – never to utter one word or syllable as to who or what I was – trusting in Providence and my own shrewdness for deliverance" (63). Northup's "true, faithful, [and] unexaggerated" (129) narrative is, in other words, punctuated by moments of indecision and fear about the consequences of asserting his true identity. The most poignant instance of Northup's anxiety about self-disclosure occurs when, after having been "in slavery nine years," he meets "with the good fortune of obtaining a sheet of paper" (175). Armed with this powerful tool of representation and potential escape, he then "succeed[s] in making ink" (175) and decides to approach Armsby, a white man also working on Epps's plantation, with a request to mail a letter. Betrayed by Armsby, Northup's only recourse is to "throw the letter in the fire" (179). At the same time as Northup must destroy the letter and the truth that is contained in it (its recovery would implicate him in any number of crimes against his master, thereby putting his survival in peril), he defends himself against Armsby's treachery by disclaiming everything related to the incident, including his access to and powers of self-representation. He reminds Epps of the ridiculousness of Armsby's charges: "How could I write a letter without any ink or paper? There is nobody I want to write to, 'cause I haint got no friends living as I know of " (178). The best way to stay alive in this context is not simply to accept the false identity created for him by his masters but to insist upon its truthfulness.

Northup's self-conscious and strategic denial of his identity as a free black man is clearly a consequence of his being kidnapped into slavery. This tactical surrender of his prior self also includes accepting the series of names given to him by his various masters and suppressing his own.[21] Like the sentimental novels that foreground the protagonist's experience of being named and renamed as a way of reflecting upon the related issue of identity, Northup's slave narrative uses the fact that the slave's last name is that of his master's, which changes with each trade, in order to make the case against the willfully produced incoherence of the slave's identity. It is instructive to compare Northup's representations of his name(s) with Pike's handling of Ida's because such textual moments help to elucidate the distinctive foundations upon which their genres are organized; to wit, while the plots of both texts rely upon the (temporary) suppression of their protagonists' names, the articulation of Northup's risks death (his is a slave narrative) and the expression of Ida's portends freedom (hers is a senti-mental novel).

The trajectory of Ida's or, more precisely, Lizzy's story is one of certain discovery, including the recovery of her name, which is why when she overhears the story of a father's search for his daughter whose "name was Ida – Ida May – rather a peculiar name, too" (196), "the name – *her name*" (197) floods the narrative. Not only does Ida "exclaim wildly, 'That's it, that's my name, – *Ida May*" (197), but the "fragment of linen . . . which Venus had the good sense to save, in hopes it might, at some time lead to a discovery" is brought out to confirm Ida's identity: "Yes, here is a name, – *the name*, – Ida May!" (200). The repeated confirmation of Ida's name is interesting from the point of view of the narrator who never fully integrates the name Lizzy into the descriptions of her protagonist. There are moments when the narrator participates in the ruse that Ida is Lizzy, occasionally using the words "said Lizzy" (109) to identify her in conversa-tion, but more often than not, Lizzy is a name that others call her as she tells Walter when he asks her, "can't you even remember your old name? What do they call you now?" and she replies, "They call me Lizzy" (107). Ida almost always remains Ida from the narrator's vantage point, even when transformed into Lizzy. Thus, even though Ida "can't remember" (107) who she is, the narrator doesn't let us forget. It is Venus who thinks she is "put[ting] her arms around Lizzy" (120–121), but it is really "Ida [who] had come to nestle in [Venus's] heart" (125). Furthermore, the tenacious hold that Ida's name has within and upon the narrative ensures that her father will know her, even after decades of separation. When they meet again, "her voice seemed to strike some chord of memory" (385) to which Mr. May murmurs "that name! always that name!" (385)

The narrator's near consistency in designating Ida as Ida points to an unwillingness to accept fully the consequences of having changed her into Lizzy. Her kidnapping is partial, temporary, reversible, and this is the case not because the story insists that all slaves (black and white) have had their freedom kidnapped from them, but because Ida is white and a terrible crime, which is not the crime of slavery, has been perpetrated. In stopping short of fully incorporating the textual effects of Ida's transformation into Lizzy, Pike dilutes the case she is trying to make against the material consequences of having one's freedom taken away. Although this account of the novel, as we shall see, doesn't do justice to Pike's anti-slavery purpose, her ideological limitations are clearly at work. Just as "de black wash off" ([129]), revealing Ida's true whiteness, Lizzy will disappear too, allowing the now white and eligible Ida to get on with the business of marrying the white and eligible Walter.

I want to use the limitations and conventions of Pike's novel to clarify the very different set of constraints under which Northup's slave narrative is organized. Let us recall that, like Ida, Northup's true identity must be revealed in order for him to become free. Like Ida, he must be recognized by someone outside of the system of slavery in order to be redeemed. And as with Ida, we know that this will happen, but we don't know how or when. And yet all of these linkages pale in comparison with the fact that Northup isn't present at the moment when his whereabouts are discovered, isn't recognized by his daughter upon his return, and comes to learn the full story of his liberation after the fact. Unlike Ida's tale, in which she is present at such key moments as when her identity as Ida, not Lizzy, is discovered, a sense of belatedness and incomplete knowledge haunts Northup's narrative.

One of the best examples of this experience of utter self-alienation occurs in New Orleans, as Northup describes the moment that he first becomes aware of his nominal transformation from Northup to Platt.

Reading from his paper, he [the trader] called "Platt." No one answered. The name was called again and again, but still there was no reply . . .
"Captain, where's Platt?" demanded Theophilus Freeman.
The captain was unable to inform him, no one being on board answering to that name.

"Who shipped *that* nigger?" he again inquired of the captain, pointing to me.
"Burch," replied the captain.
"Your name is Platt – you answer my description. Why don't you come forward?"
he demanded of me, in an angry tone.
I informed him that was not my name; that I had never been called by it, but that I
had no objection to it as I knew of.
"Well, I will learn you your name." (49)

Northup's response to receiving yet another name ("on the vessel I had
gone by the name of 'Steward'" [49]) is striking because it captures,
through withering irony, the extent to which the slave is assaulted with
experiences of dispossession at every level. His deadpan description of the
scene – "I had no objection to it as I knew of" – works both to undercut the
state of alienation he is entering (the objection of a slave is a decisively
removed speech act) and to underscore it. First, Platt is less a name than a
set of attributes noted by his purchaser. Northup is no longer a person
whose name commemorates a parental or consanguineous connection of
any kind, but rather an adult child of the slave market bearing a new first
name, with which he is unacquainted, and waiting for a last name which
will be his only by virtue of its being his master's. Furthermore, a person
doesn't need to have his/her name "learned" unless that name is unrecognizable, unless it keeps on changing, which is exactly what happens to a
slave: "More than once I heard it said that Platt Ford, now Platt Tibeats – a
slave's name changes with his change of master – was 'a devil of a nigger'"
(93). Like the earlier passage, this one calls attention to the alienating fact
that Northup both is and is not his name. The "I" of the sentence is, of
course, Northup, who conveys the experience of hearing himself referred to
not only as someone else (Platt Ford), but then as another someone else
("now Platt Tibeats").

Throughout the text, the narrating "I" remains consistent, whereas other
people identify him by names not Northup. There is, however, one bizarre
moment when this distinction breaks down, when the cumulative effects of
Northup's nominal dispossession can no longer be denied. He writes of
playing the violin at several plantations during the Christmas season, and
once again he describes a scene in which he hears his name, which is not his
name at all, being called:

The young men and maidens of Holmesville always knew there was to be a
jollification somewhere, whenever Platt Epps was seen passing through the town
with his fiddle in his hand. "Where are you going now, Platt?" and "What is coming
off tonight, Platt?" would be interrogatories issuing from every door and window,
and many a time when there was no special hurry, yielding to pressing importunities,

Platt would draw his bow, and sitting astride his mule, perhaps, discourse musically to a crowd of delighted children, gathered around him in the street. (165)

What seems so disorienting about the passage are Northup's references to himself as Platt, especially because the sentences preceding and following this description are written in the first person, thereby calling attention to the difference between Northup and Platt. This moment of nominal conflation can be read as exemplifying the success of the slave system – even Northup no longer acknowledges himself as Northup as he has relinquished his former (and free) identity – or as illustrating the success of Northup's lessons in the arts of concealment necessary to survive and escape slavery – not to "divulg[e] the secret of my real name and history . . . upon which I was convinced depended my final escape" (175).[22] It is altogether fitting that Northup responds to the name, Platt, as if he were that person, given his brutal beating at the hands of Freeman. What is odd is that Northup *stays* Platt, not resuming the first-person narrative voice for the remainder of the description. This passage first represents Northup's transformation into Platt and then instantiates it. For a brief and anomalous moment in the text, Northup and his name seem to have parted company, as if he has become unrecognizable even to himself. But this isn't necessarily a bad thing, especially within the generic context of the slave narrative, where unrecognizability often provides the foundation upon which one attacks slavery and attains freedom.[23]

In contrast to Northup, who must endure the violent instruction of repeatedly having his new name learned and then recognizing it on pain of further punishment, Ida doesn't really have to learn a new name; rather, she must recognize and remember her old one. With this recognition, her slave name vanishes (which, as we saw, didn't ever have a sure hold on the narrative) from the text and her original name assumes its rightful and now stable place as the marker of her identity, never again to be threatened by the specter of slavery. Changing Lizzy back into Ida is a relatively simple affair, requiring little more from Ida than the patience necessary for her prior self to be recognized. Changing Platt back into Northup, however, involves a list of Herculean tasks, demanding not only Northup's savvy and strength, but the efforts of many people (including Governor Hunt of New York and Supreme Court Justice Nelson, among others) determined to find him, to prove his identity as a free man, and to take on a legal system that makes such efforts almost impossible to accomplish. Northup's narrative, then, discloses the nearly unreachable divide between the past "I" of freedom and the "now Platt" of slavery.

And recognition isn't what gets someone from one to the other. Being kidnapped into slavery is, on a fundamental level, the death of Northup, a point he makes in the account of his rescue by Henry B. Northup (a relative of Northup's father's former master) and Henry Waddill, a third party interested in assisting Northup: "They were not aware that I was known only as Platt; and had they inquired of Epps himself, he would have stated truly that he knew nothing of Solomon Northup" (229–230).[24] Nor is recognition completely bestowed upon Northup even at the conclusion of his narrative. Upon his return to New York, for example, the first family member he sees is his daughter, Margaret, who "did not recognize me" (251), not having seen him since she was seven years old. Even more painful to Northup, perhaps, is the fact that when he sues the two men who initially tricked him into leaving New York and then sold him into slavery, his testimony "was rejected solely on the ground that I was a colored man – the fact of my being a free citizen of New-York not being disputed" (247). Although "the secret was out [and] the mystery was unraveled" (232), the "authors of his imprisonment" (23) remain unpunished and Northup's claims to justice unrecognized by the law.

Whereas at the conclusion of *Ida May*, Walter can sincerely assure Ida that her "trials are all over" and her "whole future life shall be free from care or sorrow" (478), no one in Northup's circle can speak those words with any degree of confidence. In fact, the final pages of *Twelve Years A Slave* illustrate the painful trials he must endure in his unsuccessful attempts to hold his kidnappers accountable for their acts, one of the most outrageous being that "the court held the fact to be established, that Burch came innocently and honestly by me, and accordingly he was discharged" (248).[25] Northup's narrative ends like Ida's – both are free – but like so many slave narratives (and unlike *Ida May*) his ends with secrets and mysteries that may never be unraveled.

Early on in the text, for example, Northup indicates that neither the names nor the intent of the two men who first lured him southward could be unmistakably determined. He writes, "their names, as they afterwards gave them to me, were Merrill Brown and Abram Hamilton, though whether these were their true appellations, I have strong reasons to doubt" (12–13). The fact that "Brown" and "Hamilton" were never found seems to confirm them as false appellations and seems to implicate them in "the great wickedness of which I now believe them guilty," though Northup concedes that "I know not" (16). In another early section of the book, Northup describes the mutinous, though unrealized, plot devised by him and two other men bound for the New Orleans slave market and directs this remark to the ship's captain: "if he is still living, and these pages should chance to meet his eye, he will learn a fact connected with the voyage of the brig, from Richmond to New Orleans, in 1841, not entered on his log-book" (46). A more significant instance of unfinished closure can be found in Northup's account of the man who was, perhaps, the individual most responsible for bringing about Northup's liberation. Northup has this to say about the Canadian man named Bass, without whom "I should have ended my days in slavery" (204): "Whither he has now gone, I regret to be obliged to say, is unknown to me. He gathered up his effects and departed quietly from Marksville the day before I did, the suspicions of his instrumentality in procuring my liberation rendering such a step necessary" (205). What interests me about these passages is the lingering sense of things not known, of people not findable, which Northup communicates *vis à vis* his own experience of bondage and liberation. Even at the time of writing his narrative, he doesn't have all the information relevant to his twelve years in slavery, which creates the impression that this experience, which is clearly his experience, both is and isn't his. He says as much in the introductory paragraph of Chapter XXI: "I am indebted to Mr. Henry B. Northup and others for many of the particulars contained in this chapter" (225). Yes, those twelve years happened to him, but the narrative is written in such a way as to suggest that he is constantly in the position of catching up with the information he requires to understand how he came to spend them in slavery and how he got out. Northup knows for sure that he was kidnapped into slavery, that his bondage lasted for twelve years (hence, the continual repetition of "twelve years" [10, 29, 40, 90, 242]), and that it's over, but a haunting sense of ellipsis characterizes his narrative.

This epistemological disjunction takes the form of a temporal one, as Northup's prose constantly, almost compulsively, calls attention to the time about which and in which he is writing. It is not unusual for passages to begin with phrases such as, "About the time of which I am now writing" (155), "In the order of events, I come now to the relation of an occurrence, which I never call to mind but with sensations of regret" (43), or "Having now brought down this narrative to the last hour I was to spend on Bayou Boeuf" (223). The "now" clearly refers to the moment in which Northup writes the narrative, demarcating the present act of representation from the past experience of self-erasure. This separation is also constructed by words such as "afterwards" (10, 12, 29, 30, 42, 60) and "since" (40, 88), and phrases such as "on my return" (75), "as I now do" (144) which are deployed in order to call attention to the years spent in slavery as opposed to the time after his liberation. Although there is a multitude of differences between those two temporal states – physical abuse v. love, unpaid labor v. market wages, to name just two – the one Northup returns to, again and again, is the knowledge differential: "as I learned afterwards" (21), "as I have since learned" (48), "as I had reason afterwards to know" (91), "I am informed" (103). Through these phrases, the reader understands Northup's experience of writing a narrative as one that has been made possible by others, that was produced through an acquisition of information that was not Northup's to begin with, even though the experience was his. Thus, even though Northup frequently conveys his knowledge of events to come ("as will appear towards the close of this narrative" [8] "as the sequel demonstrated" [177], "as will presently be seen" [93]), he just as often signals the fact that he doesn't exactly know how his freedom has been attained until after the fact.

Of course, he knows as do we that his narrative will conclude with his freedom, but he makes it clear that he was and still is, with regard to certain details, in precisely the same position with respect to his own life as the reader: "those who read these pages will have the same means of determining as myself" (16). Northup knows that he was a slave and that he is "now" free, but he doesn't exactly know how it all happened, and his narrative calls attention to the difficulties he has both in figuring out his own story and in presenting it coherently. On the most obvious level, Northup's prose abounds with self-deprecating gestures. He comments upon the "imperfectly described" (162) scenes of his life in Louisiana, or he questions his account of a specific incident, including the phrase "if I remember rightly" (71). Such phrases also draw our attention to a basic condition of slavery – which is a fundamental absence of knowledge about one's early years as a slave. In the first paragraph of Douglass's *Narrative*, for example, he confesses, "I have no accurate knowledge of my age," as well as a more pervasive "want of information" regarding the early years of his life (255). Henry Bibb maintains, "it is almost impossible for slaves to give a correct account of their male parentage" (14). Although Northup is considerably older than Douglass and Bibb when he is kidnapped into slavery, the fact that Northup's knowledge is similarly circumscribed places him in a position *vis à vis* his own life that is the starting point for many slaves. In becoming a slave, in other words, Northup's place in time reverts to childhood. As befits someone whose sense of place and time has been completely undermined, Northup's narrative registers his self-doubt: he doubts the placement of certain descriptions, wondering if "a description [of William Ford, the man to whom Northup is sold] may not be out of place" (56) and if "this may be the proper place to speak of the manner of cultivating cane" (159). Such comments are part of a larger textual pattern (or problem) that manifests itself most strikingly in Northup's inability to keep the sequence of events temporally discrete.

As early as Chapter I, for example, before any events occur which lead to Northup's kidnapping, he attests to having written a letter "twelve years afterwards . . . which was the means, in the hands of Mr. Northup, of my fortunate deliverance" (10). A more complicated instance of Northup's representation of time occurs in Chapter VIII, where he records the sale of himself to Tibeats in "the winter of 1842. The deed of myself from Freeman to Ford, as I ascertained from the public records in New-Orleans on my return, was dated June 23d 1841. At the time of my sale to Tibeats . . . Ford took a chattel mortgage of four hundred dollars. I am indebted for my life, as will hereafter be seen, to that mortgage" (75). I find this passage fascinating because Northup not only narrates the events in "the winter of 1842," but he also lurches ahead to a description of his return (as a free man) to New Orleans twelve years later when he gets access to "the deed of myself," which then supplies him with the information, in the form of dates, which he didn't have at the time of his sale. This deed also clarifies Freeman's initial sale of Northup to Ford, securing the 1841 date, which takes Northup back a year prior to the 1842 event that he is relating. Every tense is represented, as Northup travels through all of narrative time in the space of just a few sentences. These erratic temporal rhythms are not atypical of Northup's narrative. About his nemesis, Burch, Northup has this to say: "His name was James H. Burch, as I learned afterwards – a well-known slavedealer in Washington; and then, or lately, connected in business, as a partner, with Theophilus Freeman, of New Orleans. The person who accompanied him was a simple lackey, named Ebenezer Radburn . . . Both of these men still live in Washington, or did, at the time of my return through that city from slavery in January last" (21). Northup's self-conscious uncertainty about the status of the persons comprising his narrative (who then, or lately, were connected in business; who still live or did live) is undoubtedly connected to the fact that Northup "learns afterwards" the name of his torturer, as well as a host of other details about his story. What else must he wait to "learn afterwards," and after what?[26]

The uncertainty of full knowledge is matched in the narrative by the ambiguity of temporality. The "now" that signifies the act of narration and the "now" that signifies a past moment in Northup's slave experience are fully entangled, as evidenced by the following: "He [Ford] is now a Baptist preacher" (62); "I was now known as Platt" (63); "about the time of which

I am now writing" (155); "I was now in which I afterwards learned was the 'Great Pacoudrie Swamp'" (103). The temporal arrhythmia of Northup's prose is a consequence of his telling several stories at once, one of which is his descent into slavery, another which is his escape from it, and still another which is his coming to know the story of both.

IV "WHO AIN'T A SLAVE?" (*MOBY-DICK*)

Northup's experience of belatedness puts him, one might say, in a state of enforced amnesia. Ida has amnesia too, but once she awakens from the nightmare of slavery, all aspects of her life fall into place. Compared to the narrative difficulties presented by the crime perpetrated upon Northup, it's relatively easy to maintain the difference between Ida's childhood and adulthood, between her prior identity as slave and her present (and future) identity as free. Despite this fact, the language of slavery continues to permeate Pike's text and is frequently used to describe the suffering of white characters including, of course, Ida. Not only does Mr. Maynard say, "the negroes are not the only slaves" (175), while explaining to Walter the impossibility of freeing the slaves ("I am completely fettered" [174]), but his nephew similarly laments, "I am not free to act. I am completely trammeled" (296). Also, he begins his declaration of love to Ida with the phrase, "O, if I am ever a free man again" (418). What interests me most, however, are the narrator's representations of Ida's suffering, post-slavery, because at the same time as the sentimental component of the genre works to make the case for its heroine's pain by analogizing it to the slave's, the fact that she has undergone an experience of slavery (no matter how brief it may be) has the effect of challenging and even undoing the power of those analogies. Yes, her sufferings as a sentimental protagonist may be great, but if one compares them to her ordeal as a slave, they pale in comparison.

Conventional as Ida's exit from slavery is, her entry into the world of slavery is horrific and surprisingly graphic for a sentimental novel. At first, Pike manages to overcome her evident disinclination to accept fully the representational requirements of her character's enslavement. Not only does Bill, one of Ida's kidnappers, "violently strik[e] her bare shoulders" (34), but she is brutally beaten by an aged black woman named Chloe, surely one of the strangest characters in the text. Chloe guards the cavernous, Dantean place where kidnapped children are brought on their journey southward, and she gives them their initial lessons in the brutalities of slavery. About her physiognomy, the narrator writes, "her appearance was perfectly hideous. Her gray hair hung in elf locks over her neck, from under the dirty cotton handkerchief that bound her brows, and her face, tawny, and wrinkled, and seamed with age, was stamped with every bad passion" (41). Chloe's grotesque physicality is matched by her psychic disfigurement, the causes of which the narrator delineates somewhat sympathetically, the effects of which she deplores.

Chloe is the child of a slave mother, Elsie, who "had been encouraged to believe that she had a right to her own children" (37). She witnesses her mother's repeated humiliations at the hands of various masters, until Elsie is finally sold to a different master, separating mother and child forever. Chloe repeats the "sins" of her mother concentrating "the whole energy of affection in her fierce nature . . . on her children, whom she loved with a fondness that, coupled as it was with the fear of losing them, made life and love itself a torture" (40). Whereas Venus, whose experiences are quite similar to Chloe's, manages to take her torment over the loss of her children and find others, specifically Ida, to love in their stead, Chloe is unable to do anything but hate. Indeed, she relishes her position as the children's first overseer, using her opportunity to abuse them as payback for the tortures endured by her own children. She tells Ida, for example, that "I likes to hear ye [cry]" (43) and "I'll make ye pay for the blood of my child" (44). Ida's tears prompt Chloe to ask the child if she is "crying for your mammy," to which Ida mournfully replies, "poor mamma's dead" (42). Chloe's question leads us to expect that, perhaps, Ida's plight as a motherless and enslaved child will remind Chloe of her own children and thus evoke a sympathetic response. But it does precisely the opposite: "Sorry yer mammy's dead said Chloe; wish she warn't, for I knows how she'd feel to have ye toted off, – how she'd cry! – . . . How I'd like to see her, wouldn't I?" (42). Chloe's sadism, a direct consequence of her life in slavery, rocks the foundations of the sentimental genre. A mother's love for her child is not an indicator of her affection for all children, and identification doesn't lead to sympathy but rather to violence. Rather than desiring that the abuses of children end because of the sufferings of her own children, Chloe insists that others feel her pain and, like the sadist that she is, derives pleasure from administering it.

One could reasonably argue that Chloe's character is just one more demonstration of Pike's racist worldview. Chloe's actions are deplorable, her words are satanic, and as if this weren't enough, Pike compares her to "a hyena who has tasted blood and is driven from its prey" (45). To be sure, Chloe is a monster in (barely) human form. Pike, however, does such a good job not only of explaining the origins of "a hatred that might be called inhuman" (40) but of allowing Chloe to voice many of Pike's anti-slavery convictions that one can't simply dismiss this character as the product of a completely benighted authorial imagination. Interestingly, Chloe is the only character in the novel who insists on the equality of black and white flesh, and she makes the case from the perspective of the equivalence of their pain. Thus, when one of Ida's kidnappers, Bill, reprimands Chloe for whipping Ida, saying "white children a'n't to be treated like niggers" (45), Chloe retorts, "as if dey was n't de same flesh and blood as niggers" (48). She makes a similar point when Bill comments on her equally abusive treatment of black children to which Chloe replies, "dey's cried for de mammy, much as if dey was white . . . and I neber see but it [a whip] hurt nigger flesh just as quick as white flesh" (47).[27] What's so strange and distinctive about Chloe's realization of the equivalence of black and white bodies to feel pain is that this identification leads not to the dispensation of sympathy – the conventional sentimental outcome – but rather to the dissemination of additional suffering. Chloe's potentially anti-slavery observation that "dey [white children] feels jest de same tings hurtin' em dat niggers does" (48) generates only the desire to inflict the accumulated pain of her experiences upon others. Ahab-like, Chloe has been divested of an irrecoverable part of herself and her vengeance is insatiable.

Chloe is monstrous, but she is also Pike's clearest articulation of why slavery must end. She has been driven mad by slavery, specifically by the loss of her mother and her impotence to protect her children from their master's will: "when the last one was taken from her she fell down in a fit, and, from that moment, no one ever saw her manifest any trace of the kindlier feelings of our nature. Compassion had no effect upon her, and harshness she returned with a wild and defiant rage, that made cruelty itself draw back appalled" (40). Although "compassion had no effect upon her," Chloe's character elicits compassion from the reader, which is significant given the fact that she has just beaten Ida, the character with whom we are meant to identify and sympathize. The origins of Chloe's despair are narrated no fewer than two times, first by Pike and then by Chloe, as if the enormity of that suffering requires multiple tellings. In a conversation between Chloe and Bill, we learn that Chloe had seven children and saw "'em kicked, and cuffed, and 'bused, one way 'n odder, till dey was sold away from me, or I was sold away from dem; and my heart, 'pears like 't were all tore and stuck full o' thorns" (48). Upon realizing that she is pregnant with her eighth, Chloe "goes out in de cane-brake, – 'I, dat lub de little unborn baby a heap site better'n my life, and feels as if de child's mouth suckin' at my breast would draw away de dreffle pain *here*,' – and she laid her hand on her heart – 'I goes and kneels down in de night, and prays de Lord dat de little cretur may neber draw de bref of life' " (49). Chloe's capacity for sympathy is amply demonstrated in this sentimental tableau of the slave mother loving her child more than life itself, of imagining the child at her breast draining her mother's pain, of wishing that child dead so as to be spared the horrors of a life in slavery. That she becomes the haunting figure of vengeance at the mouth of the cave is the direct consequence of the brutal desecration of the sentimental bond between mother and child. It is slavery and slavery alone that explains Chloe's transformation from sympathizer to sadist.[28] Thus, in spite of the problematic elements of Pike's depiction, Chloe, who disappears from the text when Ida is purchased by Master Bell, presents us with a very different view of the bereaved slave mother. Although she is everything a mother (and a slave mother in particular) should not be, according to the protocols both of sentimental novels and of slave narratives – incorrigibly aggrieved (she laments, "dere an't no Lord" [49]), aggressive, and out of control – we not only understand how she came to be the way she is, but we sympathize with her.

Ida May, like so much sentimental fiction written by women, is a lengthy novel, the bulk of which concentrates on Ida's attachments to the Wynn family and the obstacles she and Walter must conquer in order to consummate their love in marriage. I have focused on Ida's life as a slave, even though it is dispensed with in relatively short order, because her brutal treatment at the hands of Chloe and her kidnappers serves as a benchmark for what abjection and suffering mean. Such experiences help to remind Ida (and the reader) of the differences between slavery and freedom, even when the latter begins to feel like the former. Thus, when Ida's anti-slavery opinions pit her against her guardian, Mr. Wynn, and she finds herself "subjected to [his] most imperious despotism" (328), she knows that she is free to reject his authority. She informs Mr. Wynn of her intention to free her slaves: "I claim the right to exercise liberty of conscience" (326). When Ida begins to feel sorry for herself, "murmuring at the Providence which had ordered for her such a changeful and lonely life, and made her so early fatherless and motherless," she is reminded of the obvious by an elderly female slave that "you'se *rich*, and you'se *white*, and you'se *free*" (338). The sentimental tropes, in other words, don't quite work the way they are supposed to because we (and she) have seen that her life post-slavery is absolutely different, no matter how analogically resonant, from not only the situation of the slave but Ida's situation as a slave. Her experiences with Chloe have undermined the power of that analogy. As the novel shifts from Ida's slave narrative to Ida's sentimental novel, then, Pike finds herself in the curious position of having challenged her own ability to marshal the power of sympathy on behalf of her "free" heroine having worked our sympathies so effectively on behalf of her enslaved one.

Pike has written a story that mitigates, even as it relies upon, the effectiveness of the analogy between Ida, the slave, and Ida, the suffering sentimental heroine who classically "lean[s] back in her chair so sick and faint with the violent throbbing of her heart, that it was with difficulty she sustained herself" (311). Because that analogy is instrumental in the production of readerly sympathy we find it circulating throughout the text. For example, in a conversation during which several characters consider the possibility that Ida has been sold into slavery by poor white parents, Walter wonders, "can servitude – *slavery* – be in any case the proper condition for a parent to force a child into?" (194). Later in the novel, when Mr. Wynn cruelly forbids Ida to bring a companion with her on a treacherous trip to the property she has inherited, the narrator remarks, "that he felt a perfect right to punish her disobedience; and, just as he would have imprisoned a child in a dark closet, until it promised to be good, he determined to inflict this chastisement . . . and thus coerce her into submission to his wishes with regard to her conduct" (371). It is significant that Ida's punishment follows on the heels of a scene in which Mr. Wynn applies his ideas about "family discipline" (302) to an "impudent and disobedient" (291) slave named Alfred, who ends up committing suicide, after being locked up in a closet (292) and assured that "he will be punished" severely for "being sulky and disobedient" (291). The language and treatment of the mistreated sentimental protagonist clearly parallel the condition of the abused slave, and Ida's plight enlists our sympathy precisely because of these resonances. But it is Alfred's utterly helpless situation, not Ida's bad one, that provides the catalyst for sympathy, which is a secondary consequence of and of secondary importance to our sympathy for Alfred. Alfred's pain, like Ida's earlier experience with Chloe, functions as ground zero for what suffering is and, such, it sets limits to our sympathetic response to Ida.

Lest Pike undermine completely the sympathy that we may extend to her protagonist, she has Ida endure one final trial in which her credentials as a (white) sentimental heroine are questioned, threatened, and once more defended. She must be kidnapped, or at least potentially kidnapped, a second time so that the genre to which she truly belongs will never again be in doubt. The scene is Ida's rundown property, the Triangle, located a considerable distance from the Wynn plantation. In his desire to punish Ida for criticizing his treatment of the slaves, Mr. Wynn has allowed only Venus, who is ill-equipped to act the part of Ida's protector, to accompany her on her perilous journey. Upon entering the door of a slave hut, she discovers Mr. Potter, the overseer of the plantation, preparing to whip one of the slaves and demands that he cease his actions. Ida then identifies herself as "the owner of this plantation, and of these negroes. I am Miss May!" (342). At first, her words have the desired effect, leaving Mr. Potter "fully convinced of Ida's identity" (342) and ready to treat her civilly. Moments later, however, he begins to doubt that she is who she says she is: "I don't feel right sure that you're what you pretends" (349); "I a'n't noways sure neither of yer is what you pretend to be" (357). Although Ida assures him of her identity as "owner of this property, and of that fact I can bring abundant proof" (350), the fact is that the proof is elsewhere, leaving Ida vulnerable to the clearly sexual predations of the "coarse" (353) and violent Mr. Potter. Because Ida's identity as a free, white woman cannot be established, Mr. Potter begins to treat her like the mulatto slave with whom he, Legree-like, cohabits. His declaration, "I'm master here!"(366) clearly positions Ida as his slave, and as he "cast[s] upon her glances that grew every moment more insolent" (366), Ida is back in Chloe's cave, only this time Mr. Potter is the sadist and rape is his preferred form of violence.

Unlike the first kidnapping, however, where Ida was transformed into a slave and stripped of her identity as a white sentimental heroine, even if only temporarily, here she is a slave by analogy. She is a sentimental heroine who is being treated like a slave. In contrast to the scene with Chloe, where Pike dares to allow Ida to be brutally beaten in order to establish the fact of her abjection, here the threat to Ida's virginity is just that – a threat, a convention of the sentimental novel which places its heroine in the position of a slave in order to activate our sympathies. The danger she faces in the house with Mr. Potter palpably differs from her experience with Chloe, in small part because Ida has grown into adulthood, in large part because we know no harm will come to Ida. It is purely hypothetical, because not only does sentimental convention require that she marry Walter but she cannot marry him if she is raped. In addition, the overwrought language of the scene – "the glow, the ecstasy of feeling that first sustained her, had departed" (360) – works hard to convince us of Ida's vulnerability, even as that same vulnerability, that "excitement of feeling" and that "exquisite sensation" (383), signifies her invulnerability to rape. Such sensitivity, as sentimental convention would have it, only confirms the fact that she will find a safe harbor before any crimes are committed. Ida will die before she will be raped, and she will be rescued by Walter, "her deliverer" (367), before either of those two events will happen. She is a white sentimental heroine, which is to say she is *not* a slave, and thus her dangers are more thrilling than real, more anticipatory than actual: "A wild fear thrilled her soul" (358) and "a thrill of superstitious fear stole over her" (359). It is as if, in the desire to make absolute Ida's identity as the (white) heroine of a sentimental novel, Pike has become unconscious of Ida's former life as a slave and the implications it might have for the reader's sympathies regarding her heroine's plight; to wit, this description of Ida's feelings: "Alone and helpless, she felt, as she had never felt before, a craving for affection, for support, for protection; a desire to give up all struggle; a shrinking from further sacrifice; a longing for a strong arm on which to lean, for a hand to guide her; a restless, desperate wish to free herself from the present, which girded her with realities too fearful, and to be released from the future, with whose responsibilities she felt unable to cope" (361-362). The narrative pressure, at this point, to separate Ida from her identity as a slave takes on tremendous importance, and the fascinating consequence of that pressure is that the analogy between Ida and the female slave gets pushed to its outermost limits. Ida experiences herself as vulnerable in a way "she had never felt before" (think cave) and is desperate "to free herself from the present" (think Chloe).

Pike pulls out all of the generic stops in order to activate the analogy between Ida as slave and Ida as sentimental heroine so as to cast off once and for all the possibility of her being the former. Of course, we sympathize with Ida in this situation, even though we are confident that Walter will save the day (and bring Ida's father back into his daughter's life!). The problem, however, is that our sympathy for Ida in her dire sentimental condition is both secondary and knowingly temporary. The one(s) for whom we have the "deep[est] sympathy" (307), the phrase used to describe Ida's feelings for the sufferings of slaves, are Ida, alias Lizzy, Alfred, Alfred's mother who cannot comfort him as he chooses to take his own life in the garret of the Wynn house, and Chloe – which is to say we sympathize with the slaves who are the real victims in *Ida May*.

Pike's device of having Ida kidnapped into a slave narrative has rendered problematic the deployment of one of the most basic elements of senti-mental novels, which is the reader's sympathy for the heroine. I find this aspect of Pike's text particularly compelling because it challenges conven-tional analyses of the operations of sympathy in this literature. As strenu-ously as the novel tries to convince us that Ida's existence post-slavery is as difficult and painful as her life in slavery by analogizing the two, the novel simultaneously makes clear that that's simply not true. Even when Ida is most vulnerable to Mr. Potter and thinks "how relentlessly had Death pursued her," the narrator prefaces this melancholy reflection with the rather sobering detail that Ida had "a strange, dreary pity for herself" (361). To be sure, *Ida May* begins with the premise that sympathy operates according to a structure of identification; after all, Pike's novel is predicated on the fact that Ida's own experience in slavery ignites her anti-slavery convictions. She is the spokeswoman for the power of sympathy, whether as the five-year-old "sympathizing listener" (82) of Venus's heartbreaking tale, or as the grown woman who speaks on behalf of Alfred's "right feelings" (301) and preaches the necessity of "courage and ... sympathy" (319) to those in pain. Having been a slave herself, she understands their suffering. As the novel progresses, however, a different model of sympathy begins to take shape, also based on Ida's experience in slavery, which insists that sympathy is generated for characters with whom readers (specifically a white, middle-class female audience) most likely have the least in common. Our identification with Ida as a white woman being threatened with rape produces sympathy only up until the point that we remember that we are no longer in the realm of the slave narrative where physical abuse is an absolute fact of the slave's experience, including Ida/Lizzy's. In the later scene, we are in the realm of the sentimental novel which means not only will Ida not be raped but her potential violation is a matter of effect, intending to ratchet up our feelings and fears only to have them (and Ida) restored to order by Walter's intervention. Ida's life as a slave makes her sympathize with slaves because she has shared their experience; Ida's life as a slave makes the reader sympathize with the slaves, not Ida, to the extent that their experience is different from Ida's and our own.

CHAPTER 5

Love American style: The Wide, Wide World

Most sentimental novels end in marriage, which is to say that they, by and large, conclude with an affirmation of the heroine's ability to make a contract. Although one might reasonably argue that she has no other choice than to marry, the fact is that the marital contract stands as the apotheosis of her sentimental journey, the culmination of her ability to establish loving bonds based on choice. Through this contract, she asserts her belief in the traditional reproduction of the biological family which will, she hopes, avoid the pain and disaster of the consanguineous family from which she comes.

My reading of the relation between sentimental fictions and slave narratives continues and concludes by considering Susan Warner's best-selling *The Wide, Wide World.* The chapter explores how Warner's novel, in contrast to the sentimental fictions examined thus far, presents a different and considerably less sanguine view of contract than we've seen up to this point; one which registers, to a degree surpassed, perhaps, only by slave narratives and Melville's *Pierre*, the disciplinary, psychic, and institutional restraints upon the heroine's ability to make choices, whether the context be adoption or marriage. Unlike Gerty, Ellen doesn't come to the contractual table in possession of herself, because that self always belongs to someone else, whether that someone is her mother, John Humphreys, God, or the multitude of characters who are constantly claiming ownership of her. Her virtual incarceration in Scotland represents the culmination of her experiences of abjection (some of which produce pleasure, others pain), which begins with the maternal embrace of Mrs. Montgomery, proceeds to the icy handshake of Aunt Fortune, and moves on to the confusing adoration of the Lindsays. Granted, on the face of it, *The Wide, Wide World* is a text which would seem to have nothing to do with slavery even though it was published the same year as the Compromise of 1850 became law, but as with *Ida May* the heroine, Ellen Montgomery, finds herself in a situation not unlike slavery. What might the function be, then, of what could provocatively be called "miniaturized slave narratives" in sentimental texts not explicitly about slavery?[1]

The Wide, Wide World, like *Ida May,* exemplifies the generic permeability of sentimental fictions and slave narratives, whether the points of intersection occur at the level of plot, theme, character, language, or structure. There is, as the previous chapters have delineated, what I term a "generic sympathy" that invites moments of contact as well as contrast, of proximity and distantiation. Indeed, a powerful body of literary criticism has analyzed the ideological effects of generic sympathy by considering it from the point of view of the slave narrative. Thus, we understand that slave narratives appropriate sentimental conventions in order to expand their audience, to incite readers' sympathy in the hopes of radicalizing the anti-slavery appeal, and to challenge the ideological terrain upon which racial and gendered hierarchies are being established in the antebellum period.[2] But when the notion of generic sympathy is applied to sentimental novels, they are, more often than not, found to be incapable of cultural critique, in large measure because of their allegedly incurable attachment to the bourgeois family. My analysis, however, demonstrates that this dominant reading fails to consider the very important fact that sentimental novels not only depend upon the dissolution of the biological family to get things going but then proceed to entertain the possibility, if not make the case, that consanguinity is a vastly over-rated determinant of family stability and happiness. Affection is a better bet.

In addition, just as the cultural work of slave narratives has been illuminated through their contextualization *vis à vis* sentimental fictions, particularly in the case of Harriet Jacobs's *Incidents in the Life of a Slave Girl* (to which my reading will return), the reverse is also true. The complexities of sentimental novels become more visible by reading them in conjunction with slave narratives. Doing so challenges our understanding of the relation between the genres as their textual overlaps can be understood not merely or primarily as evidence of the sentimental novel's hegemonic appropriation of the slave narrative's power to evoke sympathy, although that is the case in certain instances, but more analytically as textual moments in which the sentimental novel is meditating upon the ideological foundations that distinguish it from the genre of the slave narrative through which the novel is defining itself. In other words, if we begin to grant sentimental novels the capacity to think through the conditions that enable their ideological effects (in the same way that slave narratives have been granted this capacity), and the possibility that they do this in relation to the "hard fact" of slavery, the novels become far more diverse, interesting and intelligent. In the case of *The Wide, Wide World*, generic sympathy operates not to subvert difference but to attend to it. Just as slavery stands as the existential condition against which freedom is conceptualized, the presence of the slave narrative functions as the negative generic condition against and through which Warner's novel engages the questions of where, how, and to whom Ellen belongs.

An especially pervasive example of generic sympathy, and one that will be an important component of my reading of *The Wide, Wide World*, revolves around the question of belonging or, more precisely, the question of to whom the protagonist belongs. "Who do *you* belong to?" and versions thereof, is a question asked not only of former slaves, Jacobs, Solomon Northup, J. W. C. Pennington, and William Craft, but of Gerty, Ida, and Ellen.[3] Slave narratives and sentimental texts overlap on precisely the question and consequences of belonging. That said, the issue of belonging is also a key dividing line between the two genres. On the one hand, to be asked to whom one belongs in the context of a slave narrative is to be reminded of the brutalizing principle upon which the slave system is founded and continued – that the economic fact of belonging to one's master is also often the biological fact of being his child. The question is also to be reminded that one is deprived of the possession of oneself, is subject to physical abuse, and is denied the right to belong to one's biological family, especially one's birth mother. Indeed, the painful abrogation of family ties is usually a condition of the slave's escape from slavery, and the first step toward freedom is often the refusal to belong to anyone else except oneself. For example, when Harriet Jacobs's uncle, Benjamin, escapes, he says to his brother, "I part with all my kindred" (360). To be free is, however, also to be committed to and hopeful about the reunion with those kindred left behind, as evidenced by Henry Bibb's repeated returns to the scene of his family's enslavement in order to effect their escape. Thus, in belonging to oneself, a transformation in the meaning of belonging takes place – from economics and the law of the father to affection and the consanguineous bonds of motherly love. Belonging to oneself, then, is to refuse to be consigned to bondage because one's mother is a slave, and it is to find a place where one's biological bonds will be respected on the inextricable grounds of maternity and love. The ex-slave thus journeys toward freedom and, in doing so, comes to choose the place, whether it be Canada, America, or England, and the form of that belonging, whether it be a community of like-minded persons, a more solitary life, a marriage, or some combination thereof.

On the other hand, to be asked this question, "to whom do you belong?" in a sentimental text is to be asked the name of one's parents, which, in turn, is to be reminded that one either no longer has a mother or a father or no longer knows to which family one belongs because affections rather than consanguinity have become a competing source of familial definition.[4] The question of belonging in this case signifies biology rather than economics, unless the protagonist gets kidnapped or adopted by people who treat her like a slave along the way. Then the novel must sort out not only to whom she belongs, but in what sense she belongs, and to which genre, as we saw in the previous chapter. Because she belongs to the sentimental novel, the child journeys, not primarily toward the restoration of blood ties (although that happens too), but toward the man who has come to occupy her affections and, in doing so, she chooses to belong to him. According to the logic of much sentimental fiction, then, the heroine's freedom is measured by the progressive ownership and bestowal of her affections, and the ultimate demonstration of that freedom is marriage. To be denied the possibility of this ending, this contract (ideally) based on affection, is one of the standard ways in which sentimental novels imagine the experience of being a slave and, interestingly enough, the denial of this contract is also one of the conventional means by which slave narratives mark the cruelties of slavery.

Given what we've already seen in Hentz, Kemble, and Pike, I want to suggest that the heroine's immersion in a situation analogous to slavery, short-lived though it may be, not only ignites our sympathy for her but also establishes what, for many sentimental novels, it means to be free. Novel after novel insists that contract, specifically the marriage contract, is the clearest expression of freedom. Although antebellum feminists often maintained that marriage and slavery were two sides of the same oppressive coin, many sentimental texts represent the capacity to enter into contracts, such as marriage or adoption (or divorce, the abrogation of the marital contract, as in Kemble's case), as that which makes the two institutions irrefutably and irreconcilably different.[5] The fiction makes this point by requiring the heroine to experience a temporary, though painful, suspension of the right to make a contract, which is to say she becomes like a slave. As she experiences the effects of this analogy, the parallels accumulate. Her affections are deemed irrelevant in determining the future she desires; her memories, things, and name are rendered the possessions of others; and her identity is made alien, as she no longer knows to whom or with whom she belongs (though definitely not herself).

This description, of course, sounds perilously close to the legalized condition of coverture (and slavery), to which both Kemble's journal and Hentz's *Ernest Linwood* allude, and which was an especial target in feminist discourse, from the 1848 Declaration of Sentiments to the writings of Lucy Stone, Angelina and Sarah Grimké, and others. Although one might be tempted to argue that the heroine's eventual marriage is a repeat performance of her temporary experience in slavery – only this time its duration is permanent – the fact is that the use of the miniaturized slave narrative works to disarticulate marriage from slavery, not to claim that the two institutions are mirror images of each other. For most sentimental novels, marriage is not slavery, analogically resonant and uncomfortably alike as they may, at times, seem. The difference hinges on what may seem to be a slender, though essential, thread: marriage signifies the freedom to choose the person to whom one wishes to belong; slavery not only is having no choice in the matter but means not being able to enter into a legally binding marriage at all. Thus, given the alternative between not getting to choose to whom one belongs and choosing to whom one belongs, sentimental heroines typically choose the latter.

This, at least, is the way Warner frames the issue of Ellen Montgomery's choices in *The Wide, Wide World,* and it is materially different from Gerty's experience, as well as Gabriella's in *Ernest Linwood* and Ethelyn's in *Ethelyn's Mistake,* where the protagonist comes to possess herself in the course of her story.[6] This option is denied to Ellen, which is not to say that she is a slave, but is to say that her story speaks more to the limitations of what, as a free person capable of entering into contracts, she is able to do. If self-possession, for example, is out of the question, it seems reasonable to ask, is the absence of self-possession what it means to be a slave? Are there degrees of being a slave? "Who ain't a slave?" to quote Ishmael. Is Ellen both free and slave, and unlike Ida May, a permanent occupant of both subject positions? And, if so, might we go so far as to consider how Ellen's hybrid status resonates with the nation's in 1850?

I ELLEN'S BONDAGE

That Hentz perverts the slave narrative is to be expected given her support of slavery. That Pike installs a slave narrative at the beginning of her sentimental heroine's journey toward abolitionist practice (she announces, "I shall free my negroes as soon as they become legally mine" [281] and follows through) and marriage is also predictable given the anti-slavery intentions of the novel. But what about Ellen Montgomery, who is greeted by her Scottish uncle (and soon to be guardian), Mr. Lindsay, with these powerful and ominous words, "I am your father henceforth; – you belong to me entirely, and I belong to you; – my own little daughter"?[7] To the extent that Ellen refuses his verbal acts of mutual (at least, in this instance) appropriation, Mr. Lindsay repeats and reinforces them: "Forget that you were American, Ellen, – you belong to me; your name is not Montgomery any more, – it is Lindsay . . . you are my own little daughter, and must do precisely what I tell you" (510). Who owns Ellen comes to constitute the principal question of their relationship as Mr. Lindsay claims, yet again, "you are mine own now – my own child – my own little daughter. You shall do just what pleases me in every thing" (518), and still later, "you are mine, you must understand" (553). Elsewhere, she complains that Mrs. Lindsay has "a way of silencing her that [she] particularly disliked" (541), and also worries to herself, "I have given myself to [Mr. Lindsay]" (520). Ellen experiences her adoption by her consanguineous Scottish relations as a diminution in good times, as an eradication in bad ones, of her rights, her identity, and her freedom. The contracts based on affection that she has made with the many people who have adopted her prior to her arrival in Scotland are now being declared null and void.

Ellen's relationship with the Lindsays and, to a somewhat lesser degree, with Aunt Fortune, is not unlike that between a slave and her master, and the rhetoric of the novel reinforces the connection.[8] One need only juxtapose passages and plot lines from *The Wide, Wide World* with Jacobs's *Incidents in the Life of a Slave Girl* to make this case. Both protagonists lose their mothers and fathers at a young age and are then required to enter the wide, wide world. Jacobs is "bequeathed" (344) to Mr. Flint's five-year-old daughter, and Ellen is "sent" (101) to Aunt Fortune, who refuses to acknowledge Ellen's right to "give herself away" to the Humphreyses, because "she [Aunt Fortune] had the first right and only right to [Ellen]" (458). Like Ellen, Jacobs is constantly being watched and disciplined (362). Like Ellen, Jacobs endures a routine of continued dispossession (362). And like Ellen, Jacobs is repeatedly told by Mr. Flint "you are mine and you shall be mine for life" (408), and "He told me I was his property" (361) and "that I belonged to him" (362). Even Ellen's deployment of the Revolutionary fathers, which I shall discuss later in the chapter, is echoed as Jacobs writes, "'give me liberty, or give me death,' was my motto" (424).

There are key differences, however, one of the most significant being that Jacobs is relentlessly subjected to the sexual depredations of Dr. Flint whereas the dangers posed to Ellen's corporeal integrity are never enacted (she's threatened by Mr. Saunders, but John intervenes; Aunt Fortune threatens to whip Ellen, but Mr. Van Brunt saves her). Unlike Ellen, Jacobs has no one to save her except herself, which is why, in a decision calculated both to preserve some degree of her self-respect and to diminish some portion of Mr. Flint's mastery over her, she chooses to have sex with Mr. Sands rather than be raped by Mr. Flint. In a passage that has quite rightly drawn much critical attention for the complicated psychological and moral state to which Jacobs alludes, she frames this choice in the following way: "It seems less degrading to give one's self, than to submit to compulsion. There is something akin to freedom in having a lover who has no control over you, except that which he gains by kindness and attachment" (385). "Something akin to freedom" is the closest Jacobs gets to freedom, even when, at the conclusion of her narrative, she is legally free and has the documents to prove it: "I well know the value of that bit of paper; but much as I love freedom, I do not like to look upon it. I am deeply grateful to the generous friend who procured it, but I despise the miscreant who demanded payment for what never rightfully belonged to him or his" (512). Jacobs's articulation of her freedom is hemmed in by profound hatred and an abiding realization of all that can never be recovered.

Jacobs's narrative thus begins with her enslavement, ends with her free-dom, and observes that there are aspects of both conditions in each. This is not to imply that given the chance she would reverse her trajectory and make the claim that "something akin to freedom" is in any way equivalent to the freedom that she enjoys at the conclusion of her text. The Flint family gives her plenty of such "opportunities," and she, of course, rejects them. It is to suggest, however, that Jacobs produces a paradigm of choice (when speaking of her cramped, dark situation in the garret, she writes, "yet I would have chosen this, rather than my lot as a slave, though white people considered it an easy one" [438]) out of the experience of slavery that helps us better understand how Ellen goes about imagining and making her choices. To be sure, the stakes are dramatically different, and yet Ellen's choices, as a free sentimental heroine, are not unlike Jacobs's, as a free enslaved woman, because the choices of both are characterized by con-straint and compromise.

To this extent, Claudia Tate's reading of Jacobs's "freedom in *Incidents*" as "the result of a highly compromised, largely passive, psychological battle that is not won without considerable self-sacrifice" is as accurate an analysis of freedom in Jacobs's slave narrative as it is of Ellen's experience of bondage in Warner's sentimental novel.[9] Ellen's version of that "something akin to freedom" is much like Jacobs's in that knowing she must belong to someone (having once been possessed so fully and happily by her mother), she chooses the Humphreyses over both Aunt Fortune and the Lindsays. But whereas Jacobs arrives at a sense of freedom's limitations through her excruciating passage through slavery, out of which she is then able to critique her freedom while, nevertheless, embracing it, Ellen never really arrives at a sense of the limitations of her choices because she has accepted those limitations as constitutive of her very identity; the opening scenes with Mrs. Montgomery make clear that she has acceded to the notion of belonging to someone else right from the start.

Jacobs's relation to the issue of belonging – she's a slave and not only cannot legally belong to her parents, but can't belong to herself – is much more complicated than Ellen's. First, Jacobs has never belonged to her mother in a way that a child often belongs to her mother (the closest she comes to that is her mistress, who "had been almost like a mother to me" [343], and her maternal grandmother, "who promised to be a mother to her grandchildren" [345]), and second, Jacobs refuses to accept the premise that she belongs to her master, Mr. Flint. Even though Ellen's choices are limited as to whom she will belong, the fact is that she is one of those "happy women, whose purity has been sheltered from childhood, who have been free to choose the objects of your affection, whose homes are protected by law" (384) to whom Jacobs is referring when voicing her own very different experience as a slave for whom the objects of one's affection are deemed irrelevant and marketable. Ellen's marriage to John is, perhaps, the clearest articulation of her acceptance of the limits of freedom; Jacobs's story, which decidedly doesn't end in marriage – "my story ends with freedom; not in the usual way, with marriage" (513) – is, perhaps, her fiercest articulation of how her life in slavery has presented her with options radically different from those of a sentimental heroine. And marrying someone is not one of them. The absence of what Anne duCille calls "the coupling convention" at the conclusion of Jacobs's narrative has been read as a critique of the institution of marriage, as well as an alternative to the heterosexual bourgeois family. In other words, as subversive. Another way, however, to think about the absence of marriage at the conclusion of *Incidents* is that Jacobs still can't marry, not because the marriage contract would be fraudulent, as was the case in the south, and not because marriage would be yet another kind of enslavement, but because she remains "bound" to Mrs. Bruce. She still isn't free to be married.[10]

"It is hard to be submissive" (369), writes Jacobs, and that difficulty is evident even at the end of her narrative as she confesses, "The dream of my life is not yet realized. I do not sit with my children in a home of my own. I still long for a hearthstone of my own, however humble. I wish it for my children's sake far more than for my own" (513). Although she speaks of the "Love, duty, [and] gratitude that bind her to Mrs. Bruce's side" (513), there is no mistaking the disquieted quality of her submission. Her "own" dreams, home, and children continue to elude her, in contrast to Ellen, whose dreams are realized in her impending marriage to John. She is able to do as he says – "what God orders let us quietly submit to" (565) – not only because it's comparatively easier for Ellen than for Jacobs to submit, but Ellen has been taught to understand her submission as freedom.

Such quiet submission is, however, far from the reality when Ellen first arrives in Edinburgh "having some difficulty persuad[ing] herself that she was really Ellen Montgomery" (500). Ellen responds intensely and angrily as Mr. Lindsay demands that she surrender her name, her (national) identity, her precious time alone with her mother's gift of the Bible and John's gift of *Pilgrim's Progress*, and everything else that she understood herself to be (and own) prior to her being transferred to her "legal guardians" (561), the Lindsays. Indeed, little time passes before Ellen finds herself subject to a father figure who demands absolute obedience ("I lay my commands upon you" [526]; "I will have only obedience from you" [526]), and whose constant affection makes her feel "as if she were caught in a net from which she had no power to get free" (520). As Mrs. Lindsay remarks, "she was much too precious a plaything to be trusted to any other hands, even her own" (540). Her experiences in the Lindsay household suggest that she is both like a slave and not like a slave. She is clearly an object, "a possession," "a plaything," but a "darling" and a "dear" one (538). She is told that she cannot read the Bible and that she is no longer permitted to sleep in her own room (542) and yet "she is the pride and delight of the whole family" (528). On the one hand, she sings a Methodist hymn about being "bound for the land of Canaan . . . my happy, happy home" (546), words that resonate with the hopes of slaves dreaming of escape either northward or towards heaven, and on the other "she was petted and fondled" (538) and given "every means of improvement that masters and mistresses, books and instruments, could afford" (527).[11] Furthermore, the narrator somewhat obscurely explains what can only be described as the Lindsays' attempt to purchase Ellen and Mr. Humphreys's refusal to let them do so. Upon their sending "more than enough" money to Mr. Humphreys for the cost of Ellen's expenses while under his care, we are told that "she was sorry to have the money go; she understood the feeling with which it was sent, and it hurt her" (556).

One is left to conclude that the feeling accompanying the money is the desire to claim ownership of Ellen. Mr. Humphreys's response confirms this – "he declined utterly to accept [Mr. Lindsay's bills], telling Ellen that he looked upon her as his own child up to the time that her friends took her out of his hands" as does Mr. Lindsay's – "the bills were instantly and haughtily re-enclosed and sent back to America" (556). Ellen is caught between rival owners, and her only recourse is to wait to be rescued by "her deliverer" (401), John, the owner who "seems to have attained such an ascendancy over her" (551) and to whom she most willingly belongs.

Whereas *Ida May* makes a case for the absolute difference between adoption and slavery, even as it works that analogy in order to produce sympathy for Ida, *The Wide, Wide World* deploys the analogy between Ellen as adopted and Ellen as enslaved but seems less certain of the differences between the two and less able to extricate Ellen from Mr. Lindsay's "hand of power" (510). Ellen's slave-like experience is obviously more psychological than corporeal, and the most profound expression of the Lindsays' desire for exclusive ownership is not to threaten or punish her with physical violence but to forbid her to remember and, therefore, to own her past, on pain of the withdrawal of their love. Over and again, they demand that she not acknowledge or, better yet, repudiate the bonds she has forged with others because, as Mr. Lindsay says, "I am not satisfied to have your body here and your heart somewhere else" (534). She is repeatedly silenced by them, whether the occasion is an instance of rebellion against their wishes that she drink wine or a moment of remembrance of her earlier life without them (equivalent acts of disobedience from the Lindsays' point of view). In a predicament not unlike Northup's, she cannot say who she is, and even though "she was unaccustomed to concealments" (528), she soon finds herself trying to "screen herself from observation" (531) and searching out places where she could be "alone and free" (532). They relentlessly try to destroy her former self, the self that was Ellen Montgomery, the self that John made, in order to recreate a new one, "Ellen Lindsay" (524).

In attempting to possess her, the Lindsays unsuccessfully try to eradicate her attachments to the past – "I wish I could make her drink Lethe" (551) – including her former name. That Ellen's name comes up as a matter of debate should be expected. We have already seen several instances of the importance of naming in both sentimental novels and in slave narratives, a generic and ideological linkage that derives from their overlapping inquiries into the possibilities and limitations of self-possession. The relevant passage in *The Wide, Wide World* takes place when Ellen has momentarily relaxed her guard, having made a new acquaintance with M. Muller, a friend of Mr. Lindsay and soon-to-be French teacher to Ellen. Not having been formally introduced to her, M. Muller inquires "by what name he might remember her" to which she replies, "Monsieur, je m'appelle Ellen M—" In a Gerty-like moment, Ellen "stopped short, in utter and blank uncertainty what to call herself; Montgomery she dared not; Lindsay stuck in her throat." Their exchange continues:

"Have you forgotten it?" said M. Muller, amused at her look, "or is it a secret?"
"Tell M. Muller your name, Ellen," said Mr. Lindsay, turning round from a group where he was standing at a little distance. The tone was stern and displeased. Ellen felt it keenly, and with difficulty and some hesitation still, murmured,
"Ellen Lindsay."
"Lindsay? Are you the daughter of my friend Mr. Lindsay?"
Again Ellen hesitated, in great doubt how to answer, but finally, not without starting tears, said,
"Oui, monsieur." (524–525)

Unlike Ida who can't remember her name because of a temporary case of amnesia, Ellen can't remember her name both because she's not exactly sure what her name is (has it been legally changed to Lindsay?), and, more importantly, because if she gives the wrong name, she'll be punished for it by a withholding of affection. Her name, like Northup's, is a secret that can be disclosed only at the risk of suffering. Things are so tough for Ellen, and every conversation is an opportunity for her obedience to be tested and found wanting, that even though she gives the right answer to M. Muller, she doesn't give it in the right way, and so she incurs Mr. Lindsay's displeasure anyway. Indeed, when Mr. Lindsay tells her, "you belong to me now; and there are some things I want you to forget, and not remember" (547), Ellen finds herself in a position not unlike Northup's, where her identity as Ellen Montgomery is being purposefully erased, and she is forbidden to voice any knowledge of her past. To do so is not to incur bodily injury, as was the case with him, but it is to risk the withdrawal of the Lindsays' love. This is a consequence quite different from the physical abuse meted out to Northup should he dare disclose his identity as a free black man illegally kidnapped into slavery, but Warner works hard to make these two punishments analogous, at least during Ellen's time in Scotland. The Lindsays' affection is the whip that keeps her in the position of a slave. Its unpredictable application and abrogation determine her every move and desire. Despite their continued demands for unconditional obedience, Ellen challenges their attempt to recreate her in their image and to destroy her earlier affiliations, not by claiming the right to self-ownership but by asserting the fact of prior possession. She has, in other words, made a contract with the Humphreyses ("I have promised Alice... I have promised Mr.Humphreys" [490]) that cannot be broken.

Like most sentimental heroines, Ellen has already been transferred and transferred her affections many times over before arriving in the Lindsay household. Up until her appearance in Scotland, she has been incorporated into the many families comprising the fictional world of *The Wide, Wide World.* Most of these families, like Ellen's, are similarly fractured by death, whether it is Alice and John's dead mother, Nancy Vawse's dead mother, Ellen Chauncey's dead father, or Mrs. Montgomery's dead father. Much of the novel, therefore, charts Ellen's moral development as these families open their doors to her and she her affections to them. She finds herself a "protector" (49) in Mr. George Marshman, a "sister" (224), also called "her adopted sister" (347) in Alice Humphreys, a "new brother [who] was a decided acquisition" (279) in John Humphreys, an "adopted father" (455) in Mr. Humphreys, a "general guardian" in Mrs. Chauncey" (484) and so on. As with Gerty, virtually all adult characters come to treat Ellen as "as if she had been their own child" (384, 472, 556). Even Mrs. Gillespie, a minor character who, after escorting Ellen from America to London *en route* to her Scottish relations, confesses to her husband that "she should be rejoiced if it turned out that they might keep Ellen with them and carry her back to America; she only wished it were not for Mr. Humphreys but herself" (498).

One of the important differences, though, between Gerty's experience as an adopted daughter and Ellen's is that Gerty's multiple affiliations aren't understood as persons competing for her affections except in the case of Mr. Graham. In stark contrast, many of Ellen's adoptive parents view the relation to be exclusive, as it were. Thus Aunt Fortune's outrage when she discovers that "Ellen was to become the adopted child of the [Humphreyses's] house" (458), after she had been named "sole guardian and owner" (381) of Ellen upon the deaths of both Mr. and Mrs. Montgomery: "[Aunt Fortune] wondered who they [the Humphreyses] thought they had to deal with; did they think she was going to let Ellen go in that way?... Ellen had no more business to go and give herself away than one of her oxen" (458). Similarly, in a conversation among Ellen, Alice, and John, John declares that "Alice may have you all the rest of the year, but when I am at home you belong to me" (407). In addition, Mr. Marshman, who has known Ellen for just a brief time, says that "she must give him a large place in her heart, or he should be jealous of her 'strange friend' [an allusion to Ellen's having met his brother, George, while traveling to Aunt

Fortune's]" (332). Last but not least are Mr. Lindsay who, "when clasp[ing] her to his bosom, Ellen felt it was as *his own*; his eye always seemed to repeat, '*my own* little daughter'" (505) and Ellen's grandmother, Mrs. Lindsay, who likewise "drew her close to her bosom again, murmuring, "My own child – my precious child – my Ellen – my own darling" (502).[12] This pattern is so pervasive that even the Lindsays quarrel over Ellen when Mrs. Lindsay and her sister, Lady Keith, become jealous about Ellen's relationship with her "adopted father" (535) and think "it expedient not to let him have the whole of her" (535). The only character in *The Lamplighter* who comes close to viewing Gerty in this territorial way is Mr. Graham, and he is roundly censured by her, the narrator, and even his own daughter, Emily.

Unlike Gerty's endless round of simultaneous and flexible adoptions, Ellen's seem more permanent and ironclad, less optional and certainly less mutually agreed upon. This helps to illuminate some important but overlooked differences between the two novels, one being that Ellen's story is much more ponderous, more tortured than Gerty's, and another of which is that Ellen never attains Gerty's level of self-possession and maturity.[13] Ellen, however, not only doesn't want what her literary successor gets, but *The Wide, Wide World* insists that these attributes are vastly over-rated and irreligious anyway. Ellen's ideal psychic state is to have an experience of being possessed that most closely resembles her early, totalizing bond with her mother, and she finds this with the Humphreys, first with Alice in whose arms "she was nestling . . . both quite still for a minute" (175) and then with John whose "censorship Ellen rather loved than feared" (461).[14]

II ARE YOU MY FATHER?

Possessing Ellen involves psychological and economic stakes unknown in Gerty's world. There are two quite different reasons for this. First, Ellen has the memory of an extraordinarily intimate maternal bond that she is trying to replicate in her relationship with others; Gerty remembers neither her mother nor her father. Second, adoption in *The Wide, Wide World* elicits feelings and forms of behavior perilously similar to slavery, even though in the case of her Scottish relatives, Ellen understands that they love her as much as they wish to own her, body and soul, and that her bodily health is never in jeopardy. It is abundantly clear, though, that almost all of Ellen's adoptive relations view her as their possession, whether as a beast of burden, *pace* Aunt Fortune, or "as a recovered treasure that would not be parted with" (503) in the manner of the Humphreyses or Lindsays.

Mr. Marshman also tells Ellen that "some of these days he would take her away from her aunt, and she should have her no more" (369). To adopt Ellen is to believe and act as if one owns her exclusively (her mother writes that Mrs. Lindsay "longs to have you, and to have you as entirely her own, in all respects" [489]), which explains why, when Ellen finds herself being adopted over and over again, she has such a difficult time sorting out the question of to whom she really belongs. Whereas Gerty seems content to occupy the position of a "sort of adopted daughter," Ellen is troubled by the imprecise nature of being adopted: "I have promised Alice," thought Ellen; – "I have promised Mr. Humphreys – I can't be adopted twice . . . Oh, what shall I do! What ought I to do? . . . I have a home and a father and a brother; may I not judge for myself?" (490). Of course, there is nothing for Ellen to do except to wait until John tells her what to do. And as if we had any doubts that the answer to her final question ("may I not judge for myself?") were a resounding "no," John tells Ellen in no uncertain terms, "you have no right to choose for yourself" (561). Gerty never has such qualms because those who adopt her don't expect her to relinquish her affections or herself for any one else who has already done so. Although she is the judge of her affections, she needn't judge to whom she belongs because, as we saw, she belongs to many people at the same time, including herself. For Ellen, this last possibility doesn't exist as a viable or even ethical possibility, given that her rigorous training in Protestant submission to authority has taught her, in the words of Jane Tompkins, "the endlessly demanding attempt to achieve self-sacrifice." Indeed, everyone from her mother to John to Alice to the Lindsays is "perpetually watching, super-intending, and admonishing" (538) her every move, à la Foucault, as if she were in mortal danger of succumbing to herself and to the power of her own affections.[15]

When Ellen revisits the question of who owns her in the following passage, it is clear that the last person she might belong to is herself: "I wonder how many times one may be adopted . . . to be sure, my father and my mother have quite given me up here, – that makes a difference; they had a right to give me away if they pleased. I suppose I do belong to my uncle and grandmother in good earnest, and I cannot help myself. Well! But Mr. Humphreys seems a great deal more like my father than my uncle Lindsay. I cannot help that" (504). What "makes a difference" in altering the course of her life is not how she feels – not only can she not help that, that can't help her – but the adult who "has a right to do what he pleases with you and yours" (553). Although Ellen frequently invokes the sanctity of individual rights, for example, when it looks as if Aunt Fortune or the

Lindsays are trampling upon them, the fact is that she is speaking not on behalf of her rights but rather on behalf of John's or Alice's or, in the above passage, her parents' rights to do with her as they please. What Ellen asserts are the inalienable rights of her prior possessors, never the right of self-possession.

Indeed, the adults' desire to possess Ellen is as great as her desire to be possessed. From Ellen's perspective, the difficulty arises not in being possessed by others but rather when those others are not the desired possessors. For example, Ellen feels suffocated when she explains to John that the Lindsays "want to have me all to themselves" (563) but readily concurs with John's statement, "I think you belong to me more than to any body" by remarking, "That is exactly what I think!" (563). Similarly, immediately after the narrator tells us that Ellen felt "as if she were caught in a net from which she had no power to get free," that seeming expression of freedom's desirability is followed by the phrase, "and she longed to clasp that hand that could she thought draw her whence and whither it pleased" (520). Ellen talks a good game of republican principles. She sings the praises of the revolutionary fathers, George Washington in particular, telling Mr. Lindsay that she prefers the Scots to the French because "they would be free" (515), and criticizes Nelson, asking her uncle/father, "can a man be a truly great man who is not master of himself?" (516). Clearly, some nets and some masters are more desirable than others. Such (seeming) declarations of independence lead Mr. Lindsay to remark upon Ellen's "extraordinary taste for freedom" (515), but that is putting the case too abstractly. She doesn't want to be free; she just wants to be free from the Lindsays in order to be drawn "whence and whither" by John. Ellen's problem with her Scottish relations, then, is less their failure to respect certain corporeal and psychic boundaries or their unwillingness to allow her to belong to herself, although she uses these as evidence of their unfair treatment of her, and more her desire to be possessed by John.

Or, perhaps, Ellen's problem with her Scottish relations is that they are just that – relations. With almost pathological consistency, Ellen prefers just about any stranger who crosses her path (except the evil Mr. Saunders) to her blood relatives (except Ellen's father); Van Brunt rather than Aunt Fortune; M. Muller and Mrs. Allen over the women in the Lindsay household. What she wants to be free of, ultimately, is consanguinity, so as to be free to be possessed by contractual relations, and this is what Mr. Lindsay mistakes for an "extraordinary taste for freedom." Having "claim[ed] kindred with all the world" (529), Ellen is continuously confronted with the inadequacies of her biological family, whether those failures be moral, religious, or emotional. As the narrator says, "there was no one to take his [John's] place" (538). Needing no one else but the Humphreyses, because her chosen ties now occupy the position once held by Mrs. Montgomery, Ellen wonders, as she readies herself for her trip to Scotland, "What have I to do to seek new relations?" (496) and, once there, she asks, "am I to be separated from them for ever!" (543). Her fear of being separated from John clearly echoes her terror about that first separation from her mother. The bonds of consanguinity have been displaced and replaced by the family she has made with the Humphreyses, who now define and possess Ellen's emotional life in the way her mother had in the early pages of the novel.

Throughout her time in Scotland, Ellen defends and defines the family that she has made in America based on the absolute value of choice. In one particularly nasty confrontation with the Lindsays, she is instructed to give up the "absurd habit" of referring to Alice and John as "my brother and sister" (529), as Mr. Lindsay says, "let us hear no more of brothers and sisters. I cannot, as your grandmother says, fraternize with all the world, especially with unknown relations" (530). The conversation continues:

"I cannot conceive how Ellen has got such a way of it," said Lady Keith.
"It is very natural," said Ellen, with some huskiness of voice, "that I should say so, because I feel so."
"You do not mean to say," said Mr. Lindsay, "that this Mr. and Miss Somebody – these people – I don't know their names –"
"There is only one now, sir."
"This person you call your brother – do you mean to say you have the same regard for him as if he had been born so?"
"No," said Ellen, cheek and eye suddenly firing, – "but a thousand times more!" (530)

Ellen valorizes the claims of feeling over those of blood, as the Lindsays maintain the opposite, and this shift, as we've seen, is fundamental to the sentimental novel's project of rethinking the family. Thus, the Lindsays' defense of blood ties is nothing less than a challenge to the genre's commitment to the ideology of chosen relations. *The Wide, Wide World* demonstrates this time and again, whether Alice tells Ellen, "We will be sisters while [God] permits us to be so . . . You shall be my little sister and I will be your elder sister" (224) or John reminds her, "you know you gave me leave to be your brother" (296). Although the phrase "adopted sister" (225, 243) gets used early on to describe Ellen's relation with Alice, the term "adopted" quickly drops out, putting Ellen on the same footing as Alice. In fact, when she dies, Mr. Humphreys calls Ellen "my dear little daughter"

(497), establishing within the parental framework what has already taken place at the level of the siblings. According to sentimental convention, Ellen is convinced that because "he called me his daughter . . . I will be as long as I live, if I find fifty new relations" (497). What drives the Lindsays to especial distraction is Ellen's use of consanguineous terms when describing her relations with the Humphreyses in America, because the refusal to distinguish rhetorically between these two kinds of affiliation nullifies their right to possess her. Mr. Lindsay asks Ellen, "and what makes you call this other *your brother?*" to which Ellen replies, "his sister called me her sister – and that makes me his"(509). In the world of the sentimental novel, the act of saying such things makes them so (a matter of much significance, as we shall see in our discussion of *Pierre*), which is why the anti-sentimentalist Lady Keith is quick to dismiss Ellen's logic: "It is very absurd . . . when they are nothing at all to her, and ought not to be" (509).

Although the Lindsays appear united in their derisive attitude toward Ellen's nominal sleights of hand, the fact is that Mr. Lindsay has a similar faith in the self-fulfilling power of rhetorical consanguinity. For this reason, he is the most sympathetic character of the three Scottish relatives, as well as the one to whom Ellen is most attached and the one who first comes to accept Ellen's love for John. Mr. Lindsay is, of course, already a relation of Ellen's in the traditional sense of that term, but he desires even greater relational proximity and thinks he can get it through a series of speech acts, both his own and Ellen's. Besides compulsively referring to her as "his daughter" (510, 512, 534, 535, 536), as if saying the words will make them true – and why not, this works with Alice and John – he declares, "I will not have you call me 'uncle' – I am your father" (510) and demands, "let me hear you call me father" (518). Furthermore, after the scene with M. Muller in which Ellen has difficulty telling him that her name is Ellen Lindsay, Mr. Lindsay severely reproaches her for failing to state their parental connection. She defends herself on the grounds that she didn't want "M. Muller [to] think what wasn't true" to which Mr. Lindsay obscurely replies, "that is precisely what I wish him and all the world to think. I will have no difference made, Ellen, either by them or you . . . It is true, and if people draw conclusions that are not true, it is what I wish" (526). This final sentence sums up Mr. Lindsay's difficulty – it is both true and not true that they are father and daughter. The first phrase "it is true" seems to decide the point, except the second phrase, "if people draw conclusions that are not true," undercuts it. The untruth that is desirable from Mr. Lindsay's point of view is the fact that they are father and daughter. Ellen is quite capable of making "no difference" between chosen and consanguineous bonds when the persons involved are the Humphreyses but unable and unwilling to do so with the Lindsays, in large measure because her relationship is unalterably defined by consanguinity and cannot, in some ideal sense, enter the realm of the freely chosen. What's left for her to do is to insist on the difference between degrees of consanguinity, to keep the avuncular from devolving into the paternal (note that she has no such difficulties in transforming her brother John into her husband). The only thing she can choose is not to get any closer to Mr. Lindsay than she already is.

One must also concede that a great deal of Ellen's resistance to Mr. Lindsay derives from the fact that she doesn't really want a father at all. Mr. Humphreys will suffice because he loves Ellen from a distance, allowing the sibling love of Alice and John to do most of the work of incorporating her into the family. Ellen and Mr. Humphreys have their tender moments, but he doesn't attempt to fill the space left in Ellen's life by the death of her mother. In fact, Ellen remedies the vacancy left in his heart and home through the death of Alice. In a position quite unusual for Ellen, she possesses him more than he her. Thus, when he calls her "my dear little daughter" (note she doesn't call him her father, nor does he demand that she do so), he adds that "this house is yours, dear Ellen, as well when in Scotland as here" (497), and in the letter he writes to Ellen, which remits the money sent to him by the Lindsays, he tells her that "he owed her more than she owed him" (556). In comparison, her relation with her biological father is purely denotative and, although we have seen the power of such designations, his death easily frees her from the authority they command and her obligation to obey.

Mrs. Montgomery's death, of course, does no such thing, because the love and the loss remain. She dies but always remains Ellen's mother. It would be unimaginable for Warner to depict a scene in which Ellen is asked to call someone else her mother; the closest the novel comes is to link Alice with Mrs. Montgomery, but even this association must be tempered by making sure that Alice represents herself as a sister to Ellen. By contrast, Mr. Montgomery's death means that he is no longer her father and she is free to choose (or not) another one more to her liking. In fact, her response to her father's death is remarkable for not only its complete absence of grief but its sense of relief and release from an unpleasantly obligatory attachment:

Ellen rather felt that she was an orphan than that she had lost her father. She had never learned to love him, he had never given her much cause . . . Life had nothing now worse for her than a separation from Alice and John Humphreys; she feared her father might take her away and put her in some dreadful boarding-school, or carry her about the world wherever he went, a wretched wanderer from every thing good and pleasant. The knowledge of his death had less pain for her than the removal of this fear brought relief. (381)

This passage explains why Ellen's father has received scant critical attention. She views the death of her father as an event having less to do with the loss of him and more to do with a different definition of self; that is, before she wasn't an orphan and now she is. His death produces little feeling in Ellen, and because Ellen's feelings are essential to the fabric of the novel, their apparent absence in this case would seem to consign Mr. Montgomery to the margins of literary analysis and make her mother the only parental figure worth discussing. I think, however, that Mr. Montgomery's insignificance is quite relevant to the topic of family in *The Wide, Wide World*, especially since this description suggests a potential disjunction between consanguinity and love, which becomes the ontological foundation upon which she makes and defends her family with the Humphreyses. In a novel that gauges the spiritual development of its protagonist through the depth of her sympathy (observe that for a child so quick to tears, she doesn't cry in this scene), one should note that the narrator neither castigates Ellen for her lack of feeling nor condemns her for the feeling that she does have upon the death of her father, which is one of relief. Ellen doesn't have to love her father just because he is her father. She must obey him, but that is all.[16]

It would seem that Warner, like Cummins, has done something quite subversive by inverting the hierarchy of values attributed to consanguineous and chosen relations, but the fact is that Ellen's absolute submission to one of these paradigms of family remains unquestioned. Ellen, for example, doesn't want to undo the exclusive nature of her adoptive bonds, she just wants to ensure that she is bonded to the right family. And when she defends her choice of the Humphreyses, that choice gets registered as freedom, as we shall see when Ellen rather bizarrely begins to hold forth on the Revolutionary fathers, even though it is the freedom to be possessed by someone else. She has, in other words, simply substituted one system of authority based on blood to another based on choice, and the definitional certitude usually reserved for biological bonds gets transferred over to the ties one forges based on feeling. In addition, these new bonds carry with them the psychic weight – the expectations, the fears, the desires – of the earlier bonds. Thus, John *is* her brother (until he becomes her husband) and Mr. Humphreys *is* her father, and such designations, once made and once chosen, cannot be renounced: "I gave myself to somebody else first; – I can't undo that – and I never will!"(520). Ellen not only accepts the notion that whoever owns her owns her exclusively, but believes that she has already handed herself over to someone else. She is a *feme couverte*, one might argue, even before she marries John.[17] Given Ellen's understanding that she must belong to someone (not herself), and given the Lindsays' insistence that she belong to them, it seems logical that marriage to John comes to signify freedom or, to invoke Jacobs, "something akin to freedom."

Ellen's traumatic separations from her mother, first by geographical distance then by death, combined with an absence of feelings of love toward her father, have the effect of uprooting her actual attachments to family as well as her attachment to the conventional notion of a family based on biology. This is what freedom means to Ellen – it is to be free of consanguinity. Mrs. Montgomery's death has set in motion the necessity for Ellen, first, to find a new domestic arrangement and second, the inclination to look outside of the family when doing so. Because there is no one in her consanguineous family to replace Mrs. Montgomery, who says to her daughter, "you must not think hardly of your aunt when you find she is not your mother" (21), Ellen must turn to the wide, wide world – which is to say, *not* her family – to make a new family.

The novel situates Ellen's search for a family based on choice in the context of the many characters who have left the country in which they were born for America, the country that they choose. Thus, her world is surprisingly cosmopolitan, given that most of the action of the novel takes place in the "remote country town" (20) of Thirwall, where Aunt Fortune lives. Ellen's travels are limited, at least until her overseas departure to the Lindsays, to Alice's home in Carra-Carra (a walk away) and Mr. Marshman's home known as Ventnor (a thirty mile sleigh-ride away). We learn, for example, that Mrs. Montgomery is a Scotch woman, the Humphreyses, their domestic servant, Margery, and Mr. Marshman are British (473), and Mrs. Vawse is Swiss but "brought up in a wealthy French family" (172). This diversity of cultural influence explains why Ellen, who, "after living among a parcel of thick-headed and thicker-tongued Yankees" (505), to quote Lady Keith, knows French, has studied European geography, and speaks with an English accent. Each one of these characters has chosen to come to America, including another daughter of Lady Keith's who was "married to America some dozen or so years ago" (499), and they have been motivated primarily by affection rather than consanguinity or even economic opportunity. This scenario of people leaving the countries of their birth and adopting America as their homeland represents an adult version of Ellen's preference for chosen ties over what she views as the restrictions of biological ones.[18]

That the order of magnitude is vastly different – we are talking nations, not individuals – is unimportant in the world of the novel and, in fact, the two merge when Ellen goes to Scotland. Even before Ellen sets foot in the Lindsay household, Miss Sophia, a member of the Marshman clan, introduces the possibility that, in being adopted by the Lindsays, Ellen's national identity might be at stake with the remark "so you are going to be a Scotchwoman after all." Ellen replies, "I had a great deal rather be an American" (494). Indeed, once in residence with the Lindsays, Ellen finds herself in the position of refusing to relax her attachment not only to specific persons in America, but to the very idea of America itself. One might imagine that Ellen would welcome the chance to go to Scotland because it would provide her with an opportunity to choose her nationality in the same way that she wishes to choose her family. America is the country of her birth; Scotland could become the country of her choice. But this scenario is not to be. Ellen's unwillingness to surrender her allegiance to America involves several factors, one of the most significant being that her mother and the Humphreyses are aligned with America, despite their respective Scottish and British origins. To agree to be a Scotchwoman is to abandon those she most loves. Another, more obvious reason for her fierce defense of her nationality is that the Lindsays persistently attack it as part of their plan to remake her in their own European image, as Ellen Lindsay. Hence, Lady Keith imperially reminds Mr. Lindsay, "[Ellen] must learn to have no nationality but yours" (505), as if nationality, like family, were something to be learned (recall her thoughts about Mr. Montgomery, "she had never learned to love him" [381]). And it can be learned, as so many of the novel's "American" characters prove. Ellen, however, refuses to learn this lesson because it goes against all of the other ones she has imbibed from people whom she loves more than the Lindsays. In this last and only section of the novel not to take place in America, America comes to represent the freedom to choose everything from one's family, to one's home, to one's nation. Requiring Ellen to abandon her American nationality is the same as asking her to relinquish a condition of identity – what we might call the adoptive, with which she associates the possibility of freedom – so as to accept a new condition – what we might call the consanguineous, with which she associates the operations of unprincipled, illegitimate authority, such as they are practiced in the Lindsay household.[19]

If we needed additional evidence that Ellen's journey to Scotland is a journey back in personal time (to the place of her mother's birth) as well as national time (to the eighteenth century and the birth of America), the fact that Mr. Lindsay's first name is George (529) makes the allegory complete. A peculiar thing happens in Scotland, which is that Ellen seems to fight the Revolutionary War all over again. Not only does Mr. Lindsay call Ellen a "little rebel" (506), but they repeatedly discuss the character of George Washington and the arguments for and against America's claims for independence, with the Lindsays taking the British side and Ellen naturally the American. Only days after her arrival, the battle begins, and it is clear that their positions with respect to the Revolution replay the conflicts taking place in the household. In this first exchange on the topic, Ellen inquires of Mr. Lindsay why Lady Keith doesn't like Americans, to which he replies, "don't you know they are a parcel of rebels who have broken loose from all loyalty and fealty, that no good Briton has any business to like?" Ellen and Mr. Lindsay then get into a heated debate about King George and the Americans, whom he condemns as having "forfeited entirely the character of good friends to England and good subjects to King George." She responds that "[King George] and the English forfeited their characters first" (506). Pages later, Ellen finds herself once more defending America and Washington, in particular, to which Mr. Lindsay inquires, "are all the American children as strong republicans as yourself?" (515) Clearly, these debates about English authoritarianism and American disloyalty are versions of the conflict occurring within the Lindsay household where, instead of King George demanding absolute obedience of his American subjects, we have George Lindsay requiring the same of Ellen who "dared not disobey" (518). Ellen is caught between feeling that she "owes him a child's duty" (554) and believing that "it was her duty to disobey" (541). That it is the child's duty to disobey the father in the event of the unfair and persistent exercise of authority is, of course, one of the founding principles of the Declaration of Independence, just as "honor thy father and mother" (363) is one of the cornerstones of the Bible, that other text to which Ellen dutifully subscribes.[20] But Ellen is spared the necessity of rejecting the authority of her "adopted father" (535) as well as the teachings of her mother's religion through the timely intervention of John. She is, after all, a young woman, fourteen years old, who is conducting a war on two fronts, neither of which she can win without back-up. First, as a woman, she would not have been able to fight in the American Revolution (she remonstrates with Mr. Lindsay, "Ah, but I mean if I had been a man" [506]) and second, she is dependent upon John to extricate her from the Lindsays' tyranny so that she needn't tarnish her record with any negative act or intention toward her guardian ("she sighed for her brother" [539]).

III ELLEN'S FREEDOM; COMPROMISES, CIRCA 1850

Before John enters the scene to rescue Ellen from her trying situation with the Lindsays, there is no end in sight to their repeated efforts to dispossess her of her memories, things, and physical space in order to possess her completely. As if this weren't enough to elicit our sympathy on behalf of Ellen, her Scottish relatives are the recipients of what might be thought of as the most cutting indictment that a sentimental novel has at its disposal: "the *sympathy* was wanting" (538, emphasis Warner). Like Pierre, as we shall see in the next chapter, Ellen is surrounded by relations and destitute of sympathy as if the fact of consanguinity automatically incapacitates them from being able to dispense sympathy. Indeed, the Lindsays' conscious disregard of Ellen's feelings attests to the truth of the charge leveled against them. Not only have they restricted the time she has to read the Bible, but they force her to drink wine in the belief that she is too sober for a child her age, and Mr. Lindsay takes away John's gift of *The Pilgrim's Progress*. Each one of these acts puts Ellen in the untenable position of having to disobey at least one of her masters, John or Mr. Lindsay, leaving her to feel that "she was at war with herself" (553).[21] Incapable of escaping "the net" (520) in which she finds herself, Ellen has nothing to do but "sadly quiet herself into submission" (556). Clearly, her repeated defenses of the principles of the American Revolution don't translate into an ability to protect herself from the Lindsays' voracious appetite for her individual rights. She has none because she is theirs, a point concisely illustrated by the following exchange in which Ellen tries to get her Bunyan back. "But it is mine!" Ellen ventured to urge, though trembling," to which Mr. Lindsay replies, "Come, come! . . . and you are mine, you must understand" (553). Ellen, to return to our earlier discussion of the novel, is in a position not unlike a slave's.

The resonances and divergences are obvious: Ellen is a possession but a physically unharmed one; she is forbidden to acknowledge her identity prior to the one being foisted upon her by her Scottish owners who continually silence her by kissing her, which is "a way that she particularly disliked" (541); and she is not permitted to read the Bible (and Bunyan), although Mr. Lindsay encourages her to read anything else she pleases. There are many aspects of Ellen's experience that demonstrate the fact that she is at once like and unlike the protagonist in a slave narrative, but one of the most important points both of generic contact and departure is her structural and affective relation to family. On the one hand, she is like a slave because her biological family has come undone and, on the other, she is unlike a slave because she has no desire to see it put back together again. Thus, to the extent that the unraveling of the biological family functions as the *donnée* of both the sentimental novel and the slave narrative, the genres overlap in their commitment to seeing that their protagonists find a place and a person or community with whom they belong. Whereas sentimental novels are committed to finding that place outside of blood relations, slave narratives yearn for consanguineous reunion. The absolute difference between the genres is a function, of course, of the systematic and violent dismemberment of slave families, as in the case of Jacobs, compared with the families in sentimental novels that are broken by illness, death, or the convention of inexplicable separation. Indeed, to the extent that Ellen's development is measured according to the emotional and geographical mileage she acquires between herself and the people to whom she is consanguineously related, the generic and ideological distance between her sentimental novel and the slave narrative could not be greater. Ellen's freedom is understood as constituted outside the family; Jacobs's within it. Thus, although slave narratives also record the miles traveled by fugitive slaves pursuing their freedom, that distance signifies a mournful separation from family as much as a necessary flight from slavery. The goal, unlike Ellen's, is the affirmation of consanguineous relations that slavery, by definition, either denies or sells to the highest bidder.

Warner, furthermore, adds something to the generic mix by realigning the coordinates of freedom and slavery. Unlike the protagonists of slave narratives, who often leave America in order to find a place of greater freedom – Canada or England, for example – Ellen's freedom is in America, her enslavement overseas. In *The Wide, Wide World,* America (and we shall see that it is important to the novel that America be a monolithic entity) becomes the land of the chosen and the sentimental novel; Scotland is the land of consanguinity and the slave narrative. According to this logic, to be taken out of America is to be occupied or kidnapped by a genre to which one really doesn't belong, a dilemma familiar to readers of Pike and Northup, as well as Caroline Lee Hentz and the Crafts. It is to lose the freedom to choose one's family and it is to be governed by the imperatives of biology. Several aspects of Warner's generic splicing are fascinating, whether it be the fact that the unraveling of the biological family is usually taken to refer to the pernicious effects of slavery, not the originary condition for freedom; or the fact that slavery of the American variety never existed in Scotland; or that it is Americans in the antebellum period, not Scots, who are preoccupied with and rent apart by the institution of slavery, so much so that a civil war seems imminent.[22]

As with *Ida May*, this sentimental novel is once more imagining itself in relation to certain key topoi of the slave narrative, a genre with which it identifies and against which the sentimental defines its ideological investments. That Warner herself might have had such a connection in mind or, at the very least, a sense of the racial context informing Ellen's *Bildungsroman*, is evident in two scenes from the 1849 manuscript of *The Wide, Wide World* which were deleted when the book was published in 1850.²³ Neither of these scenes, I should add, speaks overtly to the question of slavery, but both suggest that at the time Warner wrote the novel, she was thinking about race. The first takes place in Chapter 5, after Ellen has been rescued from Mr. Saunders's rude salesmanship by an old gentleman who showers her with attention, money, as well as figs and grapes. Immediately after bidding him adieu, "a little figure came round a corner & advanced up the street towards her. It was a little black girl." This young child, Rebecca Richardson, whom the narrator and Ellen also refer to as "little blacky" in this chapter and the next, is poor, with a dress that "was miserably thin" and shoes "that had great holes through which her feet could be seen popping out." This encounter is significant because it suggests an analogy, which I've been arguing gets worked out in the remainder of the novel, between Ellen, the white sentimental heroine, and Rebecca, who, though not a slave, is black and poor: "she could not help drawing a comparison between her condition & that of her less favoured fellow creature." This moment of comparison, furthermore, produces a sympathetic response in Ellen, which leads her not only to give the other child food, but to make her a dress as well. Shortly thereafter, "blacky" arrives in Ellen's house in order to return her purse, which had dropped onto the street, and in the next chapter, another meeting between them takes place in the Richardsons' tenement-like cellar apartment, where Ellen brings Rebecca the frock, and Mrs. Montgomery informs Rebecca's mother, the impoverished washerwoman, Mrs. Richardson, "to do your duty faithfully, & trust God for the rest." Their meeting concludes, and Mrs. Montgomery reminds Ellen, "Remember Rebecca whenever you feel inclined to shrink from any disagreeable duty." Interestingly, Warner had initially wanted Rebecca's condition to serve as a marker, and a racialized one at that, for Ellen's future disinclinations.

The other relevant scene that did not make its way into future editions also occurs in the early chapters of the novel. George Marshman initially had an even larger role, in Chapters 7 and 8. In the 1849 edition, he not only replays the scenes between Ellen and her mother (and reinforces Mrs. Montgomery's Christian beliefs) in which they discuss the importance of

God, but teaches Ellen all about Robert Fulton and steamboats and, in an extended passage, tells her about his panther-hunting adventures in the south. In particular, he relates an incident in which he is terrified by one particular "panther's extraordinary behavior, for they are not generally furious unless they have been provoked." He states, "I never saw a creature behave as she did then," with "eyes flashing fire" and "making all the while the most frightful noises you ever heard." Upon encountering "a neighbor of ours with two panther cubs in his arms," Mr. Marshman soon learns the reason for the panther's behavior: "the mother had been thrown into madness by finding her young ones stolen from her." Although this story is about panthers, not slaves, it does take place in the south and represents one of the foundational moments of the experience of slavery – the separation of mothers from their children – which is also, of course, the reason that Ellen is with Mr. Marshman in the first place.[24]

I would like to conclude this chapter by suggesting how a reading of *The Wide, Wide World* that situates Ellen's bondage in Scotland with her freedom in America in the context of the conflict surrounding slavery both reflects and refracts the exigencies of Warner's historical moment. To analogize Ellen's condition with that of the slave's and then to install America as the land to which she wishes to return in order to become free introduce interpretive complexities into the novel that are of a very different order than simply trying to get her sentimental heroine married to her beloved brother/father figure (which is difficult enough). The linkage of genre and nation is, in other words, deeply problematic because of its resonances with the political turmoil of 1850; to wit, many Americans with an abolitionist perspective viewed their country as being occupied by the system of slavery, and Americans were being kidnapped by slavery, *à la* Ida May, Solomon Northup, and all of the slaves who were being treated as if they were things.

The year 1850 was a watershed in the history of the nation as Americans debated the question of their national identity. Free or slave; or, from the literary perspective, sentimental novel or slave narrative? *The Wide, Wide World* asks these questions as well and, like much of the political rhetoric of the period, goes back to the time of the Revolution to answer them. This temporal shift, however, is not about working out the entanglements of freedom and slavery that lay at the very foundation of the nation's identity – to go back to the eighteenth century is not to avoid the contradiction, but to go to its origins – but about burying the problem in a hagiographical celebration of the nation's forefathers and their commitment to American independence.[25] Thus, the novel, like the nation, invokes the

Revolutionary War as a means of attempting to establish, at least discursively, an America unified against a common enemy, England. In doing so,
the threat of disunion in 1850 gets dissolved. Warner's exportation of
slavery to Scotland, furthermore, allows America to maintain its identity
and integrity as the home of freedom. The novel fiercely makes the case for
a coherent America, even as it acknowledges in the geographical margins
the forces tearing the nation apart. The novel, like the nation, attempts to
resolve the problem of American self-definition by combining the ideology
of slavery and freedom, transforming rupture into symbiosis, deferring
conflict by compromise, producing what Jacobs calls "something akin to
freedom."

Ellen, I mean to suggest, *is* America in 1850, "at war with herself" (553),
hoping that "this may all be arranged, easily, in some way I could never
dream of" (520). As I have demonstrated with reference to *Incidents in the
Life of a Slave Girl*, Ellen, like America in 1850, is both free and not free.
Like America, hers is both a sentimental novel and a slave narrative. Like
America, she is a territory upon which/whom a battle of possession is being
waged. And like America, getting her out of her generic and ideological jam
requires a miracle or, perhaps, a compromise, not unlike the one authored
by Senator Clay of Kentucky and supported by Senator Daniel Webster of
Massachusetts that same year. Warner's takes the form of John's arrival and
the deal he is able to broker with the Lindsays while "overturning all her
[Ellen's] father's and grandmother's prejudices" (568); Clay's assumes the
far more controversial lineaments of the Fugitive Slave Law, the division of
the newly established states of California, New Mexico, and Texas into free
and slave, and the prohibition of slavery in the District of Columbia. This
conjoining of ideological antipodes is meant to diffuse the conflict into
which the nation and the novel have been heading. The political compromise postpones all-out conflict for eleven years, until the nation can no
longer withstand the irreconcilable forces pulling it apart. The novelistic
compromise releases Ellen from the burdensome responsibility and ultimate futility of opposing the Lindsays, a burden which is the slave's
existential *donnée*. For Ellen, there is little point in challenging their
authority because it is temporary, and because it is temporary, she is not
a slave or, to put the point differently, she is a slave but just for a while. The
sentimental heroine's encounter with slavery is difficult to avoid, given
how close the resemblance is between her position as orphan and the slave's
position as orphan (or the perpetual fear of being orphaned), but the
encounter can be delimited to a discrete period of time and place. Ellen's
"war," then, ends before it is fought because in the novel, slavery is

a condition of limited duration out of which the protagonist grows. In this regard, she is very much like Ida May, another white sentimental heroine who need only wait "a few years" (561), during which time she may experience things uncomfortably similar to slavery, before she, too, will be free to marry her white sentimental hero John. Through the *deus ex machina* miracle that is John's arrival in Scotland, Warner is able to painstakingly develop a conflict that is absorbed into the narrative fabric and eventually rendered invisible. The novel does what the nation can't.

The Wide, Wide World presents its readers with a generic compromise that incorporates aspects of the slave narrative into the sentimental novel in order to reject the principles of slavery and restore its heroine to the freedoms which are rightfully hers as a (white) citizen of America, marriage in particular. But, as I've been arguing, the conventional nature of this conclusion is not necessarily a basis for dismissal on the grounds that marriage is *de facto* an exemplification of the hegemonic essence of the sentimental genre itself. Such a reading would fail not only to take into account the methodical interrogation of the biological family that Warner conducts throughout the novel (which challenges the dominant understanding of the sentimental genre as implacably committed to the bonds of consanguinity) but also omit the very simple but important fact that marriage, inasmuch as it is a contract, is an institution into which a slave cannot enter. For both the sentimental novel and the slave narrative, the ability or inability to make a marriage contract often helps to demarcate the dividing line between free and not free. And while antebellum feminists, Kemble among them, are quite rightly attacking the inequities within the institution of marriage, linking its legalized erasure of female identity (*feme couverte*) and women's lack of legal protections to the condition of slave, the narratives of former slaves repeatedly express outrage about being excluded from that very institution. Even Jacobs, whose story famously doesn't end in the "usual" way of marriage, condemns, on several occasions, the laws that refuse to recognize slave marriage. Not only does she lament the fact that "even if he [her lover] could have obtained permission to marry me while I was a slave, the marriage would give him no power to protect me from my master" (373), but in the chapter describing Aunt Nancy's marriage, writes that "it was a mere form, without any legal value. Her master or mistress could annul it any day they pleased" (462).[26]

Indeed, it is as much a convention of the slave narrative to call attention to the fact that marriages aren't officially sanctioned as it is a convention of the sentimental novel to conclude either with a marriage or the promise of marriage, as is the case in Warner's novel. In *The Life and Adventures of Henry Bibb*, for example, Bibb remarks, "marriage among American slaves, is disregarded by the laws of this country. It is counted a mere temporary matter; it is a union which may be continued or broken off, with or without the consent of a slaveholder, whether he is a priest or a libertine."[27] Similarly, Pennington writes in *The Fugitive Blacksmith*: "some of my master's slaves who had families were regularly married, and others were not; the law makes no provision for such marriages, and the only provision was, that they should obtain his leave" (255). My point is not to minimize the real conditions upon which the critique of marriage is being launched at this time but rather to suggest that the conventional sentimental ending is usefully defamiliarized by juxtaposing the slave narrative's investment in marriage in relation to the sentimental novel's. Such a realignment introduces new ways of understanding the ideological work of the endings of sentimental novels. It suggests that their commitment to marriage has as much, if not more, to do with their belief that contract is the most enduring expression of one's freedom than with their commitment to the enduring life and value of the biological family, which novel after novel undermines. And then, there's *Pierre*.

CHAPTER 6

We are family, or Melville's Pierre

Running through many families are secret amours.

(Marriage: Its History, Character, and Results)[1]

Despite the fact that today Melville's reputation and readership are considerably greater than Caroline Lee Hentz's or Mary Jane Holmes's, to name just two extremely popular antebellum writers, and despite *Pierre's* insistent harangues against "the countless tribes of common novels," *Pierre* was (and is) desperate to be one of them. On the most practical level, Melville very much wanted to write a popular novel that would bring his family much-needed income. On a more theoretical level, "common novels" begin with absent parents who leave their children alone, a condition Pierre devoutly wishes for.[2] Though the separation between parent(s) and children is painful and often inexplicable (why *can't* Ellen Montgomery go overseas with her mother and father? what takes Gerty's father so long to find his daughter?), these young girls become women. If we can use *Pierre* as a piece of counter-factual evidence, they develop and flourish precisely because they have been freed from their biological parents. Gerty and Ellen grow, they learn, they live. Pierre shrivels up, deludes himself into thinking he's learned something about "the all-comprehending round of things" (111), and then dies. Why the difference?

One decisive reason is that the plots of many sentimental novels depend upon their protagonists' ability to create new affections based on the voluntary bonds of contract, which allows the scope of the novel to extend beyond the limitations of consanguinity. By contrast, Pierre tries and fails to generate contractual relations, painfully constricting the novel to a world of "blood relation" (218). For some literary critics, *Pierre's* inability to be a sentimental novel registers Melville's own success as an author of novels not plagued by the ideological and characterological problems of sentimental fictions.[3] Indeed, one of the most striking things about *Pierre* is that its failure to establish these bonds – the impossibility of producing relations that traverse the boundaries of consanguinity – has been interpreted by contemporary critics as Melville's smart and subversive indictment of the conventions and ideology of sentimental novels, undoubtedly a conclusion Melville would have been happy to embrace. His incapacity/unwillingness to author a sentimental novel is taken as a sign of his intellectual superiority, as if he were constitutionally unable to write the kind of drek that Warner, Cummins, and that undifferentiated horde of "scribbling women" so easily (allegedly) churned out. Melville's relation to sentimental novels is, however, more complicated than this scenario suggests. One look at the novel and its critical reception demonstrates that there is enough evidence to prove that *Pierre* is as much a sentimental novel as it isn't, and it seems obvious that each antithetical position is, paradoxically, correct. Because *Pierre* is neither a sentimental novel nor an anti-sentimental novel, and yet it is both, I would like to approach the text from a slightly different vantage point and argue that the story *Pierre* offers us is a pre-history of the sentimental novel. *Pierre* is the story that takes place before most sentimental texts begin, and what is absent in *Pierre* is the sentimental novel itself.

Pierre ends, in other words, where *The Lamplighter* begins but also ends so as to make *The Lamplighter*'s beginnings (nearly) unimaginable. *Pierre* is the story of why a sentimental protagonist like Gerty might be considerably happier not being enmeshed in a biological family. By the end of Melville's text, however, not only is there no alternative to biology, there is also no Gerty-figure with which to start. Pierre, Isabel and Lucy are dead, taking with them the nightmare of the biological family, which is the nightmare of *Pierre*. Thus, one might say that *Pierre* conducts an archeology of the sentimental novel, whose aim is to lay bare the foundations of its object of analysis, and, in the process, destroys it. Why?

All of the children in the novel seek to embrace an ideal of contract only to find that biology, indeed incest, awaits them. The novel thus begins to attack itself as the only available choices are negations of relation. But even the negations, it turns out, become attestations of consanguinity. Children choose not to have parents and parents choose to disown children, setting the stage for a reconstitution of family based on choice, but the "unimpairable blood-relation" (224) survives. And it is this survival that kills Pierre, the character and the novel. Unlike Ellen's or Gerty's, his is not a recovery from the loss or absence of parental relation, but a failed recovery from never having lost them. His is a deliberate flight from the consanguineous fact of parenthood, indeed from the bonds of kinship itself. From

Pierre's point of view, they and a whole host of sentimental protagonists are in the happy position of having lost their parents. They begin (or quickly become) free from parental ties, whereas Pierre must figure out a way to divest himself of his parents, indeed of all "kith and kin" (89). They get to choose new parental figures, whereas Pierre can only disown his, over and over again. Pierre's story, unlike theirs, is one where mothers refuse to go away and die, where fathers won't leave town, even though they're dead and gone. Pierre/*Pierre* can't get started because he won't be orphaned, left alone, forced to choose a new, unrelated family. All that remains for him to do is destroy the consanguineous bonds that destroy him. If Ellen thinks that reunification with her mother is her utmost desire, Pierre reveals it to be the child's worst nightmare. Indeed, what is perhaps most outrageous about *Pierre* is its utter assault on the sanctity of the parent/child relation, and the novel's (not so) underlying contention that a dead or disowned parent is better than a parent at all. *Pierre* reveals Melville's understanding of the radical origins of sentimental novels, which is to say that without the biological family in shards, they can't work, and as much as protagonists mourn the wreckage of family relations, their very lives depend upon it. To be sure, sentimental fiction cannot divulge its destructive *donnée*, but it cannot exist without it. That destructive *point d'appui* is itself *Pierre's* story, and Melville's novel can barely exist with it.

I "AND BUT BEGINNINGLY AS IT WERE" (117)

Pierre can barely begin or, more precisely, it begins again and again. There is the famously bizarre opening chapter of the novel, the story of Isabel's origins, the history of Pierre's relationship with his cousin, Glendinning Stanley, the account of Pierre as an author of sentimental fiction, and Plinlimmon's pamphlet. On the level both of plot and, as we shall see, of language, *Pierre* can be said to begin only "as it were," as it strives to conjoin the narrative continuity contained in the word "and" with the narrative suspension intrinsic to the word "but." The many beginnings of the novel consistently promise the start of a narrative, which is then blocked.[4] Indeed, the linguistic contortions of *Pierre* have been the subject of much literary criticism about the novel ever since it first appeared in 1852. George Washington Peck, for example, responded with a lengthy review which included a list of invented words that appear in the novel, such as "flush-fulness," "intermarryingly," "youngness," et al., prefaced by the following sarcastic remark: "The essence of this great eureka, this philological reform, consists in 'est' and 'ness,' added to every word to which they have no earthly right to belong. Feeling it to be our duty to give currency to every new discovery at all likely to benefit the world of literature, we present a few of Mr. Melville's word-combinations, in the hope that our rising authors will profit by the lesson, and thereby increase the richness and intelligibility of their style."[5] *Godey's Magazine and Lady's Book* seconded the negative opinion of other reviews and added its own "imitation of [Melville]'s style": "in the insignificant significances of that deftly-stealing and wonderfully-serpentining melodiousness, we have found an infinite, unbounded, inexpressible mysteriousness of nothingness" (313). If many antebellum reviewers responded to Melville's "long brain-muddling, soul-bewildering ambiguity" (308) by parodying it, more recent critics have focused on the significance of parody itself within *Pierre* from a variety of analytic perspectives, whether formalist, psychoanalytic, or cultural. In a reading that combines all three, Eric Sundquist notes that "no one can fail to be struck by *Pierre's* insanely pastoralized opening."[6] This insane opening, I want to argue, situates *Pierre* and Pierre in a temporal zone within which both novel and character have much difficulty moving, where characters "suppose it is afternoon" (14) because time is never certain, where they "swiftly pause," (3), where they are "stilly" (25, 60, 178).

Time is very much on the narrator's mind in *Pierre's* first chapter. For example, he remarks upon the strange resemblance between Mrs. Glendinning and Pierre, suggesting that "the mother seemed to have long stood still in her beauty," while the son "almost advanced himself to that mature stand-point in Time" (5). Shortly thereafter, the narrator undertakes an analysis of certain aristocratic families, like Pierre's, that manage to "imposingly perpetuate" (8) themselves in an American democracy: "if in America the vast mass of families be as the blades of grass, yet some few there are that stand as the oak; which, instead of decaying, annually puts forth new branches; whereby Time, instead of subtracting, is made to capitulate into a multiple virtue" (9). Here, the narrator draws analogies between families and natural images in order to reflect upon the capacity of time to transform subtraction into multiplication. He ambiguously calls this process a "virtue," and in the matter of oak trees, this might well be true, but when this "virtue," or aspect, of time is applied to families, the results are less certain. In the case of the Glendinnings, for example, Pierre's father, grandfather, and great-grandfather are physically dead, but like the oak, they "defy that annual decree" so that "Death itself becomes transmuted into Life" (9). And because they will not die, Pierre cannot live. "Nature [having] planted our Pierre" (13) suffers from an insufficiency of space which means that nature (and people) are not permitted to grow. "Not a flower stirs; the trees forget to wave; the grass itself seems to have ceased to grow" (3). Everything in Pierre's life at Saddle Meadows has to exist in a "half-unconscious" state because there is simply not enough room for anything more – no space, no time.

Although the narrator meditates upon these oddities of time, his narrative is clearly not immune to them. The degree to which *Pierre's* language stalls, gets obstructed, and repeats itself suggests that the "trance-like aspect" of Saddle Meadows is something with which virtually every character in the novel, including the narrator, must contend. This takes the form of words that pile up without accreting meaning and prose that has difficulty getting out of its own way. Throughout the opening chapter, for example, we read the dialogue and inner thoughts of characters who use the same words over and over again, whether it be Lucy's initial greeting to Pierre, "Pierre; – bright Pierre! – Pierre!" (4), or Mrs. Glendinning's soliloquy in which she refers to the docility of Pierre and Lucy no less than eight times in one paragraph. The characters' penchant (or compulsion) for repetition – in that same soliloquy, the words "of some dark hope forlorn" (20) occur one after another, separated by a semicolon and a dash – is also reflected in the narrative voice. Thus, the narrator refers to Pierre's grandfather as "grand old Pierre" five times in the course of a single paragraph, weirdly repeating the name and its epithets as if the personal pronoun "he" were an insufficient mode of designation: "I keep Christmas with my horses, said grand old Pierre. This grand old Pierre always rose at sunrise" (30). Such verbal excess (also known as pleonasm) signals not only the grandiosity of Pierre's grandfather's character but Pierre's subsequent diminishment. The more room taken up by the grandfather – whether on the page, in the psyche, in Saddle Meadows – the less room for Pierre. Similarly, words and their variants are repeated, as in the case of "descended" (7, 9, 17) "endless descendedness" (9), "blood-descent" (10), "far-descended" (11), "descending" (12), and "double revolutionary descent" (20), or the chapter title of Book IX, "More Light, and the Gloom of That Light. More Gloom, and the Light of That Gloom" (165).[7] The words that are *Pierre* act very much like the novel's characters, incapable of doing much more than repeating, mirroring, or descending from themselves.

Just as individual words seem to get in each other's way throughout the novel, so too the narrative of *Pierre* is constantly bumping into itself. The narrator not only frequently repeats descriptions, ideas, and passages while calling attention to those repetitions, but also has difficulty restraining the foreshadowing of the text, as if his narrative can only either circle around itself or lurch forward, unable to find a stable temporal rhythm through which to tell its story. As early as section 3 of the opening chapter, the narrator repeats himself, "It has been said that the beautiful country round about Pierre appealed to very proud memories" (8). Similarly, at the start of section 4, he asserts, "we poetically establish the richly aristocratic condition of Master Pierre Glendinning, for whom we have before claimed some special family distinction" (12). Shortly thereafter, he alludes to Pierre's grandfather as "the same grandfather several times herein-before mentioned" (13) and concludes the section with a phrase from its second paragraph, "we shall yet see again, I say, whether Fate hath not just a little bit of a word or two to say in this world" (14). The narrative is, in other words, made up of obstructions to itself, as evidenced in the following quotation from section 4: "In conclusion, do not blame me if I here make repetition, and do verbally quote my own words in saying that *it had been the choice fate of Pierre to have been born and bred in the country*" (13). This passage presents itself as a conclusion – as if the narrative has progressed from point a to point b – when in fact the passage is a citation from section 2, indicating that the narrative has circled back upon itself. But it is not as if the narrator is hiding that fact, because this "conclusion" strenuously refers to its status as a moment in the earlier part of the text. The sentence clearly acknowledges itself *as* an act of repetition, of tautology, or citationality, not only and most obviously with the italics but also through the phrase, "do verbally quote my own words in saying." The structure of the sentence enacts its meaning, which is to say that the sentence is a conclusion only insofar as it occurs last in a series of linguistic and/or conceptual repetitions. To put the point a bit differently, the conclusion and the origin are distinguishable not because of some substantive difference between them, but because of a temporal one. The conclusion is the origin repeated a bit later.[8]

The opening chapter, however, even has trouble maintaining this temporal distinction, as the narrator seems unable to tell the origins of Pierre/*Pierre* without giving away his/its conclusion. The narrator's constant use of foreshadowing supplies yet another indication of the bizarre rhythms – time grinds to a halt, repeats itself as if in a discursive stutter, or lurches ahead – of life in Saddle Meadows as well as the narrative that represents that life. The foreshadowing begins in the book's opening pages, as in this example where the narrator undertakes his description of Pierre's "romantic filial" love for his mother: "But as yet the fair river had not borne its waves to those sideways repelling rocks, where it was thenceforth destined to be forever divided into two unmixing streams" (5). Almost every paragraph in the remainder of the section ends in a similar fashion: "Pierre glance[d] along the background of his race; little recking of that maturer and larger interior development, which should forever deprive these things of their full power of pride in his soul" (6); "Pierre glide[d] toward maturity, thoughtless of that period of remorseless insight, when all these delicate warmths should seem frigid to him, and he should madly demand more ardent fires" (6); "But while thus all alive to the beauty and poesy of his father's faith, Pierre little foresaw that this world hath a secret deeper than beauty, and Life some burdens heavier than death" (7). This is foreshadowing taken to such an extreme so as to become a mockery of itself. The fictional device meant to hint at the text's future ends up in *Pierre* competing with the narration of the text's present and divulging its outcome: "Now Pierre stands on this noble pedestal; we shall see if he keeps that fine footing" (12). Indeed, the foreshadowing accretes so intensely in such a short number of pages that one cannot help but conclude that the narrator is either having an inordinate amount of difficulty restraining himself from disclosing Pierre's unhappy ending or, more likely given the narrator's hostile relationship with his main character, has absolutely no interest in self-restraint. Either way, the textual results are the same; *Pierre* can barely begin and it is over, and both happen at virtually the same time.

II "BUT NOT THUS...YET SO LIKE" (70)

Melville's novel self-destructs in a variety of ways: language coagulates, plots unravel, and characters die so as to ensure the impossibility of family reunification. There *is* a specific goal here, which is the disintegration of anything remotely representing a family, including not only the bonds of consanguinity (Pierre and his mother; Lucy and her mother; Delly and her parents), the relations that are entered into by choice (Pierre and Isabel; Pierre, Isabel, and Delly; Lucy and Pierre), but even the words on the page. From this point of view, the experimental language in *Pierre* not only calls attention to the fact that words have roots from which variations descend in a kind of philological family tree but exemplifies how those roots entangle, even strangle, the production of new words which are unable to escape what Mrs. Glendinning calls their "hereditary syllables" (287). Hence, the novel is laced with passages such as "in the minutest moment momentous things are irrevocably done" (83) or "not that at present all these things did thus present themselves to Pierre" (106), or this particularly fulsome description of Isabel's farm-house with "its ancient roof a bed of brightest mosses; its north front (from the north the moss-wind blows), also moss-incrusted, like the north side of any vast-trunked maple in the groves" (110). The words, like virtually all the characters in the novel, are related to each other, which is tantamount to a death sentence in the world of *Pierre*.

The logic and language of the biological family find their way into the very fabric of the narrative as kinship provides an especially powerful and corrosive discourse through which the narrator describes his characters' thoughts as well as his own. For example, in the chapter "Retrospective," the narrator has the following to say about Pierre's memory of his father's death-bed words, " My daughter! my daughter! . . . God! God! "(70): "into Pierre's awe-stricken, childish soul, there entered a kindred, though still more nebulous conceit" (71). At the very moment, in other words, that the text begins to engage the issue of Isabel's paternity and potential biological relation with Pierre, the word "kindred" appears as if to settle the question.[9] In a later chapter when Pierre jealously meditates upon Lucy's alleged affection for his cousin, Glendinning Stanley, the narrator once again uses the language of kinship to describe not only the content of Pierre's thoughts, which seems logical enough given the subject matter under consideration, but the very way they come into being: "Many commingled emotions combined to provoke this storm. But chief of all was something strangely akin to that indefinable detestation which one feels for any imposter who has dared to assume one's own name and aspect in any equivocal or dishonorable affair; an emotion greatly intensified if this impostor . . . be almost the personal duplicate of the man whose identity he assumes" (289). The narrator painstakingly charts the mental development of Pierre's outraged sense that an act of substitution has taken place whereby the cousins' "peculiar family resemblance" (288) has fostered a willingness on Lucy's part to accept Glen, Pierre's "kinsman" (289), as her paramour. "Indeed, situated now as he was Glen would seem all the finest part of Pierre, without any of Pierre's shame; would almost seem Pierre himself – what Pierre had once been to Lucy" (288). These reflections on Glendinning's "blood propinquity" illustrate how Pierre experiences kinship as the annihilation of his identity. To "possess a strong related similitude" (288) to someone else is the first step toward death, which is why the language of Pierre is, quite literally, both so defensively and aggressively self-referential – "self-same" (34–35); "self-willed" (41, 199);

"in me myself"(51); "self-suggested" (178, 316); "in himself absolutely" (244); "self-supposed" (294) – as if the self could remain safe only by being unrelated to anything but itself, by being its only point of reference. Naturally, this "self-conceit" (136) turns out to be a dreadful miscalculation on Pierre's part both for the simple reason that things and people *do* exist in relation to each other and for the more complex reason that as soon as one tries to cut off those relations in the novel, to "own no earthly kith or kin" (89) as Pierre contends, they, hydra-like, multiply themselves; to wit, Isabel and Lucy. Indeed, it is only a matter of time until Pierre must divide in order to establish a principle of relation, even if it is only to himself. Thus, "he himself" (63, 173) becomes "he himself, as it were" (289) or "the seeming semblance of himself" (289). Pierre's attempt to "spurn and rend all mortal bonds" (106) only necessitates that a new site of "correlativeness" (85) be produced, and that is, of course, his self.

The final point to make about the passage is its use of the term "akin" to characterize Pierre's meditations. As in the first example, where the word "kindred" describes the thought process at the same time as it insinuates the reality of Isabel's sisterly claims, here Pierre's fantasies of Lucy's alleged incapacity to distinguish between him and Glen are written so as to confirm that lack of distinction. Pierre's thoughts, in other words, are akin to an analogy produced by the narrator, which means that the experience of losing himself to Glen gets reproduced in Pierre's relation to the narrator. Indeed, in a novel of (and about) difficult relations, this is one of the most difficult. As literary critics have observed, the narrator wildly vacillates between cudgeling Pierre for his naiveté and sympathizing with his suffering. Sometimes the distance between Pierre and the narrator is absolutely clear; other times the two seem to collapse into one another. What makes the relationship between the two so hard to untangle is that in exploring a young man's attempt to make himself by unmaking his relations with others, the narrator constantly uses the language of kinship to describe that very process, which not only has the effect of undoing Pierre's attempts to strike out on his own but also recreates a family drama in the narrator's own relation with Pierre. For example, in this passage the narrator reflects upon Pierre's feelings about Lucy's "unearthly evanescence" (58) by positing a set of possibilities *not* considered by Pierre: "Not into young Pierre's heart did there then come the thought, that as the glory of the rose endures but for a day, so the full bloom of girlish airiness and bewitchingness, passes from the earth almost as soon" (58). The narrator establishes this analogy as his and not Pierre's, but the distance between them lasts for just a moment. "Pierre's thought was different from this, and yet somehow akin to it" (58).[10] Moments like this, where difference is asserted only to be absorbed by what in another context is called "catching likenesses" (330), pervade the narrative as the following examples indicate: "But not thus, altogether, was it now with Pierre; yet so like, in some points, that the above true warning may not misplacedly stand" (70); "[Pierre's father's] face was wonderful to me [Isabel]. Something strangely like it, and yet again unlike it, I had seen before . . . But one day, looking into the smooth water behind the house, there I saw the likeness – something strangely like, and yet unlike, the likeness of his face" (124); "It [the Memnon Stone] was shaped something like a lengthened egg, but flattened more; and, at the ends, pointed more; and yet not pointed, but irregularly wedge-shaped" (132). No one in the novel, and this includes the narrator, is capable of sustaining the difference between difference and similitude. The recognition of difference, which often gets registered through the use of analogies, inevitably dissipates so as to validate the primacy of "unmistakeable likeness" (351).[11] Analogies in *Pierre* work (or don't) like foreshadowing in that both fictional devices are undone by their inability to withstand the pressure of the difference upon which they are founded. That is to say, if foreshadowing implies temporal disjunction in the very act of bringing the future into the present of the narrative, in *Pierre* the effect of introducing the future is the destruction of the past. Similarly, if analogies imply likeness on the conceptual level even as they are founded on conceptual difference, here the effect of introducing similarity is the evacuation of difference. Both devices operate dysfunctionally; a failure which marks the success of the novel's attack on the conventions of the sentimental genre and the biological family that are *Pierre*'s ideological nemeses.

The narrator thus thwarts Pierre's attempts to find a haven from the heartless world of the family by linguistically arresting him in the discourse of kinship. But it seems perfectly logical in this novel of ubiquitous consanguinity that the narrator finds himself caught as well. He, too, is unable to withstand the perverse principle of "related love" (189) that governs *Pierre*, and even though phrases such as "but ignorant of these further insights" (60) or "so at least he thought" (93) appear throughout the narrative in order to accentuate the difference between his knowledge and Pierre's, the fact is that as Pierre's story progresses, Pierre and the narrator arrive at the same temporal and conceptual place. This is registered by the prolonged use of the present tense in later sections of the novel and by the fact that whereas early in the novel the narrator could confidently point to

Pierre's "ignoran[ce] at this time of the ideas concerning the reciprocity and partnership of Folly and Sense" (167), by the novel's end, "Pierre saw the everlasting elusiveness of Truth; the universal lurking insincerity of even the greatest and purest written thoughts" (339). Like Pierre and his mother, like Pierre and Isabel, like Pierre and Lucy, Pierre and the narrator merge. They must because this is the inevitable consequence of relations in this novel.

Which is why Pierre has to be an author. Although some literary critics have wondered at the plausibility of Pierre's writerly disposition, the logic of "linked correspondence" (36) makes it impossible for him to be anything else.[12] The narrator, however, does anticipate the reader's potential surprise upon learning of Pierre's authorial aspirations in a passage which features just about every peculiarity of the novel's narrative voice: "in the earlier chapters of this volume, it has somewhere been passingly intimated, that Pierre was not only a reader of the poets and other fine writers, but likewise – and what is a very different thing from the other – a thorough allegorical understander of them, a profound emotional sympathizer with them" (244). The narrator alludes to an earlier section of the novel, he deploys the terms, "likewise" and "different," as if they did not contradict each other, and he (likewise) combines "but" with "and," as if those conjunctions operated similarly. But what particularly interests me about the opening paragraphs of Book XVII, "Young America in Literature," is the narrator's methodological statement about his own writing. The desire to renounce the psychic pressure of kinship, even as it provides the very terms of that renunciation, is one that inextricably binds the narrator with his protagonist.

Among the various conflicting modes of writing history, there would seem to be two grand practical distinctions, under which all the rest must subordinately range. By the one mode, all contemporaneous circumstances, facts, and events must be set down contemporaneously; by the other, they are only to be set down as the general stream of the narrative shall dictate; for matters which are kindred in time, may be very irrelative in themselves. I elect neither of these; I am careless of either; both are well enough in their way; I write precisely as I please. (244)

Time is still very much on the narrator's mind, especially given how his narrative intentionally scorns "various conflicting modes" of writing, which he separates into two narrative categories. The first narrates events synchronically, the second diachronically. With much bravado, the narrator declines to employ either of these two modes, suggesting that he has consciously dismissed them as uninteresting and conventional. I would suggest, however, another, more skeptical reason for the narrator's election of what we might call the "careless" mode, which is that this is the only narrative mode that the story permits. To write "contemporaneously ... [or] as the general stream of the narrative shall dictate" is to be capable of sustaining the difference between events that happen at the same time and events that do not. And the narrator is telling a story about the inability to keep those differences intact, as the first chapter of *Pierre* so insistently demonstrates.[13]

When Pierre becomes an author, however, the reader begins to suspect that, perhaps, the narrator is falling victim to "this age-neutralizing Pierre" (264), as if the neutralization which the narrator had portrayed and parodied in the opening pages *vis à vis* his mother is finally neutralizing him. The final phrase of this passage – "I write precisely as I please" – might be read as the narrator's attempt to declare his independence (with feigned nonchalance) from conventional modes of writing and writers, especially Pierre, just as the text is about to plunge the narrator and Pierre into one of its most profound "infinite entanglements" (191). As critics have pointed out, it is often difficult to distinguish between Pierre's tortured book and *Pierre*, the book we are reading; to wit, the narrator writes, "It is impossible to talk or to write without apparently throwing oneself helplessly open; the Invulnerable Knight wears his visor down" (259). Ironically, the narrator's very assertion of an independent writing style could just as easily be Pierre's, who writes "careless" sentences such as "Now I drop all humorous or indifferent disguises, and all philosophical pretensions ... Away, ye chattering apes of a sophomorean Spinoza and Plato, who once didst all but delude me that the night was day, and pain only a tickle" (302). It comes as no surprise, then, that Book XVIII, "Pierre, as a Juvenile Author," finds us back in the beginning, with the narrator announcing, "It is true, as I long before said, that Nature at Saddle Meadows had very early been as a benediction to Pierre" (257). We have begun again, only now the strangulating effects of Saddle Meadows' temporality and its regime of "mutual reflections" (4) are catching up with the narrator as "the ineffable correlativeness" (85) of relationships in the novel comes closer to home.

The fact is that Pierre's authorial identity threatens to do to the narrator what Pierre's fictitious marriage to Isabel does to him; that is, "eternally entangle him in a fictitious alliance, which, though in reality but a web of air, yet in effect would prove a wall of iron" (175). Like Pierre, who "most carefully and most tenderly egg[s] [Isabel]" (189), the narrator "preambillically examine[s] [Pierre] a little further" (260). As so often happens with words in the novel, the narrator's "preamble" (260) has become "preambillical"; instead of maturing as the narrative progresses, Pierre is becoming a "little toddler" (296), "the baby toddler I spoke of" (305) who finds himself preumbillicaly (a pun Melville must have found irresistible) connected to the narrator. Thus, precisely at the moment that Pierre imagines himself to "be not only his own Alpha and Omega, but to be distinctly all the intermediate gradations" (261), the narrator turns Pierre into an utter dependent, thus discursively producing what looks to be a parental relation between himself and Pierre. Throughout the text the narrator has tried to keep himself separate from these correlations by adopting a weirdly aggressive stance toward his protagonist, which now becomes all the more important to maintain as the distinctions between the two threaten to dissolve. For example, he derides Pierre's youthful compositions as "the veriest common-place" (257), and then even as he applauds Pierre's efforts to write "his deep book" (305), he keeps his temporal and experiential distance by continuously revealing the gap between his knowledge about the writing process and Pierre's naive, "young" (244), "immature" (282), "juvenile" (257) – to use words from three of *Pierre's* chapter titles – attempts at composition. "While Pierre was thinking that he was entirely transplanted into a new and wonderful element of Beauty and Power, he was, in fact, but in one of the stages of the transition" (283). Or, "yet now, forsooth, because Pierre began to see through the first superficiality of the world, he fondly weens he has come to the unlayered substance" (285). Foreshadowing of this sort is familiar to the reader from the opening chapter, but the difference is that at this particular moment in the novel, what is being foreshadowed has everything to do with the status of the narrator *vis à vis* Pierre, rather than, say, the impending demise of Pierre and Lucy's relationship or the potential appearance of a sister for Pierre.

Thus, in what one might call the definitive paradox of the text, the narrator tries to separate himself from Pierre through the language and logic of relatedness. In other words, it can't be the case that he's Pierre if he's Pierre's father, even though the opening chapter of the novel imagines a world where this can indeed be the case. The methodological statement with which Book XVII begins, then, indicates the extent to which Pierre's dilemma has become the narrator's: "for matters which are kindred in time, may be very irrelative in themselves" (244). To be sure, events that take place at the same time may be not be related, "may be very irrelative," but the fact is that something is always "kindred," at least in the realm of temporality. This concession speaks volumes, not only because the narrator is constantly preoccupied with the breakdown and stabilization of discrete temporal frames but because his desire to maintain a theory of "irrelativity" is voiced in the language of kinship. The conceptualization of the narrative method of *Pierre* assumes the verbal lineaments of family. And because all things akin in *Pierre* must die (and because all things must become akin), the loathing and aggression that once were directed so clearly at the "pellucid and merry romance" (305) of sentimental fiction now turn inward, as *Pierre* loathes and destroys itself.[14]

III "I LOVE MY KIND" (157)

Quite early in the novel, Lucy is reunited with her brothers after a three-year separation. Her exclamation, "my darling brothers!", is reiterated and extended by Pierre's, "my darling brothers and sister!" (29). In the verbal act of translating his potential brothers-in-law into brothers, Pierre is unable to maintain an exogamous connection with Lucy. In a fictional world where even horses "were a sort of family cousins to Pierre" (21), it is simply impossible for Pierre to love someone to whom he is not related. When Isabel appears and declares herself his sister, he must believe her because he loves her; his capacity for loving her depends upon his ability to identify his feelings as signifying what he calls "our related love" (189). All love, like all language, is related. Thus, Lucy and Pierre's initial encounter, as well as the narrator's description of it, is a virtuoso mirroring perform-ance of emotions and words: "As heart rings to heart those voices rang, and for a moment, in the bright hush of the morning, the two stood silently but ardently eying each other, beholding mutual reflections of a boundless admiration and love" (4). The "mutual reflections" of the characters reflect themselves in the repetition of words. "With Lucy's hand in his, and feeling, softly feeling of its soft tinglingness; he seemed as one placed in linked correspondence with the summer lightnings; and by sweet shock on shock, receiving intimating foretastes of the etherealest delights of earth" (36). Like those "mutual reflections," Pierre's experience of "linked corres-pondence" gets registered in the narrator's description of it, as words and the sounds within words (feeling; soft/softly; tinglingness) reverberate.[15] No wonder he wants to "spurn and rend all mortal bonds" (106).

Pierre's attempted decimation of family ties – in one of his many Emersonian moments, he declares, "cast-out Pierre hath no paternity" (199) – perhaps leaves him "free to do his own self-will" (199). But "his own self-will," surely a desperate description of self-sufficiency that marks its own insufficiency, nonetheless wills itself a family in the form of Isabel, Delly Ulver, and eventually Lucy Tartan. In fact, when Lucy writes to Pierre in New York, requesting "to re-tie myself to thee" (309), Pierre not only accepts her "angelical" (311) offer without hesitation, but willingly embraces her suggestion that there may be "some indirect cousinship" (311) between them. It would seem that his decision to "spurn and rend all mortal bonds" leaves him pleasantly vulnerable, if not more willing than ever to be bound.

That Pierre's bond of choice is an incestuous relationship with his (possibly) half-sister gave antebellum readers pause. To make matters even more bizarre, Pierre insists on protecting his mother from the hypothetical knowledge of her husband's pre-marital sexual transgression by announcing that Isabel is his wife; that is, *not* his sister. In their more benign moments, Melville's reviewers were puzzled; in their more aggressive moments, they were outraged. Evert and George Duyckinck, former friends and supporters of Melville, famously dubbed *Pierre* "a literary mare's nest," and chastised him for "the supersensuousness with which the holy relations of the family are described. Mother and son, brother and sister are sacred facts not to be disturbed by any sacrilegious speculations" (301). The *American Whig Review*, in a review representative of the book's reception, begins its attack, "A bad book! Affected in dialect, unnatural in conception, repulsive in plot, and inartistic in construction" (314). Especially fulsome, apparently, was the novel's treatment of incest: "when he strikes with an impious, though, happily weak hand, at the very foundations of society, we feel it our duty to tear off the veil with which he has thought to soften the hideous features of the idea, and warn the public against the reception of such atrocious doctrines" (317). But it is precisely these atrocious doctrines to which literary critics have been drawn in their readings of *Pierre*. Leslie Fiedler, for example, asserts that "*Pierre* represents the major attempt in the history of our fiction at making of that theme [brother–sister incest] great art." Sundquist maintains that "the issue of incestuous alliances" registers the multiple crises of authority in the novel, be they familial, national, or textual. Gillian Brown has argued for an "aesthetics of incest" in which Melville, through Pierre, "discovers in incest a foundation, a familial support in the form of no family at all, for his literary economy."[16] The closed economy of incest, in other words, registers Pierre's attempted revolt against a variety of disciplinary regimes, including the sentimental family and sentimental fiction, in the name of individualism, or "his own self will."

Such atrocious doctrines were, however, not solely a feature of Melville's fictional domain. They were standard fare in the antebellum debate about family reform, and it is to this specific context that I would like to turn in order to indicate the ways in which *Pierre* engages in the critique launched by reformers during this period at the same time as it deracinates the critique.[17] The fact is that while the family home was being coronated as "the sanctuary of all that is most sacred in humanity," in the words of E. H. Chapin, author of several advice manuals including *Duties of Young Women* (1848), that same sanctuary was being condemned as the primary source of "apathy and intellectual death" with its "petty and harassing cares, with its antisocial spirit."[18] Celebrations of marital relations are ubiquitous, such as William Alcott's popular *The Young Wife, or Duties of Woman in the Marriage Relation* (1837) in which he imagines domestic bliss to be when "your souls seem to be but one, and your joys and sorrows commingle," but so are indictments, such as the one offered by T. L. Nichols and Mrs. Mary S. Gove Nichols's book *Marriage: Its History, Character, and Results*, with which this chapter begins: "Running through many families are secret amours. Children are born of these, the parents die, and the marriage of half-brothers and sisters is always possible, and doubtless of frequent occurrence."[19] A startlingly appropriate epigraph for *Pierre*.

Melville (and Pierre), in other words, are not alone in pursuing new types of community, whether one thinks of Brook Farm, New Harmony, or Oneida. Melville's comic representation of utopian communities, which he calls "Teleological Theorists and Social Reformers" (268) in Book XIX, "The Church of the Apostles," suggests his familiarity and impatience with many religious, philosophical, and dietary reform movements of the day. In an 1843 article entitled, "The Consociate Family Life," which appeared in *The New Age and Concordium Gazette*, English progressive Charles Lane offers this description of the "pure reform principles" practiced at Bronson Alcott's utopian community, Fruitlands: "Shall I sip tea or coffee? The inquiry may be. – No. Abstain from *all* ardents, as from alcohol drinks. Shall I consume pork, beef, or mutton? Not if you value health or life ... Shall I warm my bathing water? Not if cheerfulness is valuable. Shall I clothe in many garments? Not if purity is aimed at."[20] Such "insane heterodoxical notions about the economy of his body" (299) are easy targets for Melville. One group of reformers, though, seems to have particularly piqued Melville's interest, and that is the Shakers, whose communities in Hancock and Lebanon, Massachusetts he visited no less than five times in a two-year period.[21] Intriguing are the possible connections between the Shaker ritual of dancing and "the hair-shrouded form of Isabel [which] swayed to and fro with a like abandonment, and suddenness, and wantonness" (126), between the inspired visions and spiritual gifts of Shaker women and Isabel's mystical guitar in which "all of the wonders that are unimaginable and unspeakable ... are translated in [its] mysterious

melodiousness" (125). I am, however, less interested in correlating specific
Shaker belief and practice with characters and symbols in *Pierre*, suggestive
as those parallels might be, than with reading Pierre's desire and failure to
destroy the ties of consanguinity in relation to reformers of the period who
share both the desire and the failure.

When Pierre, "the young enthusiast" (175), decides to "gospelize the
world anew" (273), he naturally gravitates toward the Church of the
Apostles, a kind of half-way house for radicals in New York City. The
decrepit building – the antithesis of Pierre's home in Saddle Meadows – is
inhabited by "all sorts of poets, painters, paupers and philosophers" (269),
united by their pursuit of spiritual, corporeal, and familial reform. Because
families are few and fragmented in the Church, the building perfectly
accommodates Pierre's domestic experiments, which "take no terms from
the common world, but do thou make terms to it, and grind thy fierce
rights out of it!" (160). The narrator, for example, says about Plotinus
Plinlimmon, a guiding spirit of The Church as well as author of
Chronometricals and Horologicals, that "he seemed to have no family or
blood ties of any sort" (290). Charlie Millthorpe, Pierre's childhood friend
whose father's death leaves him responsible for his mother and sisters
(a responsibility he rather poorly fulfills), sings the praises of non-consanguinity:
"The great men are all bachelors, you know. Their family is the universe"
(281). Pierre, of course, believes this too because if everyone is related to
everyone else, then there is no such thing as incest or, more precisely,
everyone is always committing incest ("by heaven, but marriage is an
impious thing" [58]). Incest is not against the law; "it is the law" (274).
Thus, he instructs Isabel to "call me brother no more . . . I am Pierre, and
thou Isabel, wide brother and sister in the common humanity" (273). Pierre
seems to be suggesting that the difference between incestuous and exogamous love can be sufficiently marked and stabilized by dispensing with
the term "brother" and replacing it with "wide brother in the common
humanity." If this is the best Pierre can do, if this is what it means to "take
no terms from the common world," he's in trouble.

Characters in *Pierre* treat consanguineous relations as if they could be
assumed and dispensed with at will – as if a child could choose not to have a
parent, as if a mother could decide not to have a child anymore. Virtually
every character of Pierre's generation, from the ignominious Delly, whose
"own parents want her not" (163) to the angelic Lucy, whose mother
declares, "I forever cast thee off . . . I shall instruct thy brothers to disown
thee" (329), is renounced by his/her parents. Mrs. Glendinning, the character most committed to the logic of biological kinship, is most keen on its

destruction when she learns of Pierre's betrayal: "He bears my name – Glendinning. I will disown it; were it like this dress, I would tear my name off from me, and burn it till it shriveled to a crisp!" (193). Pages later, Pierre declares his sovereignty from his name in a passage that, ironically, reproduces his mother's desire to "disown" him. In the act of committing his father's portrait to the "crackling, clamorous flames" (198), Pierre proclaims, "Cast-out Pierre hath no paternity, and no past" (199). Characters are forever choosing to have or to disown biological relationships, as if these were choices to be made; as if relations that are freely and contractually entered into cannot, by definition of being chosen, be incestuous. But of course, they are. In *Pierre*, virtually all relations (with the exception of Delly and Charlie Millthorpe) are not only chosen, but they are always incestuous. The only choice one has is whether the relationship is chosen to be biological or is biological, whether one is to commit incest knowingly or unknowingly.

The domestic world Pierre creates in the Church of the Apostles follows a trajectory from utopian community to communal disintegration that is familiar to the student of antebellum reform. Like John Humphrey Noyes's (any relation to John Humphreys?) community of Perfectionists in Oneida, New York, Pierre's band of followers, which includes Isabel, Delly, and eventually Lucy, follow their leader in pursuing "the manly enthusiast cause of his heart" (167). Like Noyes, who both regarded "the whole Associate as one family, and all children as the children of the family" while striving "to get [their] freedom from any claims of kindred, etc.," Pierre's is a community organized according to blood relations in a world desperate to be free of them. And like Noyes who developed a theory of sexuality whereby men refrained from ejaculating during sexual intercourse so that "there is no risk of conception without intention," Pierre muses, "from nothing proceeds nothing, Isabel! How can one sin in a dream?" (274).[22] And like Pierre, Noyes, Mother Anne Lee, founder of the Shaker movement in America, and Joseph Smith, leader of the Mormons, were accused of everything from rape to incest. Critics taking aim at Shaker communities in New Hampshire warned, "stop these Shakers from creeping about, like the Serpent of old, destroying many a fair Eden of domestic happiness." The Mormon practice of polygamy has consequences familiar to any reader of *Pierre*: "monogamy is the true basis of all Democratic institutions . . . If that root is rendered corrupt, the whole fabric of society becomes polluted." This passage from the Reverend Hubbard Eastman's 1849 attack on Noyes could easily find its way into reviews of Melville's *Pierre*: "It [Perfectionism] not only contemplates a complete annihilation of the conjugal relations, but it designs to sever the ties of consanguinity, and its ultimate object is to make a *clean sweep* of *all* the social relations! And when all the ties of kindred are cut asunder, there must be complete submission to the will and absolute control of Mr. Noyes!" If "*Pierre* assaulted the family," as Michael Rogin correctly maintains, it was not alone in doing so.[23]

However, as much as *Pierre* is a scathing analysis of the biological family and its asphyxiating spiritualization of passions, it is also an analysis of antebellum attempts to reform it. Unlike the ideal and expanding communities imagined by reformers, where persons decide that "the[ir] neighbor is most truly our brother, – nay, more than brother, he is our other self," Pierre's world of choice ("I will no more have a father" [87]) is one of continual contraction ("I own myself a brother of the clod" [302]).[24] The Church of the Apostles contains both the experiment in reform and its inevitably disastrous consequences; inevitable because the family Pierre chooses reproduces the one he inherited. For every time that Pierre rejects the language and logic of blood ("Call me brother no more! How knowest thou I am thy brother?" [273]), he willingly re-embraces it, as in this passage where he sadly muses upon the "unrelated hands that were hired" to attend to his dead mother, "whose heart had been broken,..., by the related hands of her son" (286). Indeed, at the very moment that Pierre declares that he "will not own a mortal parent" (106), he pleads (with God?) to "bind me in bonds I can not break" (107). Those bonds assume the form of a new family, with himself as the brother/husband, and Isabel as the sister/ wife, and Lucy as the "very strange cousin" (313) whom Pierre looks upon "with an expression illy befitting their singular and so-supposed merely cousinly relation" (337). Lucy, in fact, declares Pierre to be the principle of family itself: "thou art my mother and my brothers, and all the world, and all heaven, and all the universe to me" (311). Like Pierre, who, in the very act of renouncing family produces another one, reformers desirous of challenging conventional domestic relations ended up replicating them, whether in Bronson Alcott's "consociate" family at Fruitlands, "Mother" Anne Lee, "Father" William Lee (Anne's biological brother with whom she was accused of having incestuous relations) and the "brethren" and "sisters" comprising the Shaker "families," or the institution of "complex marriage," as practiced by Noyes's followers. If their aim were the elimination of conventional family arrangements, to "engage collectively ... as children of one family," to quote Owenite Frances Wright, Pierre's experiment suggests that reformers did little more than justify and, in some cases, institutionalize (in the name of progress) the incestuous impulses within the biological family.[25] Pierre thus takes up the challenge issued by reformers like the Nicholses, who complained that "now a woman can have no brother, unless he is born such" (369), and imagines a world where brothers are not born but made only to discover that the making turns the "fictitious title" into "the absent reality" (7). Pierre, in other words, literalizes the familial metaphors governing these reform projects and in the process reveals the "nameless" and "latent" feelings, two of Melville's favorite code words for incestuous passions, at the center both of the biological family and of attempts to reform it.

The language of voluntary bonds pervades the novel, as if one could choose to make oneself a family based on a paradigm other than blood, only to reveal the "blood relation" (218) that motivates all of its characters' choices. To act as if consanguinity were capable of being destroyed is to act as if consanguinity were capable of being produced. Both actions, that is, depend upon viewing blood as if it were a matter of choice, a matter of a speech act, the only difference being whether one wants to disown it (a favorite word in the text) or choose it. Thus, Pierre's announcement that "aunts, uncles, cousins innumerable [are] dead henceforth to me" (196) or Mrs. Tartan's warning to Lucy that "I shall instruct thy brothers to disown thee" (329) is theoretically no different from his conversation with his mother where he says, "Mother, stay! – yes do sister" (96) or his claim that Lucy is "some pretty aunt or cousin" (309). Pierre conjures those relations into being as swiftly as he rejects them, which is why what someone chooses to call someone else is so crucial in the novel. For example, the strain between Pierre and his mother is twice registered by their disagreement about what to call each other, "sister me not, now, Pierre; – I am thy mother" (95) and "why don't you call me brother Pierre?" (130). Even Isabel, who in her autobiographical narration remarks upon the fact that "the word father only seemed a word of general love and endearment to me . . . it did not seem to involve any claims of any sort, one way or the other" (145), learns how powerful the words denoting consanguinity are, as well as the claims that go along with them. In her letter to Pierre, she dramatically calls attention to the act of familial designation: "yes, Pierre, Isabel calls thee her brother – her brother," and as if that weren't enough to make the relation stick, she adds, "Oh, sweetest of words . . . Dearest Pierre, my brother, my own father's child! . . . Oh, my brother!" (63–64). In Melville's novel, to call someone a brother or a sister is to make that person "thy related brother" (192) or "my best sister" (191), which is the penultimate step to committing incest. But it is also the case that the choice is a sham – one only ever chooses to make someone a brother or sister or cousin who already is one.

The proof of this is that at no point is Pierre ever tempted by Delly Ulver. Interestingly, Delly (like Charlie Millthorpe) signifies a principle of difference with which the novel ultimately can't or doesn't care to come to terms. The narrative seems utterly unconcerned with her fate as Pierre, Lucy, and Isabel lie moribund in the prison house at the conclusion of the novel. Indeed, the distance between Pierre and Delly remains surprisingly consistent for a novel that thrives on the disintegration of boundaries. Never does it cross Pierre's mind to call her sister or cousin.[26] In fact, it is in a conversation with Delly that Pierre attempts to stabilize the sexual vertigo into which the narrative has descended. The passage begins with Pierre announcing that "my cousin Miss Tartan is coming here to live with us" to which the panicked Delly replies, "Good heavens! – coming here? – your cousin? – Miss Tartan?" Sensing her confusion, Pierre restates not only the fact of Lucy's imminent appearance but the definition of their relation, "My cousin, – mind, my *cousin*, Miss Tartan, is coming to live with us" (320). Having nailed down that relation, they now turn to Isabel and Pierre's and the confirmation of that bond. Thus, Delly asks Pierre, "does Mrs. Glendin-din – does my mistress know this?" and he replies, "My wife knows all" (320). The dialogue takes a familiar turn when Pierre asks Delly, who has gone to assist Isabel and returns to the scene of interrogation, "How is my wife, now?":

Again startled by the peculiar emphasis placed on the magical word *wife*, Delly, who had long before this, been occasionally struck with the infrequency of his using that term; she looked at him perplexedly, and said half-unconsciously –
"Your wife, sir?"
"Ay, is she not?"
"God grant that she be – Oh, 'tis most cruel to ask that of poor, poor Delly, sir!"
"Tut for thy tears! Never deny it again then! – I swear to heaven, she is!" (321)

This exchange makes clear that just as Pierre's sexual radar fails to pick up Delly because of her non-consanguinity, Delly never imagines that Pierre's relationship with Isabel is anything but what they have presented themselves as being – husband and wife in "secret marriage" (202). It seems both odd and entirely proper that Delly, herself an unmarried woman who has an affair with a married man, becomes the standard-bearer of conventional notions of sexuality in the Church of the Apostles, which is to say that she remains outside of the incestuous *ménage à troising* comprising Pierre, Isabel, and Lucy.

In fact, Delly's conversation with Pierre follows an exchange between Pierre and Isabel that demonstrates just how completely unhinged relationships and the words designating them have become. Upon receiving Lucy's letter informing him of her arrival at the Church of the Apostles, Pierre breaks the news to Isabel that "some pretty young aunt or cousin" (313) is on her way. Lucy's position as cousin, however, troubles Isabel because "that is not wholly out of the degree" (313), by which she means that being a cousin doesn't keep Lucy safe from Pierre's affections. Of course not; in fact, being a cousin, even "a very strange cousin . . . almost a nun in her notions" (313), only guarantees Pierre's ardor, which is evident in his subsequent description of Lucy as having "this wild, nun-like notion in her" (313). The inability of either Pierre or Isabel to control the meaning of their words (and the "wild" passions behind them) becomes palpably obvious as Pierre instructs Isabel, "do not have any sisterly jealousy, then, my sister" (313), and Isabel later wonders, "would it be well, if I slept with her, my brother?" (314).

The insistent destabilization of the terms designating the biological family begins the process of destroying it. With relentless frequency, the language of the text suggests feelings that are not only suspect but, if and when translated into behavior, illegal. For example, the narrator muses, "much that goes to make up the deliciousness of a wife, already lies in the sister" (7). Similarly, Pierre's "romantic filial" (5) relationship with his mother tantalizes him with at least the linguistic possibility that his mother is not really his mother (or doesn't have to be his mother) and, as critics have noted, propels Pierre's demise which eventuates in his murdering those "two boiling bloods" (336), Glen and Fred. The speech act of calling a mother a sister, or a son a brother, has grave narrative consequences as the act of not calling people by their proper designations metamorphoses into an inability to know the difference between a mother and a sister, a brother and a husband, a cousin and the girl next door. As the narrator says several times in the course of the story, a "fictitious title" (7), a "fictitious alliance" (175), even (and especially) a "fictitious wife" (180) may as well be real. A "nominal conversion of a sister into a wife" (177) is a conversion. There is no such thing, in other words, as "empty nominalness" (192). *Pierre* is a novel in which what you call someone is what he/she is, which is why when Pierre "assume[s] before the world, that by secret rites, Pierre Glendinning was already become the husband of Isabel Banford" (173), it is irrelevant whether or not they have actually committed incest. The speech act has made it so. The power to designate the desired relation to someone through a speech act represents both the possibility of individual free will and the moment of its self-destruction, because the novel's logic of ubiquitous consanguinity requires that the only available names designate kinship, and so the promise of freedom turns into its nightmare.[27] Pierre and his mother can call each other anything they want, and they choose brother and sister; Pierre can name Lucy anything he wants, and he chooses cousin. Thus, *Pierre* is a novel whose protagonist is determined to end a regime of consanguinity, but whose every move seems to proliferate it.[28]

For every consanguineous relation spurned by Pierre, another and more valued one, which combines the attractions of "voluntary election [and] blood propinquity" (288), takes its place. As much as Pierre, and the "too much generous blood in his heart" (222), wants to destroy the "blood relation" (218), it refuses to go away. Blood permeates the text, whether it be the "blood in the veins of [England's] winding or manufactured nobility" (10), or the "blood-red" (92) sunrise of Saddle Meadows or the "the blood-shedding times" (75) of the French Revolution which provides the backdrop for Pierre's father's youthful indiscretions. Characters even experience their blood as a felt attribute, as if the blood in one's body could be understood as something outside of oneself. This something, of course, is the family, the "surviving blood relation" (287). Thus, for example, Pierre's mother, upon suspecting Pierre of misdeeds toward Lucy, cries out, "I feel my blood chemically changing in me" (131), and Pierre, in thinking about the "unproven fact of Isabel's sisterhood," notes that "his very blood seemed to flow through all his arteries with unwonted subtileness, when he thought that the same tide flowed through the mystic veins of Isabel" (139). Toward the end of the novel, Pierre's "very blood" is described as "rebellious" (341). The ubiquity of blood extends to representations of writing. In the case of Isabel's fateful letter to Pierre in which she declares their consanguinity, her tears famously "[assume] a strange and reddish hue – as if blood and not tears had dropped upon the sheet" (64–65). Similarly, when Pierre is at work on his masterpiece, the narrator notes that two books are being written, "the larger book...whose unfathomable cravings drink his blood; the other only demands his ink" (304). We've seen this in the language which struggles to get beyond the ubiquitous resemblance among words and in the characters who are so easily and "strangely translated" (5) into one another (Pierre, in fact, imagines Lucy as "some empty *x*" [181]). They are all "yet so like, in some points" (70), and the only way to end this regime of likeness is to "let out all thy Glendinning blood, and then sew up the vile remainder" (239). Blood is everywhere in the novel, functioning as a metonymy for the family relations which persist in spite of the text's continuous bloodletting, as the "black vein in this Glendinning" (358) opens up and "the dark vein's burst" (362). But there's always more. Even when "spatterings of his own kindred blood were upon the pavement" (360) as Glen's body lies prone, the novel ends with "more relations coming" (361) to see the imprisoned bodies of Pierre, Lucy, and Isabel.

IV "IT IS THE LAW." (274)

Isabel exists outside of the law. Had she been protected by the law (had Pierre's father not avoided it?), perhaps she would know whether she had lived in a place "five, six, perhaps, seven years" (119). Perhaps she would know if certain events took place when she was "nine, or ten, or eleven years" (122). Perhaps she would know the difference between "Virtue and Vice" (274). But it is precisely Isabel's place outside of the law that produces her unstable sense of time, as well as her inability to recognize the distinctions between moral categories. And if these attractions weren't enough for Pierre (in addition to her "wonderfully beautiful ear" [119]), her complete incomprehension of the meanings and consequences of consanguinity seals his commitment to and desire for her, thus sending him into an incestuous free-fall.

It is, however, not just Isabel who becomes the object of Pierre's desire, but it is Isabel's relation to the objects of her desire that Pierre desires. The incest taboo means nothing to her because the only distinction she is capable of making is a "general feeling of my humanness among the inhumanities" (123). From this perspective, any relation with a human being would be incestuous, which of course undercuts the *raison d'être* (exogamy) of the incest taboo, making incest itself what everyone does and therefore freeing Pierre from the constraints of the law against it. As much as Pierre wants Isabel, then, he also wants Isabel's relation to the terms that signify consanguinity. When she tells him in her narrative, "I called the woman mother" (123) and "the word father only seemed a word of general love and endearment to me . . . it did not seem to involve any claims of any sort, one way or the other" (145), she truly has no idea what kinds of claims or constraints are incumbent upon the person with whom one has that relation. To "seem not of woman born," to "never [have known] a mortal mother" (114), is the condition in which Isabel exists and to which Pierre aspires, because with it comes the inability to know the difference between virtue and vice, exogamy and endogamy.

But this knowledge, once possessed, cannot be forgotten, or in the language of the text, "disowned." "It is the law," Pierre solemnly tells

Isabel when she asks him to define virtue and vice. In response to her query, he claims that these words are meaningless, declaring them both to be "nothing" (274). Unable to dissolve the law, he instead chooses the dissolution of himself, Isabel, Lucy, and the world. Isabel will believe virtually anything Pierre tells her about these words, but rather than giving her his vision, he turns the world into a dream and words into meaningless "nothing[s]" (274). Pierre's opportunity to "gospelize the world anew" (273) has come and gone, in large measure because he has to turn the world into a dream to keep at bay the full import of having committed incest with the woman he believes is his sister. The law, however, with its "ink obliterable as the sea" (11) and its "wax ... inexorable [as] bars and bolts" (224) remains, refusing to be wiped out by Pierre's nihilism.

The tangibility of the law is confirmed by the fact that when Pierre visualizes Lucy's brother, Frederic, murdering him, he also visualizes "a jury hearing the case and declaring his innocence and Pierre's guilt: "if such a brother stab his foe at his own mother's table, all people and all juries would bear him out, accounting every thing allowable to a noble soul made mad by a sweet sister's shame caused by a damned seducer" (336). This passage is telling for several reasons, not least of which is that Pierre, "thoroughly alive to the supernaturalism of that mad frothing hate which a spirited brother forks forth at the insulter of a sister's honor," imagines the scenario as "if he were actually in the position which Frederic so vividly fancied to be his" (336). For a moment, the terms "brother and sister" have been stabilized by the law, giving Pierre a brief glimpse into the nature of his behavior, as it would be understood in court; but Pierre's imaginative appropriation of Frederic's position also begins to corrode the signifying coherence of those terms as the correspondences between Pierre and Frederic unfold and unravel. Pierre has earlier called Lucy "[his] sister" (29). Does Pierre now imagine Lucy to be his sister who must be defended against himself? And how might Isabel, his supposed sister/supposed wife fit into this domestic imaginary, especially when Pierre is his sister's "damned seducer"? If Pierre is at once himself and Frederic, at once seducer and defender of the seduced, the only option is that both die, which is exactly the conclusion Pierre reaches: "murder ... seemed the one only congenial sequel to such a desperate career" (337).

Living amongst three women who would die for him, Pierre feels himself to be in "utter isolation" (340), "utterly without sympathy from any thing divine, human, brute, or vegetable" (338). How is it that sympathy, the key affect of the sentimental novel, has no place in *Pierre*? At its most basic, sympathy in Melville's text demands the recognition of difference; more specifically the recognition that there are other people in the world not you is the precondition for sympathy. As the above example illustrates, Pierre is incapable of achieving even this most elementary step. Every aspect of the novel reveals itself to be incapable of recognizing, let alone sustaining what we might also call alterity, whether it be the narrative voice, the temporal frame, or the words on the page. The only principle the novel understands is consanguinity, which, interestingly enough, turns out to be the antithesis of sympathy. I find the novel's polarization of blood and sympathy to be fascinating because so many influential readers of the sentimental novel have insisted on its ideological limitations based on the notion that extensions of sympathy depend upon the twinned principles of identification and consanguinity. What *Pierre*, by negative example, reveals is that these sentimental novels succeed precisely because of their decoupling of sympathy and blood, sympathy and similarity. Sympathy flourishes in most sentimental texts not in spite of the fact that consanguinity is replaced by contract but because of that fact; because relations are determined not by descent but by consent. Pierre/*Pierre* escapes the "endless descendedness" (9) of its characters and its language by destroying himself/itself. Virtually everyone is dead, except for two characters whose fates are deemed narratively irrelevant given their lack of blood relation to the central characters and to each other. I am, of course, referring to Delly and Charlie Millthorpe, who possess the singular characteristic of being strangers in a book of "ineffable correlativeness" (85), and although both have rather skewed views of marriage – Delly being a fallen women, Charlie being a devoted bachelor – they survive, bearing with them the possibility of a sentimental novel to come.

Afterword

Like *Pierre, Pudd'nhead Wilson* imagines a world in which biological relations are created and uncreated through speech acts. Whereas Pierre and Isabel call each other brother and sister as well as husband and wife, thus performing incest linguistically if not literally, Roxy names her child her master, thereby relinquishing, albeit temporarily, her identity as mother and her child's as slave. She declares, as she switches her child, Valet de Chambre, with Judge Driscoll's child, Thomas à Becket Driscoll, "You's young Marse *Tom* fum dis out, en I got to practice and git used to 'memberin' to call you dat."[1] As critics have noted, Roxy's performative transformation of Chambers into her master, Tom, and herself as her child's mother into her child's slave imitates the rhetorical operations of slavery. Just as the laws of slavery deem the children of white fathers and black mothers slaves, and translate, "by a fiction of law and custom" (9), a person into a thing, Roxy mandates that Driscoll's son assume her son's fate, legally turning someone else, but a someone nevertheless, into a slave and a thing.

Pudd'nhead Wilson is an especially appropriate text with which to conclude my analysis of family, kinship, and sympathy.[2] Not only does Twain's novel explore the potential fate of sympathy in a world governed by slavery and its poisonous commodification of the slave mother/child bond, but Roxy's profoundly desperate tale of maternal strength, impotence, and defeat has very specific connections with many of the novels I have already discussed. First, there is, as has already been suggested, the problem of what a character's name is (or isn't) and the connected issue of what that character's identity might be. Second is Twain's self-conscious deployment of irony as an element in his critique of slavery. Third is the familiar theme of adoption, whether it be the narrator's assessment of Tom as "one of these late-adopted darlings" (93), or Twain's description of himself in "A Whisper to the Reader" as writing *Pudd'nhead Wilson* amidst "busts of Cerretani senators and other grandees of this line... mutely asking me to adopt them into my family, which I do with pleasure" (2).

Roxy's renunciation of her biological son releases him from the bonds of slavery in a desperate act that repeats Twain's exchange of his "remotest ancestors" for "these robed and stately antiques" (2), but without the comedy. Indeed, Roxy's switch, unlike Twain's, has many consequences, including the fact that Tom is eventually adopted by the Judge. That Roxy, in effect, adopts Chambers (he becomes her son) in the moment of the switch is a narrative strand that isn't pursued. The fact that it isn't is crucial to the workings of the novel. Let us recall that in the sentimental fictions we've discussed, adoption represents an alternate and, oftentimes, a superior model of family making. It is both an expression of sympathy and an extension of family, based not on biology but on affection. But all affection in *Pudd'nhead Wilson* goes the way of Tom, which is to say that it gets "sold . . . down the river" (115).

The perpetual questioning of the relation between naming and identity, a topic in virtually every novel considered thus far, takes on particular force in *Pudd'nhead Wilson*, with its unrelenting inquiry into how the logic of slavery forms and deforms identity. Two things make this quandary about names even more complicated, insofar as the act of telling the story is concerned. First, as with *Ida May*, the narrator never fully accepts the narrative consequences of Roxy's exchange, and second, Roxy revokes that exchange, at least in private, telling Valet de Chambers (in this passage spelled Vallet de Chambers), "You can't call me *Roxy* . . . You'll call me Ma or mammy, dat's what you'll call me" (42). What to call people is a deeply vexed issue, and it is one that frames both the beginning and the ending of the novel. "Within a week [Mr. David Wilson] had lost his first name; Pudd'nhead took its place" (6). The children of Dawson's Landing tell Tom that they "meant to call Chambers by a new name . . . 'Tom Driscoll's Nigger-pappy' to signify that he had had a second birth into this life, and that Chambers was the author of his new being" (21). At the conclusion, Tom and Chambers lose their names as Pudd'nhead declares, "we will call the children A and B" (110).

Although the narrator concedes that "this history must henceforth accommodate itself to the change which Roxana has consummated, and call the real heir 'Chambers' and the usurping little slave 'Thomas à Becket'" (17), the accommodation remains incomplete. The narrator vacillates between observing the fictional consequences of the switch (that is, calling Chambers Tom and Tom Chambers) and foregrounding the fictional consequences of the fact of the switch. Thus, the narrator begins a conversation between Roxy and "the ostensible 'Chambers'" (34) by calling attention to the fictionality of the relationship that is enunciated in their exchange. The subject is Tom's gambling debts and his dependence upon the Judge's money. Roxy asks, "Chambers, you's a jokin' ain't you?" to which he replies, "I ain't, mammy" (34). So far, their designations for each other are stable insofar as the fictional terms of their relationship are being observed by both (of course, Chambers doesn't know that Roxy is not his biological mother). This stability begins to falter, however, when Roxy accuses Chambers of being "an imitation nigger," to which he replies, "if I's imitation, what is you?" (35). Of course, "an imitation" is precisely what Chambers is by virtue of Roxy's act, which has in turn made her an imitation mother. Their language, however, becomes even more unhinged when Chambers questions Roxy's interest in Tom's fate, and she replies, "Was I his mother tell he was fifteen years old, or wusn't I? – you answer me dat" (36). This question signifies powerfully. Roxy is and isn't Tom's mother, just as she is and isn't Chambers's. In the "fiction created by herself, [Tom] was become her master" and "in her worship of him she forgot who she was and what he had been" (19). To ask Chambers, then, whether or not she is Tom's mother is to disclose the truth and fictitiousness of her identity (and his) at the same time as it is to conceal it. That Chambers doesn't answer should come as no surprise.

This same structure of disclosure and concealment takes place in the narrative voice. Prior to Roxy's meeting with Tom, in which she tells him "you hadn't no mother but me in de whole worl'" (39), Chambers is treated to a sampling of Tom's wrath. We find Tom "severe[ly] gaz[ing] upon the fair face of the young fellow whose name he was unconsciously using and whose family rights he was enjoying" (36). The narrator proceeds by describing a series of brutal kicks delivered by Tom, "the last one help[ing] the pure-white slave over the door-sill" (36). After reminding the reader, yet again, that Chambers is a white slave and Tom is a usurper, the narrator introduces Roxy in the following way: "Tom's mother entered, now, closing the door behind her" (36). "Tom's mother," as simple a phrase as it is, should give us pause because it accommodates at the same time as it doesn't. In other words, it names the characters using two different and competing modes of identification. Tom is Tom according to the fiction that Roxy has created, but according to that same fiction Roxy is not his mother; she is, as she calls herself, his "ole nigger mammy" (36, 37) – a phrase that both reveals and conceals the truth. In contrast to the phrase "nigger mammy," the term "mother," first used by the narrator and then assumed by Roxy, leaves no room for ambiguity, nor does the word son which she uses as a kind of biological weapon when she tells Tom, "you's my *son*" (41).

My point is that this narrator is very much like Roxy, who is very much like the narrators in *Pierre* and *Ida May* in their inability to "keep her [or his] distance and remember who she [or he] was" (21). Try as they might, they can't quite accommodate. Thus, the narrator of *Pudd'nhead Wilson* (inconsistently) reverts to the use of quotation marks in order to clarify who's who: " 'Chambers' came humbly in to say that breakfast was nearly ready. 'Tom' blushed scarlet to see this aristocratic white youth cringe to him" (44). Sometimes the narrative records Roxy talking to Tom, referring to him as Chambers, and then the narrator calls him Tom (42). Sometimes Tom is designated as Tom, other times as the Judge's "ostensible nephew" (67). Accommodation, in instances like this, calls attention to itself as accommodation, which has, of course, the effect of being anything but accommodating. The words on the page that designate who is talking to whom reveal that two stories are being told at once: "Now, den, Chambers, we's gwyne to talk business," and the narrator comments, "But Tom had only six dollars in the world." Roxy then asks, "Chambers, how much is you in debt?" and the narrator observes, "Tom shuddered" (42). The names dizzyingly shuttle us back and forth between Roxy's renunciation of her fiction and the narrator's continuation of it. The nominative confusion continues up to the famously devastating ending of the novel in which the narrator writes, "everybody granted that if 'Tom' were white and free it would be unquestionably right to punish him . . . but to shut up a valuable slave for life – that was quite another matter. As soon as the Governor understood the case, he pardoned Tom at once, and the creditors sold him down the river" (115). The quotation marks which had once functioned to separate the false Tom from the true Tom now do no such thing as "Tom" and Tom are the same. Although Twain hypothesizes that he has solved his authorial problem of "tell[ing] two stories at the same time" (170), by separating out the story about slavery from the story of Luigi and Angelo, clearly, the opposite is true. "Roxana's Plot," to use Carolyn Porter's phrase, itself produces two stories – neither of which can be told with or without the other, the combined effect of which is to unravel the narrative from within.[3]

In countering one fiction (the fiction that makes biology mean freedom or slavery) with another one of her own making (the fiction that makes Chambers Tom and Tom Chambers), Roxy attempts to outwit the system of slavery. Her scheme fails for several reasons, not least of which is that she reproduces all of the evils of that system; only in her version her son is master and she is his slave. That the text has a great deal of trouble accommodating itself to Roxy's act of (re)nomination can be read in the following ways: as Twain's unwillingness to sanction Roxy's fictionalization of biological identity and therefore his problematic insistence on the racial identities of the two boys, and/or as his insistence that slavery is a fiction that arbitrarily defines one category of racial identity as free and another as slave.[4] Rather than seeing these positions as mutually exclusive, I want to suggest that in not fully accommodating Roxy's plot, Twain is not exposing an essentialism regarding race so much as he is revealing his commitment to maternity as biologically understood. Roxy's plot ultimately fails not because one can't be an "imitation nigger," but because Roxy can't be an imitation mother or an adoptive one. Twain, in other words, makes his argument about the social constructedness of racial identity by biologizing maternal identity.

As hard as Twain works to represent Roxy's alienation from her bio-logical son, the fact that the narrative tells us virtually nothing about her relationship with Chambers, the child who "by the fiction created by herself" (19) is supposed to be her son, speaks volumes. Although she practices how to be a slave to Tom until she becomes "the dupe of her own deceptions" and "[forgets] who she was and what he had been" (19), she neither practices how to be a mother to Chambers nor, presumably, does she forget that he isn't her child. It is clear, in the few exchanges between Roxy and Chambers, that although "Roxy was a doting fool of a mother" (19) with regard to Tom, Chambers receives no doting at all, only "motherly curtness of speech and peremptoriness of manner" (16). Roxy cannot perform maternity, and Twain won't make her or, more import-antly, won't allow her to do so. Upon her return from St. Louis, after being gone for two years, we see nothing of her reunion with Chambers. She calls him "honey" (35) and he calls her "mammy" (34), but that's as far as the narrative will go. It can't go any further, given Twain's indictment of slavery. To imagine a loving relationship between Roxy and Chambers is to leave open the possibility that affections might flourish within the institution of slavery. Twain can't even allow a loving relationship to be performed because, according to the logic of the novel, the performance or imitation of love would be no different from the real thing.[5] The social constructedness of race allows race to be imitated. Tom becomes a "nigger" (the quotation marks indicating the cultural determinants of the term) with the knowledge that Roxy is his mother. Roxy, though, can never be anything other than Tom's mother because if maternity becomes socially constructed too, Twain's critique of slavery loses its power. Unlike "nigger," motherhood is never in quotation marks.

Twain makes it clear that Pudd'nhead is completely unaware of any of these implications. When he declares, "Valet de Chambre, negro and slave – falsely called Thomas à Becket Driscoll" (112), he is oblivious to the fact that the conjunction "negro and slave" is as false an appellation as anything else. In a text saturated with irony, perhaps none is more devastating than the fact that Pudd'nhead comprehends his victory in court, in which his expertise in fingerprinting exposes the rightful identities of the "real heir" and the "false heir," as one that means that "his long fight against hard luck and prejudice was ended" (114). We have seen how effectively irony might be deployed, especially Stowe's, in the discursive battle against slavery. Twain explicitly considers the presence (or lack) of irony in the slaveholding community of Dawson's Landing. In contrast to Pudd'nhead's predilection for "ironical form," the narrator informs us that "irony was not for those people; their mental vision was not focussed for it" (25). Pudd'nhead's irony, however, a feature which initially distinguishes him from the dunderheads of Dawson's Landing, ultimately gets used against him as Twain reserves it for himself. In the concluding courtroom scene, when Pudd'nhead reveals Tom as Judge Driscoll's killer and the fact that Tom and Chambers have been switched at birth, we see that for all of Pudd'nhead's scientific acumen and dramatic bravado, he exposes himself as the pudd'nhead he really is: "for a purpose unknown to us, but probably a selfish one, somebody changed those children in the cradle" (112). In a textual moment, deeply resonant of Melville's "Benito Cereno" in which the legal depositions that follow Melville's story of slave mutiny say nothing about the horrors of slavery against which Babo and his cohorts were revolting, Delano-like, Pudd'nhead reveals his profound blindness – "for a purpose unknown to us" (112) – of the conditions against which Roxy's actions have to be understood.[6]

"The cradles were empty" (5) in the town of Dawson's Landing. York Driscoll and his wife "had no children," (4), York's widowed sister "also was childless" (4), Pembroke Howard was a "bachelor," and Percy Driscoll's wife, after having lost her children to a variety of diseases, gives birth to Thomas à Becket Driscoll. It is a town whose population grows, in large measure, by virtue of white slaveowners, like Colonel Cecil Burleigh Essex, who rape their slaves, like Roxy, who then give birth to children, such as Chambers. Sympathy, in Dawson's Landing, means that love across races can't exist because to concede that is to open up the possibility that sympathy and slavery aren't mutually exclusive. Sympathy, in this world, means selling your mother to Kentucky rather than to Arkansas. *Pudd'nhead Wilson* represents the perversion of the sentimental novels' dream of extending family and extending sympathy through the twin forces of adoption and affection.

Notes

INTRODUCTION

1 Harriet Beecher Stowe, *Uncle Tom's Cabin or, Life Among the Lowly* (New York: Penguin, 1981; orig. pub. 1852), 624. All further quotations from *Uncle Tom's Cabin* will be from this edition and will be incorporated into the text. Herman Melville, *Pierre, or The Ambiguities* (Evanston: Northwestern University Press, 1971; orig. pub. 1852), 338. All further quotations from *Pierre* will be from this edition and will be incorporated into the text.

2 My use of the plural, "sentimental fictions," is meant to call attention not only to the sheer number of novels that fall under the rubric of sentimental fiction, but to the distinctive and different contributions made by individual texts. This is not to say, however, that in the chapters that follow, I will not be developing general claims about the genre as a whole. My aim is to make those claims based on a broader sentimental archive than has been considered by many readers of this literature, but of course, sentimentality (and analyses of it) are not the exclusive province of nineteenth-century American literature. Julie Ellison, however, correctly notes that "scholarly work on sentiment has been a disproportionately American enterprise, carried out by American critics with reference to American literature" (*Cato's Tears and the Making of Anglo-American Emotion* [Chicago: University of Chicago Press, 1999], 7). Although *Family, Kinship, and Sympathy* participates in and uses as its point of departure this "American enterprise," in order to reconfigure some of its particular manifestations and fundamental assumptions as they apply to antebellum literature, my understanding of sentimental literature has benefited from critics working in other literary fields and periods, such as David Marshall, Fred Kaplan, and Catharine Gallagher.

3 Quoted in *The Portable Hawthorne*, ed. Malcolm Cowley (New York: Penguin, 1970), 685; Ann Douglas, *The Feminization of American Culture* (New York: Avon Books, 1977), 307; Lauren Berlant, "Poor Eliza," in *No More Separate Spheres!, American Literature* 70 (1998): 663; Laura Wexler, "Tender Violence: Literary Eavesdropping, Domestic Fiction, and Educational Reform," in *The Culture of Sentiment: Race, Gender, and Sentimentality in 19th-century America*, ed. Shirley Samuels (New York: Oxford University. Press, 1992), 15; Amy

Kaplan, "Manifest Domesticity," in *No More Separate Spheres!*, *American Literature* 70 (1998): 601; Michelle Burnham, *Captivity and Sentiment: Cultural Exchange in American Literature, 1682–1861* (Hanover: University Press of New England, 1997), 140–141.

4 Saidiya Hartman, *Scenes of Subjection: Terror, Slavery, and Self-Making in Nineteenth-Century America* (Oxford: Oxford University Press, 1997), 19; Elizabeth Barnes, *States of Sympathy: Seduction and Democracy in the American Novel* (New York: Columbia University Press, 1997), 7, 92; Karen Sanchez-Eppler, *Touching Liberty: Abolition, Feminism, and the Politics of the Body* (Berkeley: University of California Press, 1993), 48. This argument can also be found in other analyses of sentimental fictions. Amy Lang writes that "the literal appropriation of the labor of slaves . . . facilitates their literary appropriation by the white artist" ("Class and the Strategies of Sympathy" in *The Culture of Sentiment*, 138). A similar slippage from identification to appropriation occurs in Christopher Castiglia's analysis of Garrison's "sympathetic abolition" ("Abolition's Racial Interiors and the Making of White Civic Depth," *American Literary History* 14 [2002], 37) in which "identifications of sympathy" (34) and "the appropriation of another's suffering" (49) are indistinguishable.

5 The influence of Adam Smith and other writers of the Scottish Enlightenment upon American literature has been well documented by literary critics, including Perry Miller and Terence Martin, and, more recently, Lori Merish, Marianne Noble, Gregg Camfield, Gregg Crane, Elizabeth Barnes, and Christopher Castiglia. My point is not to gainsay this philosophical inheritance and its significance for sentimental fictions, but to question some of the conclusions that have been drawn about how these novels go about representing sympathy, in particular claims about the hegemonic structure and ideology of sympathy. First, I want to demonstrate that these fictions deploy sympathy strategically and differently, depending upon what cultural work the text is trying to accomplish, which is to say that these novels are not merely receptors, but re-makers, of this philosophical tradition. Second, the chapters that follow demonstrate how many of these texts understand sympathy as a process (as opposed to a state of reified consciousness) that vacillates between moments of identification and distantiation, and that struggles against appropriating the suffering of others even as it may do so. Third, my reading in and of sentimental fictions has persuaded me that the sympathy/rationality (or feeling/thought) binary is far less stable than previous discussions have allowed.

6 Mary Kelley, *Private Woman, Public Stage: Literary Domesticity in Nineteenth-Century America* (Oxford: Oxford University Press, 1984), 24. Also see Mary P. Ryan, *The Empire of the Mother: American Writing about Domesticity, 1830–1860* (New York: Harrington Park Press, 1985) for a broad discussion of sentimental fiction.

7 There are, of course, some exceptions. Russ Castronovo, in his analysis of plantation fictions, considers the works of Hentz and other novelists who wrote in response to *Uncle Tom's Cabin* and contends that "the peculiar hegemonic genius of plantation sentiment was not to discount but rather to

adopt African-American textuality" ("Incidents in the Life of a White Woman: Economies of Race and Gender in the Antebellum Nation," *American Literary History* 10 [1998]: 239–265). Although our interests overlap, Castronovo isolates plantation fiction from the larger category of sentimental novels whereas I read the two in relation to each other.

8 A handful of critics do examine the ideological effects and foundations of sentimental fictions through a discussion of literary form. Susan K. Harris's *19th-Century American Women's Novels: Interpretive Strategies* (Cambridge: Cambridge University Press, 1990) carefully analyzes the plots of sentimental fictions, arguing that "their cover stories of female dependence are radically undermined by their underplots, which suggest, at the very least, that women can learn how to achieve physical, emotional, and financial independence. These were forbidden grounds for midcentury women; upon them the novels' middle portions encroach" (21). G. M. Goshgarian's *To Kiss the Chastening Rod: Domestic Fiction and Sexual Ideology in the American Renaissance* (Ithaca: Cornell University Press, 1992) uses methods from deconstruction and psychoanalysis to make the case that "passionless woman was ruled by her ruling passion, domesticity by dark forces it could not domesticate; woman suffered the division imposed by the domesticators' dual mirror structure in the impossible hope of attaining a wholeness her subjective status put out of reach" (75). Also see Erica R. Bauermeister, "*The Lamplighter, The Wide, Wide World,* and *Hope Leslie:* Reconsidering the Recipes for Nineteenth-Century American Women's Novels" (*Legacy: A Journal of Nineteenth-Century American Women Writers* 8 [1991]: 17–28), in which she argues against criticism of sentimental fiction that has "perpetuated the notion of literary homogeneity" (17) by focusing specifically on the structural and ideological differences between novels by Cummins, Warner, and Sedgwick.

9 Jane Tompkins, *Sensational Designs: The Cultural Work of American Fiction, 1790–1860* (Oxford: Oxford University Press, 1985), 178; Philip Fisher, *Hard Facts: Setting and Form in the American Novel* (New York: Oxford University Press, 1985), 108; Nina Baym, *Woman's Fiction: A Guide to Novels by and about Women in America, 1820–1870* (Ithaca: Cornell University Press, 1978), 34.

10 Orlando Patterson, *Slavery and Social Death: A Comparative Study* (Cambridge, MA: Harvard University Press, 1982); Sanchez-Eppler, *Touching Liberty,* 87. Dana D. Nelson writes the following in *The Word in Black and White: Reading "Race" in American Literature, 1638–1867* (Oxford: Oxford University Press, 1993): "*Incidents* refigures the sympathetic model in a way that shows how *contextual* identities are" (142). Other readings of Jacobs that focus on her manipulation of sentimental conventions include Lori Merish's *Sentimental Materialism: Gender, Commodity Culture, and Nineteenth-Century American Literature* (Durham, NC: Duke University Press, 2000), esp. 191–216; Burnham, *Captivity and Sentiment,* esp. 147–169.

11 Julia Stern, "To Represent Afflicted Time: Mourning as Hagiography," *American Literary History* 5.2 (summer 1998): 378–388; Gillian Brown, *Domestic Individualism: Imagining Self in Nineteenth-Century America*

(Berkeley: University of California Press, 1990), 26; *Public Sentiments: Structures of Feeling in Nineteenth-Century American Literature* (Chapel Hill: University of North Carolina Press, 2001), 18; *Home Fronts: Domesticity and its Critics in the Antebellum United States* (Durham, NC: Duke University. Press, 1977), 4, 5. Also see Franny Nudelman, "'The Blood of Millions': John Brown's Body, Public Violence, and Political Community," *American Literary History* 13.4 (winter 2001) in which she argues that "Brown's martyrdom suggests the expansive tendency of sympathy" (642).

12 My use of the term "contract" will operate both literally and metaphorically, just as it often did, according to Michael Grossberg, during this period (*Governing the Hearth: Law and the Family in Nineteenth-Century America* [Chapel Hill: University of North Carolina Press, 1985]). He calls attention to "the broader use of contract as the central metaphor for social and economic relations in early nineteenth-century America ... Contract ideology stemmed from a worldview whose lode star was the untrammeled autonomy of the individual will" (19). Amy Dru Stanley contends that "in the age of slave emancipation contract became a dominant metaphor for social relations and the very symbol of freedom" (*From Bondage to Contract: Wage Labor, Marriage, and the Market in the Age of Slave Emancipation* [Cambridge: Cambridge University Press, 1998], x). Jamil Zanaildan similarly claims that "the parent–child correlation increasingly came to be viewed as an emotionally laden contractual relationship" ("The Emergence of a Modern American Family Law: Child Custody, Adoption, and the Courts, 1796–1851," *Northwestern University Law Review* 73 [1979], 1083). Stephen Presser hypothesizes that court opinions preserv[ing] the continuity of the patrimony in the blood line" may have been a judicial reaction "against the growing trend to think of the family in what might be called 'contractual' terms" ("The Historical Background of the American Law of Adoption," *Journal of Family Law* 1 [1971], 513; n. 276). On the pliability of the marriage contract during this period, see Hendrik Hartog, *Man and Wife in America: A History* (Cambridge, MA: Harvard University Press, 2000). Furthermore, I use the term "contract" rather than "consent," because so many sentimental fictions explore the reconfiguration of the family through the presence of material contracts, particularly adoption and marriage, or their absence in the case of slavery. For a related discussion of childhood and consent, see Gillian Brown, *The Consent of the Governed: The Lockean Legacy in Early American Culture* (Cambridge, MA: Harvard University Press, 2001).

13 Gregg Crane trenchantly makes this point: "Like any tool, contract, of itself, does nothing – it is a language of intent (promises, statements of capability and agency, actions and words betokening assent) that may be used by powerful parties to expand their fortunes at the expense of the weaker parties or may be used between equals to structure their relations as equitably as they deem possible" (*Race, Citizenship, and Law in American Literature* [Cambridge: Cambridge University Press, 2002], 190).

14 *Incidents in the Life of a Slave Girl* in *The Classic Slave Narratives*, ed. Henry Louis Gates (New York: Mentor, 1987), 343.

15 It will also become clear that Kemble and Stowe use elements of sentimental fictions in their non-fictional texts: Kemble presents herself very much as a sentimental heroine in *The Journal* and Stowe deploys sentimental devices familiar to the reader of *Uncle Tom's Cabin*.

I IN LOCO PARENTIS

1 The Reverend E. H. Chapin, "A Mother's Love," in *The Mother's Assistant and Young Lady's Friend*, ed. William C. Brown (Boston: William C. Brown, 1854), vol. VII (July 1845), 9.
2 Professor George Whipple, "Dangers of Childhood, and Means of Obviating Them," in ibid., vol. VI (January 1845), 27; Mrs. M. A. R. Sargent, "The Silent Ministry of Example," in ibid., vol. VI (March 1845), 5.
3 In fact, writers such as Lydia Sigourney and Harriet Beecher Stowe were often featured in the roster of contributors to *The Mother's Assistant, Graham's Magazine*, and *Godey's Lady's Book*. "The Silent Ministry of Example" 55; "Influence of Early Instruction," in *The Mother's Assistant and Young Lady's Friend*, vol. I (January 1841), 3; Lydia Sigourney, "The First Year of Infancy," in ibid., vol. I (December 1841), 270; "Home," in ibid., vol. II (September 1842), 226; Mrs. Helen C. Knight, "The Step-Mother. – Fear and Love," in ibid., vol. VI (June 1845), 128; Mrs. Lavinia Pillsbury, "Family Education," in ibid., vol. VI (April 1845), 74. On sympathy and the family, also see Mrs. John Farrar, *The Young Lady's Friend* (New York: Samuel S. and William Wood, 1841), esp. pp. 207–209, a section entitled "Sympathy with Parents," in which she seeks to ignite "a daughter's watchful sympathy by saying: let your feelings ... be ever on the alert to sympathize where you cannot relieve" (209).
4 Jacob Abbott, "The Power of Example," in ibid., vol. I (May 1841), 100; Mrs. Elizabeth H. M'Collom, "Mental Culture," in ibid., vol. VI (May 1845), 110; "Sympathy" in ibid., vol. I (August 1841), 189.
5 In describing Eoline's break with her father (her mother is dead), the narrator of *Eoline; or Magnolia Vale* (Philadelphia: T. B. Peterson, 1852; rept. American Fiction Reprint Series, 1971) writes, "she would have suffered rather than have asked any pecuniary favors after being discarded as a daughter" (32) and again uses the term "discarded daughter" (200) later in the text. Other discarded daughters include Anna McVernon's child in Harriet Stephens's *Hagar, the Martyr; or, Passion and Reality. A Tale of the North and South* (New York: W. P. Fetridge & Co., 1854; rept. in the Fisk University Library Negro Collection, 1972), who not only does not know her mother's name, but tells people, "I'm a secret" (235), 'Lena Rivers, and, of course, all of the slave daughters of slave masters discarded/sold by their fathers. The topic of unwanted children, and the abstinence required to prevent their birth, is discussed by Henry C. Wright, the closest thing to an antebellum marriage counselor, in *The Unwelcome Child; or, The Crime of an Undesigned and*

Undesired Maternity (Boston: Bela Marsh, 1858). Intended as a manual to prepare husbands and wives for "the pure joy of a longed-for maternity" (32), Wright's jeremiad against "*an undesigned and an undesired Maternity*" (15), in which "every stage of its foetal development is watched with a feeling of settled repugnance" (45), establishes the all too frequent inadequacies of a child's biological parentage and lays the groundwork for the necessity of substitute parents.

6 These quotations are taken from several of the novels I shall be discussing. Caroline Lee Hentz, *Marcus Warland; or, The Long Moss Spring. A Tale of the South* (Philadelphia: A. Hart, late Carey & Hart, 1852), 248; Mary Jane Holmes, *'Lena Rivers* (Michigan: Scholarly Press, 1970; orig. pub. 1856), 66; Maria Cummins, *The Lamplighter* (New Brunswick: Rutgers University Press, 1988; orig. pub. 1854), 198; E.D.E.N. Southworth, *Ishmael, or in the Depths* (New York: A. L. Burt Co. 1863), 12; Herman Melville, *Pierre, or the Ambiguities* (Evanston: Northwestern University Press, 1971; orig. pub. 1851), 311; Mrs. Hornblower, *Vara; or, The Child of Adoption* (New York: Robert Carter and Brothers, 1854), 68; Mary Jane Holmes, *Meadowbrook Farm* (Chicago: M. A. Donohue & Co., 1857), 64; Stephens, *Hagar, the Martyr*, 69.

7 These quotations are from the following novels: Susan Warner, *The Wide, Wide World* (New York: The Feminist Press, 1987; orig. pub. 1850), 510; *Pierre*, 87; Mary Hayden Green Pike, *Ida May; A Story of Things Actual and Possible* (Boston: Phillips, Sampson and Co., 1854), 212; Anna S. Stephens, *Myra: the Child of Adoption, a Romance of Real Life* (New York: Beadle and Company, 1860), 55; Maria J. McIntosh, *Two Pictures; or, What We Think of Ourselves, and What the World Thinks of Us* (New York: D. Appleton and Co., 1863), 213; Mary Jane Holmes, *Dora Deane or The East India Uncle* (Chicago: M. A. Donohue & Co., 1859), 156, Caroline Lee Hentz, *Ernest Linwood; a Novel* (Boston: John P. Jewett, 1856), 95.

8 These quotations are from the following: *Marcus Warland*, 278; *Ishmael, or in the Depths*, 156; *Ida May*, 200; *The Lamplighter*, 127; *Ernest Linwood*, 107.

9 Richard Brodhead, *Cultures of Letters: Scenes of Reading and Writing in Nineteenth-Century America* (Chicago: University of Chicago Press, 1993), 22, 27. Elizabeth Barnes maintains that sympathy is produced through a recognition of familiarity which then gets registered in the discourse of family: "while the family model challenges the assumption of human rights based on economic contribution, it intensifies the psychological link between humanity and homogeneity" (97). Like Brodhead, this analysis relies on a homogeneous and misleading notion of family – "the family model" – which sentimental fictions are exploring and, I believe, exploding. Barnes's monolithic family, in turn, produces a monolithic account of sympathy. For an examination of representations of family in eighteenth-century literature and culture, see Jay Fliegelman's *Prodigals and Pilgrims: The American Revolution against Patriarchal Authority, 1750–1800* (Cambridge: Cambridge University Press, 1982). The sentimental novels' investment in non-consanguineous family relations might be read as a nineteenth-century counterpart to (or result of) what Fliegelman describes in

the following: "The 'blind fondness' of natural children for their parents is the *habit* of nature; felt and reasoned affection, whether ultimately given to blood relations or nonconsanguineous loved ones, is the *will* of nature, its only will" (51). For a discussion of the changing complexion of family in the latter part of the nineteenth-century *vis à vis* the literature of that period, see June Howard's *Publishing the Family* (Durham, NC: Duke University Press, 2001).

10 For example, Mrs. Linwood says to Gabriella that she will be "cherish[ed] … as my own daughter" (223); Edith, Ernest's sister, tells Gabriella, "only make him happy, my own dear sister" (234); and Gabriella says about Mrs. Linwood, "had I been her own daughter she could not have lavished upon me more affectionate cares" (408).

11 On Nicholas Hentz's "intense, nervous, restless personality," see Mary Kelley, *Private Woman, Public Stage: Literary Domesticity in Nineteenth-Century America* (Oxford: Oxford University Press, 1984), 164–168, 222–232. She also convincingly makes the case that Gabriella's tumultuous relationship with Ernest was based on her own marriage to Nicholas.

12 It is highly unusual for a sentimental heroine to be married an entire year and not get pregnant. This fact, I think, symbolically stands for Ernest's unwillingness to share Gabriella with anyone else.

13 Harriet Beecher Stowe, *Uncle Tom's Cabin or, Life Among the Lowly* (New York: Penguin, 1981; orig. pub. 1852), 262. All further quotations from *Uncle Tom's Cabin* will be from this edition and will be incorporated into the text.

14 We see that Topsy is (re)born in the course of the narrative through Eva's love, with Ophelia as the mother. After Eva's death, Topsy says, "I jist wish I hadn't never been born," (431), and Ophelia responds, "I can love you; I do, and I'll try to help you to grow up a good Christian girl" (432).

15 One of the best readings of Stowe's imbrication in the racial politics of the antebellum period, and her progressive position within that historical context, is Arthur Riss's, "Racial Essentialism and Family Values in *Uncle Tom's Cabin*," *American Quarterly* 46 (December 1994): 513–544. Riss persuasively makes the seemingly counter-intuitive argument that "Stowe's commitment to racial difference is precisely what enables her denunciation of slavery" (514).

16 George Fitzhugh, *Cannibals All! or, Slaves without Masters*, ed. C. Vann Woodward (Cambridge, MA: Harvard Univ. Press, 1960; orig. pub. 1857), 69; Louis McCord, "Negro and White Slavery," *Southern Quarterly Review* 20 (1851), 123. Riss puts the point nicely: "The kinship of the plantation is familial but not necessarily consanguineous, sociological rather than inevitably genealogical" (529).

17 Caroline Lee Hentz, *Rena; or, the Snow Bird. A Tale of Real Life* (Philadelphia: T. B. Peterson and Brothers, 1851), 210. All further quotations from *Rena* will be from this edition and will be incorporated into the text.

18 Mary Jane Holmes, *Ethelyn's Mistake* (Rahway: The Mershon Company, n.d.; orig. pub. 1869, 2. All further quotations from *Ethelyn's Mistake* will be incorporated into the text.

19 Holmes's *Meadowbrook Farm* (1857) is one of the few exceptions to this generic rule in that the heroine's parents actually survive well into the 300- page novel

(the dad dies on page 175, the mother survives). The novel, though, has a great deal of trouble getting started and continuing and only does so by separating Rosa from her parents whenever she threatens to come home. Maria Jane McIntosh's *Conquest and Self-Conquest* (1843) is another exception, but, perhaps, even more unusual because, although Frederick Stanley is separated from his parents by his decision to join the navy (the plot follows the rather mild tribulations that result from this choice), Captain and Mrs. Stanley survive the entire novel.

20 Leo Tolstoy, *Anna Karenina* (New York: Modern Library classics, 2000; orig. pub. 1877), 24.

21 Quoted in Mary P. Ryan, *The Empire of the Mother: American Writing about Domesticity, 1830–1860* (New York: Harrington Park Press, 1985), 101.

22 See Catherine M. Scholten, *Childbearing in American Society: 1650–1850* (New York: New York University Press, 1985), who takes these statistics from a supplementary chapter written by "a physician of New York" to Louisa M. Barwell's *Infant Treatment: With Directions to Mothers for Self-Management Before, During, and After Pregnancy.* "Statistics showed an average mortality rate of 43% under five years . . . the ratio higher in New York (50% in 1840), Philadelphia (51% in 1839), and in southern cities of Charleston, Savannah, Mobile, New Orleans 'even greater' " (130).

23 Herman Melville, *Billy Budd, Sailor* (New York: Penguin, 1986; orig. pub. 1891), 381.

24 Mary Jane Holmes, *'Lena Rivers* (New York: G. W. Dillingham Co., 1970; orig. pub. 1856), 18. All further quotations from *'Lena Rivers* will be from this edition and will be incorporated into the text.

25 This is also the case in Holmes's *Hugh Worthington. A Novel* (New York: Carleton, 1865) in which the four main female characters are named Adah (who also goes by Lily, Matilda, Adah Murdoch, Adah Hastings, Adah Gordon, and soon to be Adah Stanley), Adaline, Anna, and Alice. Alice's identity remains a secret for some time because one of the slaves in the novel calls her "Miss Ellis," in addition to which one of the evil characters has two names, George Hastings and Dr. Richards – so as to avoid the consequences of an ill-advised first marriage. Names in *Hugh Worthington* are, like those in *'Lena Rivers*, mantra-like: "Whom had he known by that name, or where had he heard it before? 'Mrs. Worthington, Mrs. Worthington,' he repeated" (76).

26 Unfortunately, little is known about Holmes's politics, especially regarding the issue of slavery. She lived in Kentucky for a few years, but most of her life was spent in Massachusetts and New York, where at the age of sixty-eight, she founded a temperance society (Kelley, *Private Woman*, 207).

27 Harry's plight is slightly more complicated than this suggests. Having secretly married Helena under the assumed name of Harry Rivers and having never revealed his true identity, he is suddenly compelled to leave her in order to care for his ailing father. He writes to Helena Rivers at their home, but not only has she has moved back home with her parents, the Nicholses, but no one by the name of Helena Rivers exists. At the same time as his letters never reach their

proper destination, he receives a letter informing him that his wife and child have died, which of course is only partly true. This makes him vulnerable to the machinations of the widower Lady Bellmont, the wealthy woman his father had wanted him to marry all along, and he becomes her husband and the father of her child, Durward Bellmont, who will eventually become 'Lena's husband.

28 In this regard, Southworth's *Ishmael, or in the Depths* is very similar to *'Lena Rivers*, although the gender of the protagonists plays a significant role in differentiating their stories. Just as the search for 'Lena's last name drives the plot, so too Ishmael has his mother's last name owing to a secret marriage, and the identity of his father must be discovered in order for the son not to be considered a bastard, for him to receive his rightful last name, and for his mother's reputation to be cleared. Southworth writes, "He had no legal name ... The human law denied him a name; the Christian law offered him one" (156). Ishmael's reputation is, however, unlike 'Lena's in that it is not in constant jeopardy. Although the behavior of both is subject to relentless scrutiny and constant innuendo (a theme taken up in D. W. Goshgarian's *To Kiss the Chastening Rod: Domestic Fiction and Sexual Ideology in the American Renaissance* [Ithaca: Cornell University Press, 1992]), Ishmael is better able to combat his enemies, in large part because he has the opportunity (both made and given) to become a lawyer and, thus, to demonstrate his intelligence and integrity. 'Lena has no such luck. Nor does she have the good fortune of having a mother whose last name was Worth.

29 For a fascinating account of marriage as an institution in transition during the antebellum period, see Hendrik Hartog's *Man and Wife in America: A History* (Cambridge, MA: Harvard University Press, 2000). He writes of the mobility of American men and its effects on marriage: "Husbands changed their minds about returning to their marriages; they found new loves; they 'remarried' in new jurisdictions; they never came back ... Who was legally married, who was not, was often uncertain, particularly across the vast reaches of an American continent" (23). Interestingly, several of Hartog's legal anecdotes overlap with the plots of sentimental novels. About separation, for example, he writes: "One might begin with the search for work, for land, for gold, for economic security ... Often couples who separated with the expectation that they would soon reunite, didn't. They fell out of love, found others to love, found that life was better alone or as part of a different community" (30). Also see Nancy F. Cott's *Public Vows: A History of Marriage and the Nation* (Cambridge, MA: Harvard University Press, 2000).

30 My book is deeply indebted to Nina Baym's *Woman's Fiction: A Guide to Novels by and About Women in America, 1820–1870* (Ithaca: Cornell University Press, 1978). In it, she writes of "the abusers of power [who] run a gamut from fathers and mothers to step-parents, aunts, uncles, grandparents, guardians, and matrons of orphanages. They are the administrators or owners of the space within which the child is legally constrained. Least guilty are the mothers; often it is the loss of the mother that initiates the heroine's woes, and the memory of her mother that permits her to endure them" (37). My goal, as

stated in the introduction, is to show that the cultural work of these "owners of the [child's] space" bears different meanings, depending upon whether the specific context is adoption law, southern slavery, or domestic reform.

31 M. J. McIntosh's *Violet; or, the Cross and the Crown* (Boston: John P. Jewett, 1856) confronts this very issue. The protagonist, Violet, survives a shipwreck and is orphaned, or so it seems. She is saved by the greedy, uncouth, and abusive Katy and Dick Van Dyke, who declare, "it's ourn" (14), and the narrator describes this claim as an "appropriation of the child" (14). She is then rescued from the Van Dyke household by the wealthy Captain Ross, who turns out to be her biological father, a fact known only to the Van Dykes, and they selfishly conceal it until, through a set of extreme circumstances, the secret is divulged. Violet quickly becomes the "adopted child" (142) of Papa Ross, the designation she uses when referring to him (Van Dyke having the claim to the title of father). Interestingly, McIntosh denounces both sides – the Van Dykes, most obviously, because they are pretending to have a biological claim to the child whom they have adopted, and Captain Ross, because even though he doesn't know Violet is his biological daughter, he does everything within his power to make his adoptive claims supersede those of her allegedly biological parents. That Mr. Merton, the trusted pastor in the novel, expresses "opposition to the adoption" (218) is the best evidence that Captain Ross's actions are wrong.

32 Harriet Beecher Stowe's *The Pearl of Orr's Island: A Story of the Coast of Maine* (Boston: Houghton Mifflin, 2001; orig. pub. 1862) 65, 82. Hagar's story is particularly interesting because although Chapter 1 seems to depict the scene of Hagar's mother's death, it turns out that her mother isn't the dying woman, but rather her aunt (and adopted mother). The remainder of the novel is, in large measure, a search for her mother which turns up some surprising suspects, including her uncle's slave, Minnie. Minnie is not Hagar's mother, although the shadow of miscegenation lingers upon Hagar until the final pages of the novel, when her biological mother reappears, claims her as "my own, own child!" (340–341), and "but a few months after establishing the birth of her child" (359) dies. As evident from my discussion thus far, adoption also plays an important part in *Vara; or, The Child of Adoption, Myra: The Child of Adoption,* Mary Jane Holmes's *Mildred, The Child of Adoption* (New York: A. L. Burt Co., n.d.), *Ernest Linwood, Violet; or, The Cross and the Crown,* and *Ishmael, or in the Depths.* Also see Alice Carey's novella, "The Adopted Daughter," in *The Adopted Daughter and Other Tales* (Philadelphia: J. B. Smith, 1860) and Mrs. Sarah Elizabeth Monmouth's *The Adopted Daughter; or, the Trials of Sabra: A Tale of Real Life* (Montreal: John Lovell, 1873; 4th edition; orig. pub. 1858). These last two texts call attention to the fact that not all members of the adoptive family treat the adopted daughter as a beloved member of their own family. Carey's Jenny, for example, laments, "They have pretended to adopted me as a child . . . that they may appear liberal in the eyes of the world; but I am, as you see, an underling and a drudge" (32). Similarly, one of Sabra's adoptive brothers reveals her status as an adopted daughter when he is angry with her (179).

33 Nehemiah Adams, *The Sable Cloud: A Southern Tale, with Northern Comments* (Westport: Negroes University Press, 1970; orig. pub. 1861), 126. All further quotations from the novel will be from this edition and will be incorporated into the text.

34 Unfortunately, there is very little information about adoption, let alone transracial adoption, in the south. Grossberg, *Governing the Hearth*, writes that "even the civil-law states Louisiana and Texas exhibited an animus against adoption" (270), and the former completely abolished the practice in 1825.

35 Adams is acutely aware of Stowe's influence as evidenced not only by the fact that he wrote *A South-Side View of Slavery* (Boston: Ticknor and Fields, 1860), his full-length reply to *Uncle Tom's Cabin*, but by his constant allusions and dismissals of Stowe in *The Sable Cloud*. Whenever Mr. North begins to feel his anti-slavery convictions slipping away, Adams has him invoke Stowe, in one case "the opening scene of 'Uncle Tom's Cabin'" (21) in order to raise his passions and deny the rational asseverations of Mr. C. Elsewhere, Mr. C. offers a reading of *Uncle Tom's Cabin* that supports slavery. He argues that Uncle Tom's religiosity is solely a function of his life in slavery and goes so far as to propose the notion that "SLAVERY MADE UNCLE TOM" (135). The pliability of the slave, in contrast to the durability of white manhood, is duly noted in this quotation: "Legree would be Legree in Wall Street, or Fifth Avenue; Uncle Tom would not be Uncle Tom in the wilds of Africa" (136).

36 This is, after all, a romance. The best account of adoption in the south is Peter Bardaglio, *Reconstructing the Household: Families, Sex, and the Law in the Nineteenth-Century South* (Chapel Hill: University of North Carolina Press, 1995), which suggests that adoption law proliferated in the postbellum period (as opposed to the north which saw the development of domestic relations law in the antebellum period): "in short, when evaluating the rights of adoptive parents, southern courts remained committed for the most part to a narrow construction of adoption statutes. But toward the end of the nineteenth century the courts also became recognizably more sensitive to the welfare of the child" (169–170). Although Bardaglio does not explicitly connect this seeming reluctance to accommodate adoption with the institution of slavery, it is hard to imagine how a culture defined by consanguinity (the child shall follow the condition of the mother) could easily embrace a reconstitution of the family based on affection, which is what adoption implies.

37 Lydia Maria Child, *A Romance of the Republic*, ed. Dana D. Nelson (Lexington: University of Kentucky Press, 1997; orig. pub. 1867) 40, 150, 244, 354, 416. All further quotations from the novel will be from this edition and will be incorporated into the text.

38 Mrs. Delano's connection to Flora might usefully be compared to Ophelia's relation with Topsy as one means of distinguishing between Stowe's novel and Child's. After Eva's death, for example, Ophelia tells Augustine, "I want her [Topsy] to be mine legally" (445). Unlike Mrs. Delano, who adopts Flora as a way of beginning the process of setting her free, Ophelia buys Topsy. This is important because in purchasing Topsy, rather than adopting her, Stowe

consistently drives home the point that adoptive mothers can't take the place of the slaves' biological mother. In contrast to Flora, who is constantly referring to Mrs. Delano as her mother (and happily so), Topsy will never confuse Ophelia with a biological mother.

2 "A SORT OF ADOPTED DAUGHTER": FAMILY RELATIONS IN *THE LAMPLIGHTER*

1 Maria Cummins, *The Lamplighter*, ed. Nina Baym (New Brunswick: Rutgers University Press, 1988), 38, 58. All further quotations from *The Lamplighter* will be from this edition and will be incorporated in the text.
2 Michael Grossberg, *Governing the Hearth: Law and the Family in Nineteenth-Century America* (Chapel Hill: University of North Carolina Press, 1985), xi.
3 June Howard, "What is Sentimentalism?" *American Literary History* 11:1 (spring 1999), 63; Amy Kaplan, "Manifest Domesticity," in *No More Separate Spheres!*, *American Literature* 70 (1998), 599.
4 Amy Schrager Lang, "Class and the Strategies of Sentiment," in *The Culture of Sentiment: Race, Gender, and Sentimentality in Nineteenth-Century America*, ed. Shirley Samuels (Oxford: Oxford University Press, 1992), 131. Gerty is no slave, though, and as much as the abuse heaped upon her by Nan Grant may look like slavery, the fact that the child is not owned by Nan marks a crucial difference between the arrangements of Gerty and those of a slave. Gerty chooses and slaves don't. Her narrative of legal self-possession and the possession of her sympathy depends, in other words, upon the fact that she is not a slave. The coalescence of sentimental novels and slave narratives is the subject of Chapters 3, 4, and 5. It is also important to distinguish Gerty from her sentimental predecessor, Ellen Montgomery of *The Wide, Wide World*, whose life experiences, according to Jane Tompkins, require "an extinction of her personality so complete that there is literally nothing of herself that she can call her own" (*Sensational Designs: The Cultural Work of American Fiction, 1790–1860* [Oxford: Oxford University Press, 1985], 179). In sympathizing with Ellen, the reader is meant to learn the folly of self-reliance and the necessity of religious belief. Gerty's education is, of course, fundamentally Christian as well, but the model of sympathy Cummins advances is not one of self-abnegation but rather self-possession. Domestic self-possession has been convincingly linked to the workings of the marketplace by Gillian Brown, who reads "the logic of sympathetic proprietorship [in *Uncle Tom's Cabin*] . . . as symptomatic of a problem within possessive individualism; the problem being that such proprietorship, while domesticating the experience of ownership, is nevertheless fundamentally invested in the practice of ownership – and therefore reproduces the structure and ideology of slavery (*Domestic Individualism: Imagining Self in Nineteenth-Century America* [Berkeley: University of California Press, 1990], 41). Sympathetic proprietorship represents Stowe's well-intentioned but doomed effort to challenge a system in which "human beings are treated as transferable,

as commodities" (41). *The Lamplighter*, on the contrary, doesn't have a problem with this transferability. Gerty's adoptions, in fact, are based on the benefits gained by transferability. It is the source of her sympathy and the foundation for her eventual self-possession. In other words, not being possessed (biologically) doesn't mean being a possession, or a slave. In a suggestive reading of the plantation novel, Russ Castronovo argues that "adoption is the patriarchal act par excellence" ("Incidents in the Life of a White Woman: Economies of Race and Gender in the Antebellum Nation," *American Literary History* 10 [1998], 247). By contrast, adoption in the world of *The Lamplighter* works to undermine patriarchy by disarticulating authority from its biological bonds.

5 Quoted in Morton Horowitz, *The Transformation of American Law, 1780–1860* (Cambridge, MA: Harvard University Press, 1977), 185.

6 The idea of contract, as legal historians have demonstrated, helped to reorganize the family (see my introduction, n. 12, p. 194 below). Interestingly, it is the relative absence of material contracts (except in the case of Miss Patty Pace's will, which I discuss at the end of this chapter) and the presence of metaphorical ones, and the no less real obligations inherent in the latter, that best describes the project of family formation in Cummins's novel. On the role of contract in late nineteenth-century law and realist literature, see Irene Tucker's fine discussion of Henry James's *What Maisie Knew* in the context of the nineteenth-century "model of contractual obligation" (*A Probable State: The Novel, the Contract, and the Jews* [Chicago: University of Chicago Press, 2000], 133), and Brook Thomas's analysis in which he registers "the persistence of status in a world claiming to be ruled by contract" (*American Literary Realism and the Failed Promise of Contract* [Berkeley: University of California Press, 1997], 3). The ambiguous relation between status v. contract is also present in *The Lamplighter*, but we might think of the problem as the persistence of contract in a world claiming to be ruled by status. For an analysis of these issues (the family, the marriage contract, and the significance of acquiring names) as they operate in early twentieth-century literature, see Walter Benn Michaels's "The Contracted Heart," *New Literary History* 21 (1990): 495–531. On the importance of names in antebellum fiction, see Wai Chee Dimock's reading of *The Deerslayer* in which proper names "figure, above all, as signs, signs of something gone awry and of an ensuing sequence of retribution" (*Residues of Justice: Literature, Law, Philosophy* [Berkeley: University of California Press, 1996], 37). Although Dimock's reading of the law is meant to focus on the "self-imposed singularity of reference in criminal law" (25), her analysis gestures toward a more abstract account of the relation between law and literature: "The law was spatialized in the nineteenth century; it had a specific locale and a specific set of boundaries. Henceforth its sphere of operation was to be narrow, precise, sharply delimited" (23). In correcting new historical analyses which read the novel as the apotheosis of disciplinary regimes, Dimock emphasizes the novel's "allusive, elastic, circuitous" (24) qualities. As a consequence, the law assumes literature's disciplinary function, and its discursive capability becomes "narrow, precise, sharply delimited." My reading of antebellum domestic

relations law suggests that, like the novel, the law's significations can be "allusive, elastic, circuitous."

7 William Whitmore makes this point in his analysis of Massachusetts adoption law: "The statutes generally seem to be silent as to the transfer of an adopted child to a second adopter. It may be inferred that as the general rule is to place an adopted child in the position of one lawfully born to the adopter, the new parent may dispose of this child to a second adopting parent, and so indefinitely. Whenever the law prescribes that the lawful parent, by consenting to the act of adoption, severs all his previous natural relations with it, a second adoption would be an easy method of terminating his responsibilities" (*The Law of Adoption in the United States, and Especially in Massachusetts* [Albany: Joel Munsell, 1876], 76). Far from being worried about the possibility of endless adoptions, *The Lamplighter* celebrates it.

8 Ibid., 2–3. It is also worth noting that the adoption law of 1851 was passed in conjunction with another law that sought to simplify the procedure whereby one's name was changed. An editorial in the *Boston Daily Advertiser* noted: "As usual, the names of a large number of persons have been changed by acts of the legislature, but a law has been passed by which persons may hereinafter have their names changed by authority of the judges of probate without the necessity of application to the legislature" (quoted in Jamil Zanaildan, "The Emergence of a Modern American Family Law: Child Custody, Adoption, and the Courts, 1796–1851," *Northwestern University Law Review* 73 (1979): 1044). Stephen B. Presser, "The Historical Background of the American Law of Adoption," *Journal of Family Law* 1 (1971), goes so far as to hypothesize that "the men in Massachusetts might not have thought of adoption as much more than a change of name for the adopted child" (471). Also see Presser and Grossberg, *Governing the Health*, for an analysis of antebellum adoption laws in Massachusetts and elsewhere.

9 Whitmore, *The Law of Adoption*, 3.

10 Grossberg, *Governing the Hearth*, 273.

11 Lewis Hochheimer, *A Treatise on the Law Relating to the Custody of Infants* (Baltimore: John Murphy, 1887), 11. This murky state of affairs is also evident in the legal writings of Joel Bishop, whose chapter "Custody of Children" begins with the following series of pronouncements and hesitations: "At common law the father is, in some sense, the guardian of his children, though in precisely what sense, the books do not seem perfectly to agree." If fathers are "in some sense" guardians (mothers, according to common law, become guardians when fathers die), then how is one to distinguish between the sense in which a biological parent is a guardian and a third party, appointed either by the court or parent, is a guardian? The term guardianship, like adoption, is ambiguous right from the start in that it can apply to any person, biological parent or not, "entrusted by law with the interests of another, whose youth [and] inexperience . . . disqualify him from acting for himself in the ordinary affairs of life" (*Commentaries on the Law of Marriage and Divorce* [Boston: Little Brown, 1852]), 5. Hochheimer suggests that the fundamental difference

between "mere guardian[ship]" (11) and parenthood is "the presumption that the promptings of natural affection are the strongest guarantee of the proper fulfillment of their [the parents'] charge" (12). The "natural affection" of a parent, however, wasn't always the "strongest guarantee" that the child's best interests were being served.

12 *Commonwealth* v. *Hamilton*, 6 Mass. 273 (1810), 274.

13 *Commonwealth* v. *Hammond*, 10 Pick 274 (Mass. 1830), 274.

14 *Mercein* v. *People ex. rel. Barry*, 25 Wend. 65 (N.Y. 1840), 70, 80. For a related reading of this case, see Chapter 7, "John Barry and American Fatherhood," in Hendrik Hartog, *Man and Wife in America: A History* (Cambridge, MA: Harvard University Press, 2000), 193–217. It should be noted that the paramount right of the father to custody of the children was almost always invoked as a feature of Common Law, even when judges went on to award custody to the mother. See *State* v. *Smith*, 6 Me. 462 (1830), *Commonwealth* v. *Maxwell*, 6 Mon. L. Rep. 214 (Mass 1843), *Dumain* v. *Gwynne*, 92 Mass 10 Allen, 270 (1865).

15 *Mercein* v. *People ex. rel. Barry*, 71, 100, 80, 86. Leo Albert Huard observes, "the 'best interests' formula has consistently been honored by our courts and is a uniquely American contribution to the law of adoption" ("Adoption: Ancient and Modern," *Vanderbilt Law Review* 9 [1956], 749). Connecticut, as early as 1796, had established a version of the "best interests of the child" in *Nickols* v. *Giles*. "the child was well provided for; and said Nickols having no house and very little property, and very irregular in his temper and life, his wife had left him and went and lived with her father, where both she and her child were well provided for" (*Nickols* v. *Giles*, 2 Root 461 [Conn. 1796], 462). Even in the case of *Commonwealth* v. *Addicks*, where the child's mother was living in adultery, the court could not "avoid expressing our disapprobation of the mother's conduct, although so far as regards her treatment of the children, she is in no fault. They appear to have been well taken care of in all respects. It is to *them*, that our anxiety is principally directed" (*Commonwealth* v. *Addicks*, 5 Binn [Pa. 1813], 521). Also see *Commonwealth* v. *Maxwell*.

16 *Commonwealth* v. *Maxwell*, 6 Mon. L. rep 214 (Mass 1843), 218. Grossberg notes, "gradually a father's custody power evolved from a property right to a trust tied to his responsibilities as a guardian; his title as father thus became more transferable … [this] was yet another example of the antipatriarchal ethos embedded in republican family law" (236).

17 Zanaildan, "The Emergence of a Modern American Family Law," 1057.

18 *State* v. *Smith*, 6 Greenleaf 426 (Me. 1830), 469, 464.

19 Grossberg, *Governing the Hearth*, 388, n. 56.

20 Ibid., 24.

21 Hochheimer, *A Treatise*, 29.

22 Zanaildan, "The Emergence of a Modern American Family Law," 1083.

23 *Gilkeson* v. *Gilkeson*, Wall. Phila. Rep. 194 (Allegheny County Dist. Ct. 1851), 194.

24 *Gilkeson* v. *Gilkeson*, 195–197.

25 *Pool* v. *Gott*, 14 Mon. L. Rep. 269 (Mass. 1851), 269. Zanaildan, "The Emergence of a Modern American Family Law," observes, "within the doctrine of child custody, then, an adopter maintaining custody for a lengthy period of time might acquire a customary right upon evidencing a superior ability to meet the child's critical needs. Under the decisions in *Gilkeson* and *Gott* as well, an adopter might also reap a Common Law right through an explicit or implicit transfer" (1083).

26 *Mercein* v. *the People ex. rel. Barry*, 71.

27 *Pool* v. *Gott*, 269–272.

28 *Pool* v. *Gott*, 270.

29 Nina Baym, *A Guide to Novels by and about Women in America, 1820–1870* (Ithaca: Cornell University Press, 1978), 165. Elizabeth Barnes makes a similar point about the conclusion of the novel but does not read the resolution in the context of developing domestic relations law (*States of Sympathy: Seduction and Democracy in the Early American Novel* [New York: Columbia University Press, 1997]), 84–91.

30 G. M. Goshgarian interestingly discusses the incestuous subtext of *The Lamplighter*, as well as other sentimental novels, and argues that the "real stakes of the novel [have to do with] Gerty's (re)union with her biological father" (*To Kiss the Chastening Rod: Domestic Fiction and Sexual Ideology in the American Renaissance* [Ithaca: Cornell University Press, 1992], 168). I agree that Gerty's reunion with her father is an attempt to install biology as the definitive paradigm for identity, but given that the novel works equally hard to authorize contract, there are mutually competing "real stakes." Glenn Hendler also discusses this literature's ineluctable fascination with incest, suggesting that even as "sympathy imagines that the term 'family' can designate something chosen rather than a given set of biological or legal relations," sentimental novels "contain this ambiguity by raising the specter of incest as the family's internal limit" ("The Limits of Sympathy: Louisa May Alcott and the Sentimental Novel," *American Literary History* 8 [1996], 688). Both Goshgarian and Hendler claim that the possibility of incest ultimately functions to arrest the chosen affections of the heroine, limiting her choices, problematizing her sympathy, and, as Hendler contends, producing "a kind of agency predicated on selflessness" (690). The limitations installed by incest, though significant, don't convincingly account for Gerty's agency in the text, which, if anything, is predicated on an increasing capacity for self-possession rather than selflessness. The novel's refusal to allow Gerty to consummate her relationship with her father doesn't mean that her agency is mitigated to the point of eradication.

31 Although Cummins manages to tie up the loose ends of *The Lamplighter*'s plot and stabilizes her characters' names, long enough for Gerty to marry, the imprecision of family identifications continues at the end of the novel when Kitty, Gerty's friend, has married and "the child she held by the hand was [her husband's] orphan niece, and just like a daughter to him" (414).

32 *Gilkeson* v. *Gilkeson*, 196–197.

33 One may ask whether in waiving his parental rights, Amory establishes his right to be Gerty's suitor, which would make "closer than kindred" – a relation that embraces and exceeds both contract and biology. Gerty's marriage to Willie (a "brother," but not a brother), I would suggest, illustrates her authority to define the father/daughter "arrangement," as well as the principle of "sufficient discretion."

3 THINKING THROUGH SYMPATHY: KEMBLE, HENTZ, AND STOWE

1 Harriet Beecher Stowe, *Uncle Tom's Cabin or, Life Among the Lowly* (New York: Penguin, 1981; orig. pub. 1852), 624. All further quotations from *Uncle Tom's Cabin* will be from this edition and will be incorporated into the text. The potentially "disconcerting aspects" (180) of sympathy are delineated in David Marshall's *The Surprising Effects of Sympathy: Marivaux, Diderot, Rousseau, and Mary Shelley* (Chicago: University of Chicago Press, 1988), which analyzes Adam Smith's theory of the theatrical structure of sympathy in order to argue for its potential vulnerability to "misrepresentation and misinterpretation" (181). Stowe, like the authors Marshall discusses, is keenly aware of sympathy's threatening plasticity and, in *A Key*, we see her buttressing the power of sympathy with the *imprimatur* of facts. What it means to be a fact is, of course, a subject of inquiry in itself. Mary Poovey, for example, unfolds the many social causes and consequences of the fundamental ambiguity at the core of what she denominates "the modern fact" or "the epistemological unit that organizes most of the knowledge projects of the past four centuries" (xiii): "the modern fact could be represented either as mere data, gathered at random, or as data gathered in the light of a social or theoretical context that made them seem worth gathering" (*A History of the Modern Fact: Problems of Knowledge in the Sciences of Wealth and Society* [Chicago: University of Chicago Press, 1998], 96). Poovey's work illuminates my reading of the debate surrounding the authenticity of *Uncle Tom's Cabin* because defenders of slavery attacked Stowe's facts as false, in part on the grounds that her critique of slavery – the social context – disqualified their accuracy as facts or "data." Interestingly, Stowe doesn't respond in *A Key* with numbers, the modern fact par excellence, according to Poovey, but rather with a barrage of different kinds of narratives gathered from court documents, legislation, and individuals' correspondence designed to validate her facts and the anti-slavery sympathy that results from them. Indeed, when she graphs the number of papers consulted, slaves and lots advertised, runaways described, she remarks: "we present the result of this estimate, far as it must fall from a fair representation of the facts, in a tabular form" (*A Key to Uncle Tom's Cabin; Presenting the Original Facts and Documents upon which the Story is Founded. Together with Corroborative Statements Verifying the Truth of the Work.* [Boston: John P. Jewett, 1853], 142. All further quotations from *A Key* will be from this edition and will be incorporated into the text).

2 I realize that sympathy is not usually understood as having much to do with facts. Catharine Gallagher, for example, argues that it is precisely the quality of fictionality or the "nobodiness" (xix) in novels written by women primarily during the eighteenth century that generated sympathy within readers: "[Fiction] bypasses the stage at which the sentiments perceived in other bodies are mere matters of fact and gives us the illusion of immediately appropriable sentiments" (*Nobody's Story: The Vanishing Acts of Women Writers in the Marketplace, 1670–1820* [Berkeley: University of California Press, 1994], 171). Gallagher is working within a Humean framework whereby matters of fact are unimportant in the development of sympathy. In a *Treatise of Human Nature* (ed. L. A. Selby Bigge [Oxford: Oxford University Press, 1978]), Hume argues, "moral distinctions are not the offspring of reason. Reason is wholly inactive, and can never be the source of so active a principle as conscience, or a sense of morals" (458). Stowe, however, is willing to take her chances that when presented with the facts of slavery, reason will be activated and an anti-slavery conscience will be produced. While recognizing the influence of eighteenth-century philosophers of sympathy on Stowe, literary critics have mistakenly minimized her strategic deployment of "mere matters of fact" as a means of activating anti-slavery sympathy, especially in *A Key*. This is the case for other reasons as well: *Uncle Tom's Cabin* has been taken to be her sole statement on sympathy, and most readings of sympathy don't entertain the possibility that facts might be expressions of sympathy. Even Philip Fisher's aptly titled *Hard Facts: Setting and Form in the American Novel* (New York: Oxford University Press, 1985) quickly dispenses with Stowe's commitment to representing the "hard facts" of slavery in order to argue for the greater importance of Stowe's softer side; that is, the tears which allegedly "represent the fact that only a witness who cannot effect action will experience suffering as deeply as the victim" (108). This chapter, by contrast, will demonstrate Stowe's quite literal investment in the discourse of "facts," and her growing sense that the anti-slavery case must be made by riveting feeling to fact. For fine accounts of the influence of eighteenth-century moral philosophy on Stowe, see Gregg Camfield, "The Moral Aesthetics of Sentimentality: A Missing Key to *Uncle Tom's Cabin*," *Nineteenth-Century Literature* 43 (1988): 319–345 and Gregg Crane, *Conscience, Consent and Citizenship in Nineteenth-Century American Law and Literature* (Cambridge: Cambridge University Press, 2002).

3 The connections between Hentz and Stowe are intriguing. Not only did they know each other during their years in Cincinnati's Semi-Colon club (Joan D. Hedrick mentions this briefly in *Harriet Beecher Stowe: A Life* [New York: Oxford University Press, 1994], 83), but both experienced the death of a child, both followed husbands from one academic job to another, and both resided, in their later years, in Florida. Especially intriguing, though, is the possibility that, early on in Hentz's career, she and Stowe might have shared certain political leanings. Hentz's patronage of George Moses Horton, during her years in Chapel Hill, suggests that her defense of slavery evolved and became increasingly adamant as she spent more time in the south. For example, she was the

force behind the April 9, 1829 publication of Horton's anti-slavery protest, "Liberty and Slavery," in her Massachusetts hometown newspaper, the *Lancaster Gazette.* Their mutual affection is also evident in her portrayal of him in her novel *Lovell's Folly* (1833), and his for her in the poem "Eulogy," and also in Horton's *The Life of the Author,* which precedes *The Poetical Works of George M. Horton, The Colored Bard of North Carolina* (1845). For additional information about their relationship, see the essays in M. A. Richmond's *Bid The Vassal Soar; Interpretive Essays on the Life and Poetry of Phillis Wheatley and George Moses Horton* (Washington, DC: Howard University Press, 1974).

4 In making an argument for the political effectiveness of *Uncle Tom's Cabin,* I am returning to and revising the pathbreaking reading by Jane Tompkins in *Sensational Designs: The Cultural Work of American Fiction, 1790–1860* (Oxford: Oxford University Press, 1985), although by analyzing its effects through the works of Kemble, Hentz, and Stowe, our primary texts as well as our methods differ.

5 Lauren Berlant, "Poor Eliza," in *No More Separate Spheres!, American Literature* 70 (1998): 646. Whereas Berlant privileges what she calls "postsentimentality [or] a resistant strain of the sentimental domain" (655), which is to be found in a set of contemporary texts, my point is that Stowe's sentimentalism, once viewed through the lens of southern strains of sentimentalism, is more ideologically complicated (and progressive) than Berlant allows. Her critique of Stowe's sentimental politics has its antecedents in a redoubtable tradition beginning with antebellum responses to *Uncle Tom's Cabin,* continuing in James Baldwin's essay "Everybody's Protest Novel," through the present. For an excellent analysis of antebellum readings of Stowe, particularly the debate between Frederick Douglass and Martin Delany, see Robert S. Levine, " *Uncle Tom's Cabin* in *Frederick Douglass' Paper*: An Analysis of Reception," rept. in *Uncle Tom's Cabin,* ed. Elizabeth Ammons (New York: Norton, 1994), 523–542. Levine writes, "that a figure such as Douglass truly believed Stowe's novel could counteract the effects of the Compromise of 1850 should temper our skepticism about Stowe's large intentions and achievements and about her complicity in the power structure" (541). Louis J. McCord, "Uncle Tom's Cabin," *Southern Quarterly Review* 23 (January 1853): 118.

6 Frances Anne Kemble, *Journal of a Residence on a Georgian Plantation in 1838–1839,* ed. John A. Scott (Athens: University of Georgia Press, 1984), 74. All further quotations from the *Journal* will be from this edition and will be incorporated in the text.

7 The *Journal* was not published until 1863 because Kemble was desperately trying to save her marriage and keep her children. She believed that publishing the *Journal* would jeopardize both; however, not releasing it didn't help. She and Butler ended up divorcing, and he got custody of their children. For a more detailed account of these events, see Scott's introduction, especially pages xlv–liii.

8 In a short review of Kemble's *Record of a Girlhood,* that appeared in the December 12, 1878, issue of the *Nation,* Henry James notes, "she is naturally a writer, she has a style of her own which is full of those felicities of expression that

indicate the literary sense" ("Frances Anne Kemble" rept. in *Henry James: Literary Criticism: Essays on Literature, American Writers, English Writers* [New York: The Library of America, 1984], 1069). Kemble's work has been singled out primarily by historians for its effective portrayal of southern culture and has recently been the subject of two books by Catherine Clinton, *Fanny Kemble's Civil Wars* (New York: Simon and Schuster, 2000) and *Fanny Kemble's Journals* (Cambridge, MA: Harvard University Press, 2000). Additional references to Kemble can be found in Eugene D. Genovese's *Roll, Jordan Roll: The World the Slaves Made* (New York: Vintage, 1976) in which he writes, "among the harshest of contemporary indictments [of planters] was Fanny Kemble's. High-spirited, intelligent, sharp-tongued and sharp-penned, although certainly not always fair or accurate, she had lived as a planter's wife and was at her considerable best in studying the character of the men of the master class" (95). In *Goodbye to Uncle Tom*, J. C. Furnas ferociously (and unfairly) uses Kemble to illustrate many of Stowe's deficiencies: "it is notable further that Fanny Kemble encouraged none of the other tendentious errors that Uncle Tom saddled on the nation" (New York: William Sloane Associates, 1956), 37. Also see Elizabeth Fox-Genovese, who writes, "Fannie Kemble, with her literary gifts, her flare [*sic*] for the dramatic, and her antislavery passion, was capable of exaggeration, but she grasped a central truth about plantation households: Missus was not Massa" (*Within the Plantation Household: Black and White Women of the Old South* [Chapel Hill: University of North Carolina Press, 1988], 132).

9 Evidence of this warfare over words abounds in the debate over slavery, and it is not just limited to fiction. In *An Inside View of Slavery: or a Tour Among the Planters* (Boston: John P. Jewett, 1855), an ethnographic study of slavery, C. G. Parsons quotes the following passage from "a foreigner, whose letters have been read with much interest" (107): "'I am now writing,' said Mrs. D., 'by a *candlestick* that cost *seven hundred dollars*.'" Parsons, anti-slavery activist and traveler to the south, does some detective work which reveals Mrs. D's semantic devilry: "a slaveholding clergyman who spake as knowing the fact . . . that the wonderful candlestick was nothing more nor less than *Cuffee, holding a flambeau!*" (108). In Chapter 2 of *An Appeal in Favor of that Class of Americans Called Africans* (ed. Carolyn L. Karcher [Amherst: University of Massachusetts Press, 1996]), Lydia Maria Child writes, "this extraordinary use of the word *migrate* furnishes a new battering ram against the free colored class, which is everywhere so odious to slave owners. A *visit* to relations in another State may be called migrating; being taken up and detained by *kidnappers*, over ninety days, may be called *migrating*; – for where neither the evidence of the sufferer nor any of his own color is allowed, it will evidently amount to this" (64). Even something as seemingly uncontroversial as corn becomes subject to definitional debate. In the section "Privations of the Slaves – Food," from Weld's *American Slavery As It Is: Testimony of a Thousand Witnesses* (New York: Arno Press, 1968; orig. pub. 1839) it turns out that when southerners use the word "corn" they mean one thing and northerners mean quite another. He writes, "as a quart of southern corn weighs at least five ounces less than a quart of northern corn, it requires

little arithmetic to perceive, that the daily allowance of the slave fed upon that kind of corn, would contain about one third of a pound less nutriment than though his daily ration were the same quantity of northern corn" (32).

10 Although Kemble's body registers the pain of the slaves, she is keenly aware of her differences from them, such as in this passage where she contrasts the slave's "deadly dread" of losing her family with her own "blessed security, safe from all separation but the one reserved in God's providence" (135). Her sympathy, that is, does not lead, in the words of Saidiya Hartman, to an obliterating identification of "approximation [that] overtakes the proximity essential to ethical conduct" (*Scenes of Subjection: Terror, Slavery, and Self-Making in Nineteenth-Century America* [Oxford: Oxford University Press, 1997], 35). Also see Hartman for a brief allusion to Kemble, which, while acknowledging her eloquent description of the plight of slave women, nevertheless denounces her "callous[ness] when confronted with the inescapable normativity of rape" (87). My reading, in this chapter and the next, shows the inadequacy of this account.

11 The narrative of relentless repetition is also evident in a brief scene recounting the death of a new-born. Kemble notes that the slave mother "merely repeated over and over again: 'I've lost a many; they all goes so' " (130).

12 Thomas Gossett, *Uncle Tom's Cabin and American Culture* (Dallas: Southern Methodist University Press, 1985); Caroline Lee Hentz, *The Planter's Northern Bride* (Chapel Hill: University of North Carolina Press, 1970; orig. pub. 1854), 10–11. All further quotations from *The Planter's Northern Bride* will be from this edition and will be incorporated in the text. For a fine reading of Hentz's southern partisanship, see Elizabeth Moss, *Domestic Novelists in the Old South: Defenders of Southern Culture* (Baton Rouge: Louisiana State University Press, 1992) who similarly maintains that Hentz's "excellent mimicry of Stowe's style and skillful manipulation of the northern novelist's message lent Hentz's interpretation a freshness and vigor that distinguished it from the spate of replies issued by less talented writers" (112). I should add that it is not the case that all of Hentz's novels arrive at this ingenious structural defense of slavery via the valorization of the stepmother. *Linda, or the Pilot of the Belle Creole*, for example, features the archetypally cruel stepmother but, then again, *Linda* is not a rebuttal to *Uncle Tom's Cabin*.

13 Interestingly, Fanny Fern asks this question in an April 4, 1857 *New York Ledger* article entitled "Has a Mother a Right to her Children?" Like Hentz's character, Claudia, Fern doesn't have slave law in mind, but custody laws, which deny a mother, "who [has] suffered martyr-like, these crucifying pains – these wearisome days and sleepless nights…her sweet reward" (*Ruth Hall and Other Writings*, ed. Joyce W. Warren [New Brunswick: Rutgers University Press, 1986], 283).

14 George Fitzhugh, for example, writes in *Sociology for the South*, "the free laborer is compelled by capital and competition to work more than he ever did before, and is less comfortable. The organization of society cheats him of his earnings, and those earnings go to swell the vulgar pomp and pageantry of the ignorant

millionaires" (quoted in Paul Finkelman, *Defending Slavery: Proslavery Thought in the Old South: A Brief History with Documents* [Boston: Bedford, St. Martin's, 2003], 194). James Henry Hammond, senator of South Carolina, asserted in his infamous 1858 "Mudsill Speech," "your whole hireling class of manual laborers and 'operatives,' as you call them, are essentially slaves. The difference between us is, that our slaves are hired for life and well compensated . . . yours are hired by the day [and] not cared for" (Finkelman, *Defending Slavery,* 87).

15 John R. Thompson, *Southern Literary Messenger,* October 1852:631. George F. Holmes, in a review of *Uncle Tom's Cabin,* also refers to "the mazes of its misrepresentation" (*Southern Literary Messenger,* December 1852:724). These reviews and many others can be found at Stephen Railton's comprehensive website – www.iath.virginia.edu/utc – *Uncle Tom's Cabin* and American Culture. Also see my essay, "*Uncle Tom's Cabin* and the South," in *The Cambridge Companion to Harriet Beecher Stowe,* ed. Cindy Weinstein (Cambridge: Cambridge University Press, 2004), 39–57.

16 The serial version of *Uncle Tom's Cabin* had as its subtitle "the Man that was a thing," as opposed to the novel's subtitle, "Life among the Lowly."

17 Robert S. Levine, in his introduction to the Penguin edition of *Dred: A Tale of the Great Dismal Swamp,* makes a compelling case for reading *Dred,* whose original publication date is 1856, as Stowe's response not only to the anti-Tom novels that quickly followed in the wake of *Uncle Tom's Cabin,* but "an even more crucial inspiration was the response of African Americans to *Uncle Tom's Cabin*" (xv). I agree with his analysis, although this chapter focuses on how Stowe began responding to readings of *Uncle Tom's Cabin* as early as 1853, the year *A Key* was published.

18 Stowe's punctuation is an important component in her argument against the perversions of language required by slavery. I am using double quotation marks here to signal that Stowe herself puts these words in quotation marks.

4 BEHIND THE SCENES OF SENTIMENTAL NOVELS: *IDA MAY* AND *TWELVE YEARS A SLAVE*

1 Much groundbreaking literary criticism has concentrated on the relation between these two genres either in order to analyze how slave narratives use the conventions of sentimental novels so as to make the story of the sexually violated female black slave more palatable to a middle-class audience (while simultaneously critiquing the assumptions of that audience) or to argue that abolitionist writers create an insidious correspondence between female slaves and white women which engages the sympathies of the latter on behalf of the former and, in the process, erases the crucial distinctions between them. The deployment of sentimental conventions, in the first case, leads to a powerful critique both of slavery and of bourgeois morality, whereas the deployment of elements of slave narrative results in the mindless reproduction of dominant ideology. The texts under consideration in this chapter challenge these

explanations of generic relation and demonstrate the extent to which senti-mental fictions, like slave narratives, not only are capable of understanding the difference between analogy and appropriation but are able to activate that difference for the purposes of ideological critique. For the earliest and best examples of both schools, see Hazel Carby's *Reconstructing Womanhood: The Emergence of the Afro-American Woman Novelist* (Oxford: Oxford University Press, 1987) and Karen Sanchez-Eppler's *Touching Liberty: Abolition, Feminism, and the Politics of the Body* (Berkeley: University of California Press, 1993).

2 Frederick Douglass, *Narrative of the Life of Frederick Douglass*, in *The Classic Slave Narratives*, ed. Henry Louis Gates, Jr. (New York: Mentor, 1987; orig. pub. 1845), 300.

3 Nina Baym, *Woman's Fiction: A Guide to Novels by and about Women in America, 1820–1870* (Ithaca: Cornell University Press, 1978), 268.

4 These quotations are from the January 18, 1855, edition of *The National Era*. Interestingly, when *Ida May* first appeared, a *New York Evening Post* reviewer attributed the novel to Stowe. *The National Era* writes on November 16, 1854, "we believe he is mistaken," and on November 30, 1854, includes this notice from Phillips, Sampson, and Co., Pike's publisher: "the pen that sketched the grand outlines of Uncle Tom might surely a second time delight the world; but it is due to all parties to say that *Ida May* is the production of an author as yet unknown to fame." In addition to *Ida May*, Pike wrote two other novels: the anti-slavery *Caste: A Story of Republican Equality* and a historical novel of the Revolutionary period, *Agnes* (1858). *Caste* is an interesting novel to read along-side *Ida May* because the story of Helen Dupré is the inverse of Ida's. Unlike Ida, whose blackness turns out to be a ruse, Helen is a mulatta whose whiteness turns out to be a ruse. In the course of the narrative, whose plot anticipates elements of Child's *A Romance of the Republic*, Helen learns that she is the child of a slave mother and a plantation owner, she comes to terms with her blackness, and her white fiancé (who had initially spurned her upon learning of her origins) eventually decides to take her to Europe, where he marries her against the wishes of his family.

5 Being "kidnapped" into a genre is obviously a provocative way to frame the issue of generic hybridity. I use this term, however, to register a cultural preoccupa-tion with the possibility that slave traders are routinely kidnapping white children in order to sell them on the slave market. *Ida May* clearly uses this anxiety in order to help make its anti-slavery case, but Pike's text is by no means alone in doing so. William and Ellen Craft's slave narrative begins with a list of such cases, implying that everyone is at risk of becoming a slave: "I have myself conversed with several slaves who told me that their parents were white and free; but that they were stolen away from them and sold when quite young" (*Running A Thousand Miles for Freedom; or, the Escape of William and Ellen Craft from Slavery*, in *Great Slave Narratives*, selected and introduced by Arna Bontemps [Boston: Beacon Press, 1969], 272). According to the March 12, 1855 edition of Douglass's *Paper*, "we daily see white fugitives, and the cupidity of a slaveholder

would suffer him to keep anyone, even his mother in slavery. When white men learn this, and that their own liberties are in danger, then they will see the reasonableness of an unconditional emancipation."

6 The March 16, 1855 edition of Douglass's *Paper* includes the headline, "The Arrival of Solomon Northup, and 'Little Ida May.'" About the "real 'Ida May,'" a *New York Times* article (reprinted in the *Paper*) has this to say: "the child was exhibited yesterday to many prominent individuals in the City, and the general sentiment, in which we fully concur, was one of astonishment that she should ever have been held a slave. She was one of the fairest and most indisputable white children that we have ever seen," in addition to which a Boston correspondent for the paper reports, "Northup and 'Ida' visited both branches of the Legislature on Saturday." I am grateful to Robert S. Levine for alerting me to the presence of reviews of *Ida May* in Douglass's *Paper*.

7 Frances Anne Kemble, *Journal of a Residence on a Georgian Plantation in 1838–1839*, ed. John A. Scott (Athens: University of Georgia Press, 1984; orig. pub. 1863), 272. All further quotations will be from this edition and will be incorporated in the text.

8 In his discussion of the complexities of married women's property rights in the south, Peter Bardaglio acknowledges the judicial inclination to enlarge women's property rights, but adds "by no means did this legislation intend to place women in an equal position with men; granting women special treatment under the law, the married women's property acts provided equity, not equality" (*Reconstructing the Household: Families, Sex, and the Law in the Nineteenth-Century South* [Chapel Hill: University of North Carolina Press, 1995], 32). In *Within the Plantation Household: Black and White Women of the Old South* (Chapel Hill: University of North Carolina Press, 1988), Elizabeth Fox-Genovese explains that "slaveholding women might inherit households from their fathers or husbands, but they almost invariably turned the management over to men in practice, even if a will or marriage settlement had left them legally in the woman's control" (203). She argues that "the management of slaves remained inextricably intertwined with political power" (206) which meant that, except in the rarest of circumstances, men were in charge. On the Kemble/Butler marriage, Catherine Clinton writes, "Butler reasoned that, according to marital law, any money his wife earned was rightfully his" (*Fanny Kemble's Civil Wars* [Oxford: Oxford University Press, 2000], 72).

9 Quoted in Norma Basch, *In the Eyes of the Law: Women, Marriage, and Property in Nineteenth-Century New York* (Ithaca: Cornell University Press, 1982), 48.

10 Mary Hayden Green Pike, *Ida May; A Story of Things Actual and Possible* (Boston: Phillips, Sampson and Company, 1854), 89. All further quotations from *Ida May* will be from this edition and will be incorporated into the text.

11 My reading of the relation between sentimental fictions and slave narratives is indebted to Amy Dru Stanley's illuminating analysis of nineteenth-century debates about contract in relation to slavery in *From Bondage to Contract: Wage Labor, Marriage, and the Market in the Age of Slave Emancipation* (Cambridge: Cambridge University Press, 1998).

12 Descriptions of Venus, for example, are particularly offensive: "in that genial light, Aunt Venus looked intelligent, and even showed that once she might have been almost handsome. But if the smile deepened into a laugh, all the somber dignity of her appearance vanished, and her gums, garnished with broken teeth, displayed in a broad grin, her head ducked down between her shoulders, and the indescribable comical giggle that convulsed her whole figure, transformed her into something very much resembling a baboon" (70).

13 I do not mean to suggest that *Ida May* is unique among sentimental and anti-slavery fiction in representing trans-racial adoption – clearly Lydia Maria Child's *The Romance of the Republic* and Stowe's *Uncle Tom's Cabin* considered this topic – but adoption in Pike's text epitomizes the governing tension of contract v. slavery between the two genres and within antebellum culture(s). A much streamlined version of Pike's tale is told by Child in her 1834 short story "Mary French and Susan Easton." See Carolyn Karcher, *The First Woman in The Republic: A Cultural Biography of Lydia Maria Child* (Durham, NC: Duke University Press, 1994), esp. 165–170.

14 When Venus "took the child" from Mr. Bell, he asks her to "take her home" and reminds her that she has successfully "raised many a child as sick as she [Ida] is" (71).

15 Until Venus belongs to Ida: Ida becomes Venus's child "in some degree," but Venus becomes Ida's, in no uncertain terms, upon her eighteenth birthday, "the time fixed for her majority in Mr. Maynard's will" (230).

16 For a related discussion of how the analogy with slavery operates in antebellum fiction and culture, with specific reference to Melville's *White Jacket* and naval flogging, see Samuel Otter's *Melville's Anatomies* (Berkeley: University of California Press, 1999), in which he writes, "the specter of racial slavery echoed through antebellum debates on marriage, family, citizenship, work, social structure, military practice, and national character. The analogy was crucial but also volatile. Its terms, once animated, released unaccountable desires and fears and suggested unsettling links between white and black Americans" (58).

17 Solomon Northup, *Twelve Years a Slave*, ed. Sue Eakin and Joseph Logsdon (Baton Rouge: Louisiana State University Press, 1968; orig. pub. 1853), 252. All further quotations will be from this edition and will be incorporated into the text.

18 *The Life and Adventures of Henry Bibb, An American Slave* (Madison: University of Wisconsin Press, 2001; orig. pub. 1849), 1.

19 Elsewhere, Northup writes, "it is not safe to contradict a master, even by the assertion of a truth" (174). Most famously, Douglass provides readers with a powerful account of how the slave's very survival depends upon concealment and dishonesty.

20 Toward the end of his narrative, Northup writes at length upon this subject: "I am often asked, with an air of incredulity, how I succeeded so many years in keeping from my daily and constant companions the knowledge of my true name and history. The terrible lesson Burch taught me, impressed indelibly upon my mind the danger and uselessness of asserting I was a freeman. There

was no possibility of any slave being able to assist me, while, on the other hand, there *was* a possibility of his exposing me. When it is recollected the whole current of my thoughts, for twelve years, turned to the contemplation of escape, it will not be wondered at, that I was always cautious and on my guard. It would have been an act of folly to have proclaimed my *right* to freedom ... It was important, therefore, not only as regarded my hope of deliverance, but also as regarded the few personal privileges I was permitted to enjoy, to keep from him [Epps] the history of my life" (211–212).

21 The issue of naming is of central importance to the slave narrative. Most famously, Harriet Jacobs published *Incidents in the Life of a Slave Girl* under the pseudonym Linda Brent. *The Narrative of Sojourner Truth* begins, "The subject of this biography, Sojourner Truth, as she now calls herself, but whose name was originally Isabella" (New York: Dover Publications, 1997; orig. pub. 1850), 1. William Wells Brown poignantly explains the origin of his name in *Clotel; or, The President's Daughter: A Narrative of Slave Life in the United States*, ed. Robert S. Levine (Boston: Bedford/St. Martin's 2000; orig. pub. 1853), 63. Douglass's explanation of his name gives us a sense of the slave's detached relation to his name. He states, "I gave Mr. Johnson [of New Bedford] the privilege of choosing me a name, but told him he must not take from me the name of 'Frederick.' I must hold on to that, to preserve a sense of my identity. Mr. Johnson had just been reading the 'Lady of the Lake,' and at once suggested that my name be 'Douglass.' From that time until now I have been called 'Frederick Douglass,' and as I am more widely known by that name than by either of the others, I shall continue to use it as my own" (322–323).

22 This passage is also a moment of performance. By referring to himself in the third person, Northup is clearly "performing" his identity as a slave, as Platt Epps. In an earlier part of the narrative, Northup runs away from Tibeats, who is trying to kill him, and "adopted a ruse that proved entirely successful. Assuming a fierce expression, I walked directly towards [the white man], looking him steadily in the face ... He looked upon me as some infernal goblin, just arisen from the bowels of the swamp!" (106). On the subversive potential of performance within the context of antebellum slavery, see Saidiya Hartmann's *Scenes of Subjection: Terror, Slavery, and Self-Making in Nineteenth-Century America* (Oxford: Oxford University Press, 1998).

23 The plots of slave narratives often hinge on the necessity of unrecognizability. See Jacobs's *Incidents in the Life of a Slave Girl*. Also see *Running a Thousand Miles for Freedom; or, the Escape of William and Ellen Craft from Slavery*, *The Fugitive Blacksmith, or Events in the History of James W. C. Pennington*, and *Narrative of the Life of Henry Box Brown*.

24 See Orlando Patterson, *Slavery and Social Death* (Cambridge, MA: Harvard University Press, 1982).

25 In their introduction to Northup's narrative, Eakin and Logsdon write of the years following Northup's enslavement: "Justice, therefore, never came to Solomon Northup, either in the South or in the North. He had no choice

but to try and pick up his life where he had left it in 1841. He had received only a pathetic recompense for the stolen years – three thousand dollars for selling the copyright of his memoirs . . . His simple, moving wish at the conclusion of the narrative was never honored; he does not rest in the churchyard where his father sleeps" (xxii–xxiii).

26 Many other examples can be found: "Having now brought down this narrative to the last hour I was to spend on Bayou Boeuf . . . I must now beg the reader to go back with me to the month of August" (223); "since my return, I learned that he [Clem Ray] had escaped from bondage, and on his way to the free soil of Canada, lodged one night at the house of my brother-in-law in Saratoga" (40).

27 A similar exchange takes place between Chloe, Bill, and Nick, the other kidnapper: "it don't do to whip white children like they were niggers. Yes, responded Bill, white folks is white folks, and niggers is niggers. Niggers is niggers, is dey? rejoined Chloe. I neber could see, fur my part, but de nigger flesh feels jest de same tings white flesh does" (53).

28 This transformation is usually reserved for white women (Sophia Auld in Douglass's *Narrative* would be the most famous example) or black men (Sambo and Quimbo in *Uncle Tom's Cabin*). That a female slave would respond to being abused by abusing others is not often represented because to do so is to risk losing the reader's sympathy for the character. Pike's depiction of Chloe is interesting in this regard because our sympathy for her remains, even though she does terrible things.

5 LOVE AMERICAN STYLE: *THE WIDE, WIDE WORLD*

1 Although my analysis focuses on *The Wide, Wide World*, one can find other examples of these "miniaturized slave narratives" in sentimental novels, including *Ruth Hall, Ishmael, or in the Depths, Hagar the Martyr, Marcus Warland*, and, of course, *Ida May*. Anne duCille encourages this kind of "dialogic reading" and reminds us, using the case of *Clotel*, "if Brown's text talked back to the novels of Harriet Beecher Stowe, Catharine Maria Sedgwick, Lydia Maria Child, and E.D.E.N. Southworth, *all* of these writers also listened to and drew from the Josiah Hensons, Henry Bibbses, Frederick Douglasses, Harriet Jacobses, Mary Princes, and Ellen Crafts of their times" (*The Coupling Convention: Sex, Text and Tradition in Black Women's Fiction* [Oxford: Oxford University Press, 1993], 24). In his introduction to Harriet E. Wilson's *Our Nig; or, Sketches from the Life of a Free Black* (New York: Vintage, 1983; orig. pub. 1859), Henry Louis Gates demonstrates the usefulness of reading Frado's story in terms of its generic mixture of slave narratives and sentimental fiction.

2 In addition to the critics discussed in the last chapter, see Lori Merish, *Sentimental Materialism: Gender, Commodity Culture, and Nineteenth-Century American Literature* (Durham, NC: Duke University Press, 2000)

and Franny Nudelman, "Harriet Jacobs and the Sentimental Politics of Female Suffering," *English Literary History* 59 (1992): 939–964.

3 J. W. C. Pennington, *The Fugitive Blacksmith, or Events in the History of James W.C. Pennington, Pastor of a Presbyterian Church, New York, Formerly a Slave in the State of Maryland, United States,* in *Great Slave Narratives* ed. Arna Bontemps (Boston: Beacon Press, 1969; orig. pub. 1849), 220. The exact phrasing in *Running a Thousand Miles for Freedom, or The Escape of William and Ellen Craft from Slavery* is, "Boy, do you belong to that gentleman?" (in *Great Slave Narratives*; orig. pub. 1860, [301]). All further quotations from Pennington and the Crafts will be from this edition and will be incorporated into the text. Pennington's opening chapter also focuses on the issue of belonging: "My parents did not both belong to the same owner: my father belonged to a man named —; my mother belonged to a man named —. This not only made me a slave, but made me the slave of him to whom my mother belonged; as the primary law of slavery is, that the child shall follow the condition of the mother" (207). Mrs. Sands asks this question about Jacobs's son, Benny: "Whom does he belong to?" (457), and Dr. Flint is continually telling Jacobs and others that "she don't belong to me" (407), while nevertheless insisting, "you are my slave, and shall always be my slave" (390).

4 Slave narratives often make the point that one's master is often one's father. Part I of the Crafts' narrative includes the following: "My wife's first master was her father, and her mother his slave, and the latter is still the slave of his widow" (271). Also see Frederick Douglass, *Narrative of the Life of Frederick Douglass,* in *The Classic Slave Narratives,* ed. Henry Louis Gates, Jr. (New York: Mentor, 1987; orig. pub. 1845).

5 I would contend that many slave narratives also view the right to contract as the constitutive difference between freedom and slavery. In fact, Jacobs, Douglass, Bibb, Northup and others represent as a turning point in their lives their refusal to accept slavery as a negation of their contractual rights and their decision to view slavery as a condition which one consents to or contests.

6 Unlike Gerty, though, Gabriella's and Ethelyn's mistake is that they marry prior to their self-possession, and, as a consequence, they must separate from their husbands in order to own themselves and, their stories imply, to be happily married the second time around.

7 Susan Warner, *The Wide, Wide World* (New York: The Feminist Press, 1987; orig. pub. 1850), 504. All further quotations from *The Wide, Wide World* will be from this edition and will be incorporated into the text.

8 Jane Tompkins makes this point in her Afterword to the Feminist Press edition of *The Wide, Wide World.* Not only does she characterize Ellen's behavior as a refusal to "rebel against the injustice of her masters" (598), but in using Susan Griffin's explanation of "the basic pornographic situation, in which one person is robbed by another of everything that makes him or her a human being and is reduced to the status of an object" (599) to describe Ellen's, Tompkins similarly views Ellen as a slave. Also see Patricia Crain's *The Story of A: The Alphabetization of America* from *The New England Primer* to *The Scarlet Letter* (Stanford:

Stanford University Press, 2002), which also argues that "Ellen is, literally, chattel" (156), not, however, in order to examine the complexities of Ellen's story in relation to the slave narrative, but rather to demonstrate how Ellen is the blank page upon which John writes her into existence: "John insists on being Ellen's only textbook to sexuality or to any other kind of emotional adventure – indeed, any kind of interior existence at all" (165).

9 Claudia Tate, *Domestic Allegories of Political Desire: The Black Heroine's Text at the Turn of the Century* (Oxford: Oxford University Press, 1992), 27.

10 Elizabeth Freeman interestingly extends Tate's reading of Jacobs to suggest that "Brent's distinctly nonmarital sense of mutual obligation – with her children, female benefactors, and grandmother – represents a set of bonds that competed with the middle-class, couple-centered model of marriage for African Americans in the antebellum era" (*The Wedding Complex: Forms of Belonging in Modern American Culture* [Durham, NC: Duke University Press, 2002], 73). Freeman's analysis of the illegality of interracial marriage suggests yet another mechanism that prevents Jacobs from entering into marriage (should she wish to do so), even when she is free.

11 In the introduction to *Narrative of the Life of Henry Box Brown*, Richard Brown points out that "it is now well-known that the slave songs or Negro Spirituals are full of allusions to escape . . . for example, Canaan is Canada; the Jordan is the Ohio River (the dividing line between the slave and free states); and the many references to travel (shoes, wheels, chariots, trains) are all about running away" (Oxford: Oxford University Press, 2002; orig. pub. 1851), xviii.

12 This has everything to do with her maternal bonds, which literary critics have correctly described as close to the point of suffocation and exclusion from the rest of the world: "if you were to tell me black is white, mamma, I should think my eyes had been mistaken . . . And I am glad to think I belong to you, and you have the management of me entirely, and I needn't manage myself, because I know I can't; and if I could, I'd rather you would, mamma" (18). Ellen has this totalizing connection with her mother against which to validate or condemn later affiliations. Gerty doesn't, which I think helps explain the ease with which she incorporates alternative models of kinship. For a more positive reading of Ellen's attachment to her mother, see Nancy Schnog's "Inside the Sentimental: The Psychological Work of *The Wide, Wide, World*," *Genders* 4 (1988): 11–25.

13 Nina Baym points out that "the most significant difference between *The Wide, Wide World* and *The Lamplighter* is that the guardians and caretakers in the latter book are kind and loving . . . Cummins replaces the Warner world of human cruelty and exploitation with one of mutual support and guidance" (*Woman's Fiction: A Guide to Novels by and about Women in America, 1820–1870* [Ithaca: Cornell University Press, 1978], 165). Erica R. Bauermeister's "*The Lamplighter, The Wide, Wide World,* and *Hope Leslie*: Reconsidering the Recipes for Nineteenth-Century American Women's Novels," *Legacy: A Journal of Nineteenth-Century American Women Writers* 8 (1991): 17–28 uses Sedgwick's *Hope Leslie* in order to explicate the differences between Cummins's

and Warner's texts. Another key distinction between the two is that religion
plays a far less central role in *The Lamplighter* than in *The Wide, Wide World*.
For an excellent analysis of religion in Warner's text, see Jane Tompkins,
Sensational Designs: The Cultural Work of American Fiction, 1790–1860
(Oxford: Oxford University Press, 1985), esp. 147–185.

14 Several other passages allude to Alice's maternal relationship with Ellen: "Ellen
rested her head on [Alice's] bosom as she had been wont to do of old time on
her mother's" (219); "She could go through with the next hymn, though it had
been much loved and often used, both by her mother and Alice" (453). Alice
herself, however, makes it clear that there is no maternal substitute. She says to
Ellen, "I am afraid I shall be a poor substitute for your mother" (238).

15 Tompkins, Afterword, 586; see Richard Brodhead, "Sparing the Rod: Discipline
and Fiction in Antebellum America," *Representations* 21 (winter 1988): 67–96.

16 Elizabeth Barnes puts the point nicely: "The interactions between Mr.
Montgomery and his wife and daughter are devoid of feeling or, more
precisely, devoid of the expression of feeling. In his presence, the narrative
practically comes to a halt; there is action but no reaction" (*States of Sympathy:
Seduction and Democracy in the Novel* [New York: Columbia University Press,
1997], 107). Warner's willingness to let Ellen's lack of feeling go uncorrected is
surely related to her own troubled relations with her father whose financial
indiscretions involved them in a devastating series of lawsuits (not unlike the
lawsuit with which *The Wide, Wide World* begins) that catapulted the once
comfortable, middle-class Warner family into dire poverty. The consequence
was that Susan and Anna Warner became prolific writers, supporting themselves and their economically reckless father with income from their literary
endeavors. Biographies of the Warner family include Edward Halsey Foster,
Susan and Anna Warner (Boston: Twayne Publishers, n.d.) and Anna B.
Warner, *Susan Warner* (New York: G. P. Putnam's Sons, 1909).

17 In her reading of the place of sentimental masochism in *The Wide, Wide World*,
Marianne Noble also links Ellen's behavior to "the ideal of the feme-covert,
both in its advocacy of female subordination to male subjectivity and in its
implication that a woman cannot trust her own body and its sensory input"
(*The Masochistic Pleasures of Sentimental Literature* [Princeton: Princeton
University Press, 2002], 97).

18 The question of citizenship never comes up, so it isn't clear whether these
characters have formally abrogated their ties to the nation of their birth and
become American citizens or if they simply live in America and have maintained citizenship in the country of their birth. Alice describes herself in the
following way: "I am English born, Ellen, but you may count me half American
if you like, for I have spent rather more than half my life here" (174). It would
seem that Mrs. Vawse would have to be a citizen, given that so much of her life
has been spent in America. Alice explains this character's complicated heritage:
"Her real name is Vosier. She was born a Swiss, and brought up in a wealthy
French family, as the personal attendant of a young lady to whom she became
exceedingly attached. This lady finally married an American gentleman; and so

great was Mrs. Vawse's love to her, that she left country and family to follow her here. In a few years her mistress died; she married" (172).

19 The notion that one can learn to be an American is also evident in an early, prize-winning essay written by Warner under her pseudonym, Elizabeth Wetherell, "American Female Patriotism" (New York: Edward H. Fletcher, 1852), in which the husband of the piece urges his wife to "Dare to be American!" (26). Although she is American-born, she suffers from a bad case of Europeanism, and thus he gives her lessons on how to re-acquire her national identity. The essay thus suggests that one needn't be born in America to be American. One can make the choice and then educate oneself in the principles of Americanism, which is, of course, something that many of the characters do in *The Wide, Wide World*.

20 For a psychological analysis of the generation following the Revolutionary fathers, and the difficulties they faced in creating a cultural identity of their own, see George Forgie, *Patricide in the House Divided: A Psychological Interpretation of Lincoln and his Age* (New York: W. W. Norton, 1979). On the familial (and anti-familial) rhetoric deployed in the Revolutionary War, see Jay Fliegelman, *Prodigals and Pilgrims: The American Revolution against Patriarchal Authority* (Cambridge: Cambridge University Press, 1982).

21 Ellen's difficulty in knowing which of her masters has priority resonates with the predicament in which Jacobs's brother, Willie, finds himself: "One day when his father and his mistress both happened to call him at the same, he hesitated between the two; being perplexed to know which had the strongest claim upon his obedience" (345).

22 That Ellen's defense of American republicanism takes place in Scotland rather than England allows Warner to make the connection between England's imperial relation to both colonies. Scotland's colonization by England is also referenced by Colonel Munro in *The Last of the Mohicans* (New York: Penguin, 1986), when defending his marriage to Cora's mother, a West Indian woman whose mother was a slave: "Ay , sir, that is a curse entailed on Scotland, by her unnatural union with a foreign and trading people" (159). For an interesting essay that delves into the literary consequences of the American/ Scottish analogy, see Homer Brown, "Why the Story of the Origin of the (English) Novel is an American Romance (If Not the Great American Novel)," in *Cultural Institutions of the Novel*, ed. Deidre Lynch and William B. Warner (Durham, NC: Duke University Press, 1996), 11–43.

23 I am deeply grateful to Marianne Noble for drawing my attention to the scene with Rebecca Richardson or "little blacky," and I also want to thank the Huntington Library for permission to quote from the 1849 hand-written manuscript.

24 Exactly why these scenes were deleted is currently not known. Two reasons come to mind. The first is that Warner's editor (and perhaps Warner herself?) decided that in the interests of making the novel as marketable to the broadest audience possible, it was best to omit references to anything overtly racial or connected to the issue of slavery. The second is that these scenes, especially the

one when Ellen and Mrs. Montgomery visit Rebecca and her mother, suggest a world outside of the one occupied by Ellen and her mother. What is so powerful, as many critics have noticed, about those opening chapters is the insulating and insular quality of the love between Ellen and her mother. Susan Williams considers Warner's revisions and deletions (specifically, a passage from that early scene with Mr. Marshman, only in this part of it, he is showing her around the boat) and arrives at this conclusion, with which I agree: "readers influenced the terms of their [Susan and Anna's] writing and, at times, appeared to suppress a literary will toward increased worldliness" ("Widening the World: Susan Warner, Her Readers, and the Assumption of Authorship," *American Quarterly* 42 [1990]: 575).

25 A commitment which was, of course, terribly fraught given that many were themselves slaveholders. The classic analysis of the mutual dependence between freedom and slavery is Edmund S. Morgan, *American Freedom, American Slavery: The Ordeal of Colonial Virginia* (New York: Norton, 1975).

26 Amy Dru Stanley's *From Bondage to Contract: Wage Labor, Marriage, and the Market in the Age of Slave Emancipation* (Cambridge: Cambridge University Press, 1998) analyzes the various ways in which the marriage contract was understood, upheld, and critiqued in the antebellum period.

27 *The Life and Adventures of Henry Bibb, An American Slave*, ed. Charles Heglar (Madison: University of Wisconsin Press, 2001; orig. pub. 1849), 38.

6 WE ARE FAMILY, OR MELVILLE'S *PIERRE*

1 A The full title of T. L. Nichols and Mrs. Mary S. Gove Nichols's book is *Marriage: Its History, Character, and Results; its Sanctities, and its Profanities; its Science and its Facts. Demonstrating its Influence, as a Civilized Institution, on the Happiness of the Individual and the Progress of the Race* (New York: T. L. Nichols, 1854), 325.

2 Herman Melville, *Pierre, or The Ambiguities* (Evanston: Northwestern University<?A3B2 tlsb=t Press, 1971), 141. All further quotations from *Pierre* will be from this edition and will be incorporated into the text.

3 Richard Brodhead makes a similar point about Melville's complicated relation to the sentimental novel: "The odd combination of straightforwardness and secret mockery inherent in his handling of the style, characters, and characteristic situations of sentimental romance is evidence of his ambivalence, his desire both to make use of this genre and to assert his independence from it. The distortedness and chaos of *Pierre* are products of a tension, present from the first and explosive at the end, between the author and the literary form he has chosen to work in" (*Hawthorne, Melville, and the Novel* [Chicago: University of Chicago Press, 1973], 164). For an account of Melville's subversive use of the conventions of "life writing," see Jennifer DiLalla Toner's "The Accustomed Signs of the Family: Rereading Genealogy in Melville's *Pierre*," *American Literature* 70 (June 1998): 237–263. Shelia Post-Lauria interestingly argues that

antebellum reviewers read *Pierre*, not through the lens of sentimental fiction, but in relation to French sensational fiction (*Correspondent Colorings: Melville in the Marketplace* [Amherst: University of Massachusetts Press, 1996]). She insists that "*Pierre* is no *sentimental* romance"; rather, it is a sensational novel, and, as such, challenges "notions of Melville's reputed remoteness from his culture" (141). It isn't clear why *Pierre* can't be contextualized in relation to both sentimental and sensational fictions, especially given that virtually all of Melville's novels transgress generic boundaries, and just because *Pierre* isn't sentimental (although this chapter argues that the novel has a much more complicated relation to sentimentalism than Post-Lauria suggests) doesn't mean that Melville isn't engaged in a profound inquiry into the meanings and effects of sentimentalism.

4 Samuel Otter notes a similar effect in *Pierre*, describing the novel as "filled with structures that entice and recede" (*Melville's Anatomies* [Berkeley: University of California Press, 1999], 244).

5 *Melville, The Critical Heritage*, ed. Watson G. Branch (London and Boston: Routledge & Kegan Paul, 1974), 319. All further quotations will be from this edition and will be incorporated into the text.

6 Eric J. Sundquist, *Home as Found: Authority and Genealogy in Nineteenth-Century American Literature* (Baltimore: Johns Hopkins University Press, 1979), 150.

7 Readers of *Moby-Dick* are well acquainted with Melville's use of verbal repetition. Passages in "The Doubloon," for example, when juxtaposed with *Pierre* help illuminate the comparison. Upon looking at the doubloon, Ahab has difficulty getting past the notion (and the words) that "all are Ahab": "The firm tower, that is Ahab; the volcano, that is Ahab; the courageous, the undaunted, and victorious fowl, that, too, is Ahab" (*Moby-Dick or the Whale* [Evanston and Chicago: Northwestern University Press and the Newberry Library, 1988], 431). Similarly, Pip's response is marked by repetition. Three times, he conjugates the verb to look, "I look, you look, he looks; we look, ye look, they look" (434), and then ends his observations with a minstrel-like performance, "Cook! ho, cook! and cook us! Jenny! hey, hey, hey, hey, hey, Jenny, Jenny!"(435). Whereas this degree of repetition is anomalous and primarily reserved for Ahab and Pip, the madmen of the novel, it pervades *Pierre* and does so because the narrator of *Pierre*, unlike Ishmael, is incapable of getting beyond the linguistic tautologies of his characters.

8 The narrator repeats himself most insistently in the early sections of *Pierre*, but repetition occurs throughout: "It has been said, that always when Pierre would seek solitude in its material shelter and walled isolation, then the closet communicating with his chamber was his elected haunt" (86); "Wonderful, indeed, we repeat it, was the electrical insight which Pierre now had into the character of his mother" (90); "In the earlier chapters of this volume, it has somewhere been passingly intimated" (244); "Not seldom Pierre's social placidity was ruffled by polite entreaties from the young ladies that he would be pleased to grace their Albums with some nice little song. We say that here his social placidity was ruffled" (250).

9 Sacvan Bercovitch convincingly argues, "whether or not Isabel is literally related to Pierre, she is his sister metaphorically, and he is right to claim her as part of his patrimony, and right to want to redress her wrongs" (*Rites of Assent: Transformations in the Symbolic Construction of America* [New York: Routledge, 1993], 296).

10 The narrator uses this device in his description of Pierre's correspondence with Glen about the use of his New York house: "Now, if it were not conscious considerations like the really benevolent or neutral ones first mentioned above, it was certainly something akin to them" (223).

11 As Plotinus Plinlimmon puts it, "by their very contradictions they are made to correspond" (212). The text calls attention to its bizarre use of analogies when Pierre offers the following comment on Isabel's hand: "But hard and small, it by an opposite analogy hints of the soft capacious heart that made the hand so hard with heavenly submission to thy most undeserved and martyred lot" (165).

12 See Brian Higgins and Hershel Parker, "The Flawed Grandeur of Melville's *Pierre*," in *New Perspectives on Melville*, ed. Faith Pullin (Kent: Kent State University Press, 1978), 162–196. For a comprehensive analysis of the composition of *Pierre* and Melville's decision to make Pierre a writer, see Parker's splendid biography *Herman Melville: A Biography*, vol. II: *1851–1891* (Baltimore: The Johns Hopkins University Press, 2002), especially pp. 76–89. Although the chapters about Pierre's authorship were written later, in a second round of fast and furious composition, my reading demonstrates that those additions make perfect conceptual sense given the novel's inability to maintain differences between characters, words, and voices. Elizabeth Renker similarly notes the difficulties in separating the narrative voice from Pierre's, although she explores this through the novel's tropes of vision (*Strike through the Mask: Herman Melville and the Scene of Writing* [Baltimore: The Johns Hopkins University Press, 1996], esp. 24–48).

13 For an alternate reading of this passage, see Priscilla Wald's *Constituting Americans: Cultural Anxiety and Narrative Form* (Durham, NC: Duke University Press, 1995), esp. 148–149. Wald's point that "Pierre lacks the language in which to tell his story" (153) is well taken, but I think the case is more complicated in that the language Pierre has to tell his story cancels it out.

14 At this point in the novel, not only have the distinctions between the narrator and Pierre become blurred beyond recognition, but Melville, too, appears to have fallen victim to his novel's relentless logic of "seeming semblance" (289) and "catching likenesses" (330). Thus, when the narrator tells us that Pierre "seems to have directly plagiarized from his own experiences, to fill out the mood of his apparent author-hero, Vivia" (302), we recognize that passages from *Pierre*, especially those sections having to do with the composition and the reception of Pierre's work, have been plagiarized from Melville's own authorial experiences. "Corporations have no souls" (302) is one particularly bizarre autobiographical detail. Clearly, Pierre has less reason to be thinking about corporations than Melville whose negotiations with Harper's for the

publication of the novel were proving difficult, indeed. Unlike his earlier dealings with the publishing house, this contract didn't offer Melville the financial and psychological boost he had been anticipating. According to Hershel Parker, the fact that the Harper's contract for *Pierre* "stipulate[d] that for the first 1,190 copies sold . . . the author was to receive no royalties," may have "enforced upon him the realization that he might have to abandon the hope of earning a living as a writer" ("Why *Pierre* Went Wrong," *Studies in the Novel* 8 [1976]: 12–13). This realization is precisely Pierre's once he receives the note from the publishing firm of Steel, Flint & Asbestos labeling him "a swindler" and demanding that he pay the "bill for printing thus far, and also for our cash advances" (356). The contract negotiations with Harper's both for *Moby-Dick* (they refused to give Melville an advance in contrast to advances given for his earlier novels) and for *Pierre* are clearly propelling Melville to collapse the distinctions between himself, narrator, and protagonist.

15 My argument in this chapter is indebted to Wai Chee Dimock's point that "a figure of difference" is impossible in *Pierre*, which "affirm[s] a world of likeness, a world of kinship and only kinship" (*Empire for Liberty: Melville and the Poetics of Individualism* [Princeton: Princeton University Press, 1989], 173). In contrast to Dimock's focus on the constitution of Pierre's self with respect to antebellum theories of individualism, my reading adopts a more formalist perspective and establishes how the very grammar of the text struggles with this principle of kinship. Also see Brook Thomas, "The Writer's Procreative Urge in *Pierre*: Fictional Freedom or Convoluted Incest?", *Studies in the Novel* 11 (1979): 416–430.

16 Leslie Fiedler, *Love and Death in the American Novel* (New York: Dell, 1966), 420; Sundquist, *Home as Found*, 177; Gillian Brown, *Domestic Individualism: Imagining Self in Nineteenth-Century America* (Berkeley: University of California Press, 1990), 152, 161.

17 See Wyn Kelley's essay "*Pierre*'s Domestic Ambiguities," in *The Cambridge Companion to Herman Melville*, ed. Robert S. Levine (Cambridge: Cambridge University Press, 1998), 91–113.

18 E. H. Chapin, *Duties of Young Women* (Boston: George W. Briggs, 1850; orig. pub. 1848), 169; quoted in Mary P. Ryan, *The Empire of the Mother: American Writing about Domesticity, 1830–1860* (New York: Harrington Park Press, 1982), 82.

19 William A. Alcott, *The Young Wife, or Duties of Woman in the Marriage Relation* (Arno: New York, 1972; orig. pub. 1837), 58. Nichols, *Marriage: Its History*, 325.

20 Charles Lane, "The Consociate Family Life," *The New Age and Concordium Gazette* 1 (1843): 116, 120.

21 Merton M. Sealts, Jr., "Melville and the Shakers," *Studies in Bibliography*, ed. Fredson Bowers, vol. 2 (1949): 105–114.

22 John Humphrey Noyes, *Bible Communism; a Compilation From the Annual Reports and other Publications of the Oneida Association and its Branches; Presenting, in Connection with their History, a Summary View of their Religious and Social Theories* (Brooklyn: Office of the Circular, 1853), 13, 17, 51.

23 Hubbard Eastman, *Noyesism Unveiled: A History of the Sect Self-Styled Perfectionists; with a Summary View of their Leading Doctrines* (Brattleboro: B. D. Harris and Co., 1849), 117; Michael Paul Rogin, *Subversive Genealogy: The Politics and Art of Herman Melville* (New York: Knopf, 1983), 160.

24 Parke Godwin, *A Popular View of the Doctrines of Charles Fourier* (New York: J. S. Redfield, 1844), 28.

25 Frances Wright, *Course of Popular Lectures, as Delivered by Frances Wright* (New York: Office of the Free Enquirer, 1829), 45. Myra Jehlen persuasively argues that it is both Pierre's and Melville's inability to produce a social, familial, or novelistic order different from the one they have inherited that leads to Pierre's (and *Pierre's*) tragic ending. She reaches the conclusion that "Pierre cannot imagine reform, but it emerges in Melville's novel as a fatally missing term" (*American Incarnation: The Individual, The Nation, and the Continent* [Cambridge, MA: Harvard University Press, 1986], 204). This chapter argues, by contrast, that reform is very much at the center of *Pierre*, quite explicitly in chapters such as "Young America in Literature" and "The Church of the Apostles," which Brodhead (*Hawthorne, Melville, and the Novel*) has identified as "enormously expand[ing] Melville's book's frame of reference; each chapter here provides a new context and a new order of meaning in terms of which to make sense of the enthusiastic youth's crusade" (182).

26 Other reasons help to explain Pierre's attitude toward Delly, such as her class affiliation (although she and Isabel may share this) and her adulterous affair. But one can imagine a plot line whereby in identifying Isabel with Delly's bastard child (who dies), Delly would become the structural analogue of Isabel's mother, which would put Pierre and his desires on very familiar emotional turf. The fact that Pierre or the narrator, who is so quick to question and insinuate his protagonist's every motive, doesn't even entertain the possibility of an attraction between Pierre and Delly suggests that his certainty of their familial unrelatedness guarantees his sexual disinterestedness.

27 Marc Shell writes, "Between perfect liberty and death, which the optimistic American revolutionary Patrick Henry set forth as comedic alternatives, there is, tragically, no essential difference – as probably there was not for Melville himself" (*Children of the Earth: Literature, Politics and Nationhood* [Oxford: Oxford University Press, 1993], 16).

28 Through a close reading of the scene in which Pierre's hand is blackened at the Black Swan Inn, Robert S. Levine intriguingly links the presence of blood and other moments of racialized discourse in *Pierre* with anti-slavery accounts of the miscegenated origins of American society and Western culture in general. This analysis intersects with and supports my argument about slavery's instrumental place in the imagination of sentimental fictions. In tracing the novel's obsessive interest in racial mixture and purification, Levine is careful to note that Melville "points more generally to the ultimate reality of miscegenated (and unknown) genealogies rather than offering some specific 'proof' of Pierre's 'black' blood" ("Pierre's Blackened Hand," *Leviathan: A Journal of Melville Studies* 1 [1999]: 34–35). It seems entirely correct to argue that the

ubiquitous presence of blood has to do with the matter of race, but I believe that this is only one among many of Pierre's anxieties regarding blood. Black or white, consanguinity must be decimated.

AFTERWORD

1 Mark Twain, *Pudd'nhead Wilson and Those Extraordinary Twins*, ed. Sidney Berger (New York: Norton, 1980; orig. pub. 1894), 14–15. All further quotations from *Pudd'nhead Wilson* will be from this edition and will be incorporated into the text.

2 Although published in 1894, a full fifty years later than many of the novels I have discussed, the story begins in 1830 and concludes in 1853, after Pudd'nhead reveals that the children were separated at seven months and had each lived the other's life for twenty-three years.

3 An alternate reading of this issue of naming can be found in Myra Jehlen's "The Ties that Bind: Race and Sex" in *Mark Twain's* Pudd'nhead Wilson: *Race, Conflict, and Culture*, ed. Susan Gillman and Forrest G. Robinson (Durham, NC: Duke University Press, 1990). Michael T. Gilmore calls Tom "a principle of illegibility," (*Surface and Depth: The Quest for Legibility in American Culture* [Oxford: Oxford University Press, 2003], 167), an illegibility that is, perhaps, most evident by the fact of his fluctuating names. Even fluctuating names fluctuate, as demonstrated by the fact that Valet de Chambers is also spelled Vallet de Chambers. It is also worth recalling that Pudd'nhead refers to the children as "A and B" (110).

4 This split in the novel has been analyzed by many critics. See essays by Michael Rogin, Eric J. Sundquist, and Susan Gillman in *Mark Twain's* Pudd'nhead Wilson, ed. Gillman and Robinson.

5 George E. Marcus discusses Chambers's absence in "Doubled, Divided, and Crossed Selves" (ibid.), but rather than connecting it with Twain's maternal essentialism, he argues that Twain accepts an argument about the dehumanizing effects of slavery (Chambers doesn't exist as a human being given his insertion into slavery) and, that had Twain "doubled the double . . . he might have achieved a thoroughly postmodernist work" (207).

6 Carolyn Porter makes this point as well in her fine essay "Roxana's Plot": "[Pudd'nhead's] intelligence is proven, and his ascension to authority vindicated in the end, but only after what amounts to Twain's extended humiliation of him as a detective who is remarkably dull-witted when it comes to reading his evidence" (ibid., 132).

Select bibliography

Adams, Nehemiah, *The Sable Cloud: A Southern Tale, with Northern Comments*, 1861. Westport: Negro University Press, 1970.
A South-Side View of Slavery. Boston: Ticknor and Fields, 1860.
Alcott, William A., *The Young Wife, or Duties of Woman in the Marriage Relation*, 1837. New York: Arno Press and the *New York Times*, 1972.
Bardaglio, Peter, *Reconstructing the Household: Families, Sex, and the Law in the Nineteenth-Century South*. Chapel Hill: University of North Carolina Press, 1995.
Barnes, Elizabeth, *States of Sympathy: Seduction and Democracy in the American Novel*. New York: Columbia University Press, 1997.
Basch, Norma, *In the Eyes of the Law: Women, Marriage, and Property in Nineteenth-Century New York*. Ithaca: Cornell University Press, 1982.
Bauermeister, Erica R., "*The Lamplighter, The Wide, Wide World,* and *Hope Leslie*: Reconsidering the Recipes for Nineteenth-Century American Women's Novels." *Legacy: A Journal of Nineteenth-Century American Women Writers* 8 (1991): 17–28.
Baym, Nina, *Woman's Fiction: A Guide to Novels by and about Women in America, 1820–1870*. Ithaca: Cornell University Press, 1978.
Bercovitch, Sacvan. *Rites of Assent: Transformations in the Symbolic Construction of America*. New York: Routledge, 1993.
Berlant, Lauren, "Poor Eliza." *No More Separate Spheres!, American Literature* 70 (1998): 635–668.
Bibb, Henry, *The Life and Adventures of Henry Bibb, an American Slave*, 1849. With a new introduction by Charles Heglar. Madison: University of Wisconsin Press, 2001.
Bishop, Joel, *Commentaries on the Law of Marriage and Divorce*. Boston: Little Brown, 1852.
The Black Bard of North Carolina: George Moses Horton and his Poetry. Edited by Joan R. Sherman. Chapel Hill: University of North Carolina Press, 1997.
Branch, Watson G., ed., *Melville: The Critical Heritage*. London and Boston: Routledge & Kegan Paul, 1974.
Brodhead, Richard, *Cultures of Letters: Scenes of Reading and Writing in Nineteenth-Century America*. Chicago: University of Chicago Press, 1993.
Hawthorne, Melville, and the Novel. Chicago: University of Chicago Press, 1973.

Brown, Gillian, *The Consent of the Governed: The Lockean Legacy in Early American Culture*. Cambridge, MA: Harvard University Press, 2001.

Domestic Individualism: Imagining Self in Nineteenth-Century America. Berkeley: University of California Press, 1990.

Brown, Henry Box, *Narrative of the Life of Henry Box Brown, written by Himself*, 1851. With an introduction by Richard Newman and a Foreword by Henry Lewis Gates, Jr. New York: Oxford University Press, 2002.

Brown, Homer, "Why the Story of the Origin of the (English) Novel is an American Romance (If Not the Great American Novel)." In *Cultural Institutions of the Novel*, edited by Deidre Lynch and William Warner, 11–43. Durham, NC: Duke University Press, 1996.

Brown, William Wells, *Clotel; or the President's Daughter: A Narrative of Slave Life in the United States*, 1853. Edited by Robert S. Levine. Boston: Bedford/St. Martin's, 2000.

Burnham, Michelle, *Captivity and Sentiment: Cultural Exchange in American Literature, 1682–1861*. Hanover: University Press of New England, 1997.

Camfield, Gregg, "The Moral Aesthetics of Sentimentality: A Missing Key to *Uncle Tom's Cabin*." *Nineteenth-Century Literature* 43 (1988): 319–345.

Carby, Hazel, *Reconstructing Womanhood: The Emergence of the Afro-American Woman Novelist*. New York: Oxford University Press, 1987.

Carey, Alice, "The Adopted Daughter." In *The Adopted Daughter and Other Tales*, 9–86. Philadelphia: J. B. Smith & Co., 1860.

Castronovo, Russ, "Incidents in the Life of a White Woman: Economies of Race and Gender in the Antebellum Nation." *American Literary History* 10 (1998): 239–265.

Chapin, E. H., *Duties of Young Women*, 1848. Boston: George W. Briggs, 1850.

Child, Lydia Maria, *An Appeal in Favor of that Class of Americans Called Africans*. Edited by Carolyn L. Karcher. Amherst: University of Massachusetts Press, 1996.

A Romance of the Republic, 1867. Edited by Dana D. Nelson. Lexington: University of Kentucky Press, 1997.

Clinton, Catherine, *Fanny Kemble's Civil Wars*. New York: Simon and Schuster, 2000.

Fanny Kemble's Journals. Cambridge, MA: Harvard University Press, 2000.

Cooper, James Fenimore, *The Last of the Mohicans*, 1826. With an introduction by Richard Slotkin. New York: Penguin, 1986.

Cott, Nancy, *Public Vows: A History of Marriage and the Nation*. Cambridge, MA: Harvard University Press, 2000.

Cowley, Malcolm, ed., *The Portable Hawthorne*. New York: Penguin, 1970.

Craft, William and Ellen, *Running a Thousand Miles for Freedom, or the Escape of William and Ellen Craft from Slavery*, 1860. Reprinted in *Great Slave Narratives*, selected and introduced by Arna Bontemps, 269–331. Boston: Beacon Press, 1969.

Crane, Gregg, *Race, Citizenship, and Law in American Literature*. Cambridge: Cambridge University Press, 2002.

Cummins, Maria Susanna, *The Lamplighter*, 1854. Edited by Nina Baym. New Brunswick: Rutgers University Press, 1988.

Dimock, Wai Chee, *Empire for Liberty: Melville and the Poetics of Individualism.* Princeton: Princeton University Press, 1989.

   Residues of Justice: Literature, Law, Philosophy. Berkeley: University of California Press, 1996.

Douglas, Ann, *The Feminization of American Culture.* New York: Avon Books, 1977.

Douglass, Frederick, *Narrative of the Life of Frederick Douglass,* 1845. In *The Classic Slave Narratives.* Edited by Henry Louis Gates, Jr., 243–331. New York: Mentor, 1987.

duCille, Ann, *The Coupling Convention: Sex, Text, and Tradition in Black Women's Fiction.* New York: Oxford University Press, 1993.

Eastman, Hubbard, *Noyesism Unveiled: A History of the Sect Self-Styled Perfectionists; with a Summary View of their Leading Doctrines.* Brattleboro: B. D. Harris and Co., 1849.

Ellison, Julie, *Cato's Tears and the Making of Anglo-American Emotion.* Chicago: University of Chicago Press, 1999.

Farrar, Mrs. John, *The Young Lady's Friend.* Newyork: Samuel S. & William Wood, 1841.

Fern, Fanny [Sara Willis Parton], "Has a Mother a Right to her Children?", 1857. In *Ruth Hall and Other Writings.* Edited by Joyce W. Warren, 282–283. New Brunswick: Rutgers University Press, 1986.

Fiedler, Leslie, *Love and Death in the American Novel.* New York: Dell, 1966.

Finkelman, Paul, *Defending Slavery: Proslavery Thought in the Old South: A Brief History with Documents.* Boston: Bedford/St. Martin's, 2003.

Fisher, Philip, *Hard Facts: Setting and Form in the American Novel.* New York: Oxford University Press, 1985.

Fitzhugh, George, *Cannibals All! or, Slaves without Masters,* 1857. Edited by C. Vann Woodward. Cambridge, MA: Harvard University Press, 1960.

Fliegelman, Jay, *Prodigals and Pilgrims: The American Revolution Against Patriarchal Authority, 1750–1800.* Cambridge: Cambridge University Press, 1982.

Forgie, George, *Patricide in the House Divided: A Psychological Interpretation of Lincoln and his Age.* New York: W. W. Norton, 1979.

Foster, Edward Halsey, *Susan and Anna Warner.* Boston: Twayne Publishers, n.d.

Fox-Genovese, Elizabeth, *Within the Plantation Household: Black and White Women of the Old South.* Chapel Hill: University of North Carolina Press, 1988.

Furnas, J. C., *Goodbye to Uncle Tom.* New York: William Sloane Associates, 1956.

Gallagher, Catharine, *Nobody's Story: The Vanishing Acts of Women Writers in the Marketplace, 1760–1820.* Berkeley: University of California Press, 1994.

Genovese, Eugene, *Roll, Jordan Roll: The World the Slaves Made.* New York: Vintage, 1976.

Gilmore, Michael T., *Surface and Depth: The Quest for Legibility in American Culture.* New York: Oxford University Press, 2003.

Godwin, Parke, *A Popular View of the Doctrines of Charles Fourier.* New York: J. S. Redfield, 1844.

Goshgarian, G. M., *To Kiss the Chastening Rod: Domestic Fiction and Sexual Ideology in the American Renaissance.* Ithaca: Cornell University Press, 1992.

Gossett, Thomas, *Uncle Tom's Cabin and American Culture.* Dallas: Southern Methodist University Press, 1985.

Grossberg, Michael, *Governing the Hearth: Law and the Family in Nineteenth-Century America.* Chapel Hill: University of North Carolina Press, 1985.

Harris, Susan K., *19th-Century American Women's Novels: Interpretive Strategies.* Cambridge: Cambridge University Press, 1990.

Hartman, Saidiya, *Scenes of Subjection: Terror, Slavery and Self-Making in Nineteenth-Century America.* New York: Oxford University Press, 1997.

Hartog, Hendrik, *Man and Wife in America: A History.* Cambridge, MA: Harvard University Press, 2000.

Hedrick, Joan D., *Harriet Beecher Stowe: A Life.* New York: Oxford University Press, 1994.

Hendler, Glenn, "The Limits of Sympathy: Louisa May Alcott and the Sentimental Novel." *American Literary History* 3 (1991): 685–706.

Public Sentiments: Structures of Feeling in Nineteenth-Century American Literature. Chapel Hill: University of North Carolina Press, 2001.

Hentz, Caroline Lee, *Eoline; or Magnolia Vale, a Novel,* 1852. Reprinted in *American Fiction Reprint Series* from the T. B. Peterson edition. Freeport: Books for Libraries Press, 1971.

Ernest Linwood; a Novel. Boston: John P. Jewett, 1856.

Linda; or, the Young Pilot of the Belle Creole. Philadelphia: T. B. Peterson & Brothers, 1869.

Marcus Warland; or, The Long Moss Spring. A Tale of the South. Philadelphia: A. Hart, late Carey & Hart, 1852.

The Planter's Northern Bride, 1854. With an Introduction by Rhoda Coleman Ellison. Chapel Hill: University of North Carolina Press, 1970.

Rena; or, the Snow Bird. A Tale of Real Life. Philadelphia: T. B. Peterson & Brothers, 1851.

Higgins, Brian and Hershel Parker, "The Flawed Grandeur of Melville's *Pierre.*" In *New Perspectives on Melville,* edited by Faith Pullin, 162–196. Kent: Kent State University Press, 1978.

Hochheimer, Lewis, *A Treatise on the Law Relating to the Custody of Infants.* Baltimore: John Murphy, 1887.

Holmes, George F., "Review of *Uncle Tom's Cabin.*" *Southern Literary Messenger* 18 (1852): 722–731.

Holmes, Mary Jane, *Dora Deane or the East India Uncle.* Chicago: M. A. Donohue & Co., 1859.

Ethelyn's Mistake, 1869. Rahway: The Merson Co., n.d.

Hugh Worthington. New York: Carleton, 1865.

'Lena Rivers, 1856. New York: G. W. Dillingham Co., 1970.

Meadowbrook Farm. Chicago: M. A. Donohue & Co., 1857.

Mildred: The Child of Adoption. New York: A. L. Burt Co., n.d.

Hornblower, Jane Elizabeth Roscoe, *Vara; or, The Child of Adoption.* New York: Robert Carter and Brothers, 1854.

Horowitz, Morton, *The Transformation of American Law, 1780–1860.* Cambridge, MA: Harvard University Press, 1977.

Horton, George Moses, *The Poetical Works of George M. Horton, The Colored Bard of North Carolina, to which is Prefixed the Life of the Author, Written by Himself,* 1845. Electronic edition, University of North Carolina. *Documenting the South, or, the Southern Experience in 19th-century America,* 1997.

Howard, June, *Publishing the Family.* Durham, NC: Duke University Press, 2001.

"What is Sentimentalism?" *American Literary History* 11 (1999): 63–81.

Huard, Albert Leo, "Adoption: Ancient and Modern." *Vanderbilt Law Review* 9 (1956): 743–763.

Hume, David, *A Treatise of Human Nature,* ed. L. A. Selby Bigge. Oxford: Oxford University Press, 1978.

Jacobs, Harriet, *Incidents in the Life of a Slave Girl Written by Herself,* 1861. In *The Classic Slave Narratives.* Edited by Henry Louis Gates, Jr., 333–515. New York: Mentor, 1987.

James, Henry, "Frances Anne Kemble," *Nation,* December 12, 1878: 1069–1071. In *Henry James: Literary Criticism: Essays on Literature, American Writers, English Writers.* New York: The Library of America, 1984.

Jehlen, Myra, *American Incarnation: The Individual, the Nation, and the Continent.* Cambridge, MA: Harvard University Press, 1986.

"The Ties that Bind: Race and Sex." In *Mark Twain's* Pudd'nhead Wilson: *Race, Conflict, and Culture,* edited by Susan Gillman and Forrest G. Robinson, 105–120. Durham, NC: Duke University Press, 1990.

Kaplan, Amy, "Manifest Domesticity." *No More Separate Spheres!, American Literature* 70 (1998): 581–606.

Kelley, Mary, *Private Woman, Public Stage: Literary Domesticity in Nineteenth-Century America.* New York: Oxford University Press, 1984.

Kelley, Wyn, "*Pierre's* Domestic Ambiguities." In *The Cambridge Companion to Herman Melville,* edited by Robert S. Levine, 91–113. Cambridge: Cambridge University Press, 1998.

Kemble, Frances Anne, *A Journal of a Residence on a Georgian Plantation in 1838–1839.* Edited and with an introduction by John A. Scott. Athens: University of Georgia Press, 1984.

Lane, Charles, "The Consociate Family Life." *The New Age and Concordium Gazette* 1 (1843): 116–120.

Lang, Amy, "Class and the Strategies of Sympathy." In *The Culture of Sentiment: Race, Gender, and Sentimentality in 19th Century America,* edited by Shirley Samuels, 128–142. New York: Oxford University Press, 1992.

Levine, Robert S., "Pierre's Blackened Hand." *Leviathan: A Journal of Melville Studies* 1 (1999): 23–44.

"*Uncle Tom's Cabin* in *Frederick Douglass' Paper*: An Analysis of Reception." Reprinted in *Uncle Tom's Cabin,* edited by Elizabeth Ammons, 523–542. New York: Norton, 1994.

Marcus, George E., "Doubled, Divided, and Crossed Selves." In *Mark Twain's Pudd'nhead Wilson: Race, Conflict, and Culture*, edited by Susan Gillman and Forrest G. Robinson, 190–210. Durham, NC: Duke University Press, 1990.

Marshall, David, *The Surprising Effects of Sympathy: Marivaux, Diderot, Rousseau, and Mary Shelley*. Chicago: University of Chicago Press, 1988.

McCord, Louisa S., "Negro and White Slavery – Wherein do they Differ?" *Southern Quarterly Review* 20 (1851): 119–132.

"*Uncle Tom's Cabin.*" *Southern Quarterly Review* 23 (1853): 81–120.

McIntosh, Maria Jane, *Conquest and Self-Conquest; or, Which Makes the Hero?*, 1843. *American Fiction Reprint Series*. Freeport: Books for Libraries Press, 1969.

Two Pictures; or, What We Think of Ourselves, and What the World Thinks of Us. New York: D. Appleton and Co., 1863.

Violet; or, the Cross and the Crown. Boston: John P. Jewett, 1856.

Melville, Herman, *Billy Budd, Sailor (An Inside Narrative)*. With an introduction by Frederick Busch. New York: Penguin, 1986.

Moby-Dick, or the Whale, 1851. Vol. VI of *The Writings of Herman Melville*, edited by Harrison Hayford, Hershel Parker, and G. Thomas Tanselle. Evanston and Chicago: Northwestern University Press and the Newberry Library, 1988.

Pierre, or the Ambiguities, 1852. Vol. VII of *The Writings of Herman Melville*, edited by Harrison Hayford, Hershel Parker, and G. Thomas Tanselle. Evanston and Chicago: Northwestern University Press and the Newberry Library, 1971.

Merish, Lori, *Sentimental Materialism: Gender, Commodity Culture, and Nineteenth-Century American Literature*. Durham, NC: Duke University Press, 2000.

Michaels, Walter Benn, "The Contracted Heart." *New Literary History* 21 (1990): 496–531.

Monmouth, Sarah Elizabeth, *The Adopted Daughter; or, the Trials of Sabra. A Tale of Real Life*, 1858. Montreal: John Lovell, 1873.

Morgan, Edmund S., *American Freedom, American Slavery: The Ordeal of Colonial Virginia*. New York: Norton, 1975.

Moss, Elizabeth, *Domestic Novelists in the Old South: Defenders of Southern Culture*. Baton Rouge: Louisiana State University Press, 1992.

The Mother's Assistant and Young Lady's Friend. Edited by William C. Brown. Boston: William C. Brown, 1841–54.

Nelson, Dana D., *The Word in Black and White: Reading "Race" in American Literature, 1638–1867*. New York: Oxford University Press, 1993.

Nichols, T. L. and Mrs. Mary S. Gove Nichols, *Marriage: Its History, Character, and Results: Its Sanctities, and its Profanities; its Science and its Facts. Demonstrating its Influence, as a Civilized Institution, on the Happiness of the Individual and the Progress of the Race*. New York: T. L. Nichols, 1854.

Northup, Solomon, *Twelve Years a Slave. Narrative of Solomon Northup, a Citizen of New-York, Kidnapped in Washington City in 1841, and Rescued in 1853, from a Cotton Plantation Near the Red River, in Louisiana*, 1853. Edited by Sue Eakin and Joseph Logsdon. Baton Rouge: Louisiana State University Press, 1968.

Noyes, John Humphrey, *Bible Communism; a Compilation from the Annual Reports and other Publications of the Oneida Association and its Branches; Presenting, in Connection with their History, a Summary View of their Religious and Social Theories.* Brooklyn: Office of the Circular, 1853.

Nudelman, Franny, " 'The Blood of Millions': John Brown's Body, Public Violence, and Political Community." *American Literary History* 13 (2001): 639–670.

"Harriet Jacobs and the Sentimental Politics of Female Suffering." *English Literary History* 59 (1992): 939–964.

Otter, Samuel, *Melville's Anatomies.* Berkeley: University of California Press, 1999.

Parker, Hershel, *Herman Melville: A Biography*, vol. II: *1851–1891.* Baltimore: The Johns Hopkins University Press, 2002.

"Why *Pierre* Went Wrong." *Studies in the Novel* 8 (1976): 7–23.

Parsons, C. G., *An Inside View of Slavery: or a Tour among the Planters.* Boston: John P. Jewett, 1855.

Patterson, Orlando, *Slavery and Social Death.* Cambridge, MA: Harvard University Press, 1982.

Pennington, J. W. C., *The Fugitive Blacksmith, or Events in the History of James W. C. Pennington, Pastor of a Presbyterian Church, New York, Formerly a Slave in the State of Maryland*, 1849. Reprinted in *Great Slave Narratives*, selected and introduced by Arna Bontemps, 193–267. Boston: Beacon Press, 1969.

Pike, Mary Hayden Green [Sydney Story, Jr.], *Caste: A Story of Republican Equality.* Boston: Phillips, Sampson and Co., 1856.

[Mary Langdon], *Ida May: A Story of Things Actual and Possible.* Boston: Phillips, Sampson and Company, 1854.

Poovey, Mary, *A History of the Modern Fact: Problems of Knowledge in the Sciences of Wealth and Society.* Chicago: University of Chicago Press, 1998.

Porter, Carolyn, "Roxana's Plot." In *Mark Twain's* Pudd'nhead Wilson: *Race, Conflict, and Culture*, edited by Susan Gillman and Forrest G. Robinson, 121–136. Durham, NC: Duke University Press, 1990.

Presser, Stephen B., "The Historical Background of the American Law of Adoption." *Journal of Family Law* 1 (1971): 443–516.

Renker, Elizabeth, *Strike through the Mask: Herman Melville and the Scene of Writing.* Baltimore: Johns Hopkins University Press, 1996.

Riss, Arthur, "Racial Essentialism and Family Values in *Uncle Tom's Cabin.*" *American Quarterly* 46 (1994): 513–544.

Rogin, Michael Paul, *Subversive Genealogy: The Politics and Art of Herman Melville.* New York: Knopf, 1983.

Romero, Lora, *Home Fronts: Domesticity and its Critics in the Antebellum United States.* Durham, NC: Duke University Press, 1997.

Ryan, Mary P., *The Empire of the Mother: American Writing about Domesticity, 1830–1860.* New York: Harrington Park Press, 1982.

Sanchez-Eppler, Karen, *Touching Liberty: Abolition, Feminism, and the Politics of the Body*. Berkeley: University of California Press, 1993.

Schnog, Nancy, "Inside the Sentimental: The Psychological Work of *The Wide, Wide World*." *Genders* 4 (1989): 11–25.

Sealts, Merton M. Jr., "Melville and the Shakers." *Studies in Bibliography*, ed. Fredson Bowers, vol. 2 (1949): 105–114.

Shell, Marc, *Children of the Earth: Literature, Politics and Nationhood*. New York: Oxford University Press, 1993.

Southworth, E.D.E.N., *Ishmael, or in the Depths*. New York: A. L. Burt Co., 1863.
Self-Raised, or From the Depths, 1876. New York: Grosset & Dunlap, n.d.

Stanley, Amy Dru, *From Bondage to Contract: Wage Labor, Marriage, and the Market in the Age of Slave Emancipation*. Cambridge: Cambridge University Press, 1998.

Stephens, Ann, *Myra: The Child of Adoption, a Romance of Real Life*. New York: Beadle and Company, 1860.

Stephens, Harriet Marion, *Hagar, the Martyr; or, Passion and Reality. A Tale of the North and South*, 1854. Reprinted in the *Black Heritage Library Collection*. Freeport: Books for Libraries Press, 1972.

Stern, Julia, "To Represent Afflicted Time: Mourning as Hagiography." *American Literary History* 5 (1998): 378–388.

Stowe, Harriet Beecher, *A Key to Uncle Tom's Cabin; Presenting the Original Facts and Documents Upon which the Story is Founded. Together with Corroborative Statements Verifying the Truth of the Work*. Boston: John P. Jewett, 1853.
Dred, A Tale of the Great Dismal Swamp, 1856. Edited by Robert S. Levine. New York: Penguin, 2000.
The Pearl of Orr's Island: A Story of the Coast of Maine, 1862. With a foreword by Joan D. Hedrick. Boston: Houghton Mifflin, 2001.
Uncle Tom's Cabin or, Life Among the Lowly, 1852. Edited with an introduction by Ann Douglas. New York: Penguin, 1981.

Sundquist, Eric J., *Home as Found: Authority and Genealogy in Nineteenth-Century American Literature*. Baltimore: Johns Hopkins University Press, 1979.

Tate, Claudia, *Domestic Allegories of Political Desire: The Black Heroine's Text at the Turn of the Century*. New York: Oxford University Press, 1982.

Thomas, Brook, *American Literary Realism and the Failed Promise of Contract*. Berkeley: University of California Press, 1997.

Tolstoy, Leo, *Anna Karenina*, 1877. New York: Modern Library Classics, 2000.

Tompkins, Jane, *Sensational Designs: The Cultural Work of American Fiction, 1790–1860*. New York: Oxford University Press, 1985.

Toner, Jennifer DiLalla, "The Accustomed Signs of the Family: Rereading Genealogy in Melville's Pierre." *American Literature* 70 (1998): 237–263.

Truth, Sojourner, *The Narrative of Sojourner Truth*, 1850. New York: Dover Publications, 1997.

Tucker, Irene, *A Probable State: The Novel, the Contract, and the Jews*. Chicago: University of Chicago Press, 2000.

Twain, Mark, *Pudd'nhead Wilson and Those Extraordinary Twins*, 1894. Edited by Sidney Berger. New York: Norton, 1980.

Wald, Priscilla, *Constituting Americans: Cultural Anxiety and Narrative Form.* Durham, NC: Duke University Press, 1995.

Warner, Anna B., *Susan Warner.* New York: G. P. Putnam's Sons, 1909.

Warner, Susan [Elizabeth Wetherell], *American Female Patriotism. A Prize Essay.* New York: Edward H. Fletcher, 1852.

    The Wide, Wide World, 1850. Afterword by Jane Tompkins. New York: The Feminist Press, 1987.

Weld, Theodore Dwight, ed., *American Slavery As It Is: Testimony of a Thousand Witnesses,* 1839. Reprint. New York: Arno Press and the New York Times, 1969.

Whitmore, William, *The Law of Adoption in the United States, and Especially in Massachusetts.* Albany: Joel Munsell, 1876.

Williams, Susan S., "Widening the World: Susan Warner, Her Readers, and the Assumption of Authorship." American Quarterly 42 (1990): 565–586.

Wilson, Harriet, *Our Nig; or, Sketches from the Life of a Free Black,* 1859. Introduction and notes by Henry Louis Gates, Jr. New York: Vintage, 1983.

Wright, Frances, *Course of Popular Lectures, as Delivered by Frances Wright.* New York: Office of the Free Enquirer, 1829.

Wright, Henry C., *The Unwelcome Child; or, the Crime of an Undesigned and Undesired Maternity.* Boston: Bela Marsh, 1858.

Zanaildan, Jamil, "The Emergence of a Modern American Family Law: Child Custody, Adoption, and the Courts, 1796–1851." *Northwestern University Law Review* 73 (1979): 1038–1089.

Index

Printed in the United States
76878LV00005B/1-9